D1542031

BLACKS IN THE NEW WORLD: *August Meier, Series Editor*

A list of books in the series appears at the end of this volume.

FATHER DIVINE
and the Struggle for Racial Equality

FATHER DIVINE
and the
Struggle for Racial Equality

ROBERT WEISBROT

UNIVERSITY OF ILLINOIS PRESS

Urbana   Chicago   London

This book is printed on acid-free paper.

Photographs courtesy of the Peace Mission movement.

LIBRARY OF CONGRESS CATALOGING IN PUBLICATION DATA

Weisbrot, Robert.

Father Divine and the struggle for racial equality.

(Blacks in the New World)
Bibliography: p.
Includes index.
1. Divine, Father. 2. Afro-Americans—Civil rights.
3. United States—Race relations. 4. Church and
race relations—United States. I. Title.
BX7350.A4W44   299'.93   82-2644
ISBN 0-252-00973-8   AACR2

To Milton I. Vanger and Rudolph Binion

Preface

Robert Murciano first sparked my interest in Father Divine ten years ago while we were students at Brandeis University. Amid one of our countless discussions that so enjoyably helped shape my views of history and human nature, he suggested that I would find Divine a fascinating religious figure about whom little scholarly work had been done. I've never received happier counsel. Later, as a graduate student at Princeton University, I wrote a seminar paper on Divine's Harlem ministry for James McPherson's course on black history. I had intended, at first, simply to explore why urban blacks would join an "escapist" religious cult, as Divine's popular Peace Mission movement was widely portrayed during the 1930s. In examining black journals, however, I discovered that Divine stood for a socially progressive religion tied to a cooperative ethic and to demands for racial equality. I found this minister's complex leadership intriguing and, aided by Professor McPherson's perceptive criticisms, eventually returned to the subject for my dissertation. Immersing myself in sermons and letters by Father Divine, which I would now gauge as voluminous but at the time seemed endless, I crystallized a view of the man as strongly impelled by a passion for justice. In his basic aims and values he seemed to me to reflect a great deal about Afro-American leadership and, more broadly, American reform movements during the Great Depression.

Frank Freidel guided my dissertation at Harvard University, combining sage advice and valued encouragement. A fellowship from the Du Bois Institute for Afro-American Research at Harvard University enabled me to complete the dissertation, in 1980. It further gave me the chance to become acquainted with four scholars at the institute—Evelyn Brooks-Barnett, Gerald Gill, Jacqueline Grant, and Valerie Smith—who each enriched my perspectives of black history and culture. During this time I also attended the meetings of a seminar group, including Randall Burkett, Richard Newman, Edwin Redkey, Preston N. Williams and David Wills, whose sessions on Afro-American religion I found delightful as well as most illuminating for my study of Father Divine.

In the year I spent revising the dissertation, August Meier proved an ideal editor, whose penetrating criticisms and extraordinary knowledge of black history immeasurably enhanced my efforts. Working with him both resulted in a far better book and afforded me a deeply rewarding experience.

My efforts at revision also benefited greatly from the aid of several readers who gave generously of their time and ideas. I was fortunate to have Elliott Rudwick contribute incisive advice for strengthening sections on Afro-American history. Preston N. Williams, who read the dissertation at Harvard, helped me to rethink varied points relating to black religion, particularly the interaction between Divine and other ministers. My good friend and colleague Jonathan Sarna examined the dissertation with characteristic insight and a rare sensitivity to broader theoretical questions in history and other fields. Elana Shavit kindly read the revised thesis, as both a patient proofreader and a skillful stylistic critic. I am also grateful to Bonnie Depp and John A. Clark for carefully checking the manuscript.

Colby College notably facilitated the work of revision. Through the Mellon Foundation, the college generously financed my travels to research additional chapters; and the college manuscript typist, Julie Cannon, produced a flawless typescript of my revised study.

Finally, I would like to express a personal word of appreciation to Eric Goldman, who has inspired me as a teacher and friend; to Stephen Zwick, for his kind interest in my work and the example of his own searching study of Father Divine; to Dolita, for her creative ideas on religion; and to my parents, whose encouragement and aid in many ways have made this project a family endeavor.

Contents

Abbreviations Used in Notes

AA	*Baltimore Afro-American*
Age	*New York Age*
CD	*Chicago Defender*
ND	*New Day*
NYAN	*New York Amsterdam News*
PC	*Pittsburgh Courier*
SW	*Spoken Word*
Times	*New York Times*

FATHER DIVINE
and the Struggle for Racial Equality

Introduction

Father Divine and the Black Religious Tradition

Father Divine, known to thousands during the Depression as God on earth, was nearly lynched, by his own account, on some thirty-two occasions. Whether or not strictly true, the claim reveals Divine as a cult deity self-consciously forged by suffering rather than privilege. He spent his youth in the rural South after Reconstruction, confined by a caste system that kept people of his dark complexion in want and fear. As a sharecropper's son bearing hunger, exhaustion, and frustrated ambitions, Divine learned firsthand the need for a society that offered opportunity to all people. In the same harsh way, he developed his passion for racial justice as the victim of segregation and at least one incident of violence, which left a scar on the back of his head and likely deepened other, inner wounds as well.

If, as Martin Luther King, Jr., once observed, "[t]he central quality in the Negro's life is pain,"[1] then religion has been the Negro's central organized means of responding to that pain. When blacks had little chance to improve their status, as in Father Divine's early years, the church offered mainly the solace of fiery evangelical services. Often such worship centered on charismatic preachers who, like Divine, were seen as heavenly messengers coming to assure the poor, the powerless, and the uprooted of their closeness to God. Yet the church also imparted a moral sanction and institutional base crucial to movements for social progress and protest. Typically, as blacks organized more aggressively for reform, the role of the church as a force for change expanded as well. The Negro church, in brief, was inherently neither progressive nor conservative, militant nor escapist, but rather a mirror and realistic defender of evolving black hopes and values.

Father Divine's sharply checkered evangelical career, beginning in the late nineteenth century, epitomized the way black religion has adapted

3

to changing communal needs. As a young exhorter, Divine at first implicitly defied the Jim Crow campaigns violently sweeping the South, by preaching a message of God-given equality and present-centered hope to black people. He gathered disciples who hailed him as the embodiment of God on earth, come to deliver them from evil; but his attitudes proved ill suited to the times. White authorities and alarmed Negro ministers more than once charged him with subversion, and he met arrest, imprisonment, and, on one occasion, detention in an insane asylum. Far from uprooting the hated caste system and the prejudice on which it fed, Father Divine remained among its embittered victims.

In 1915 Divine arrived in the major Negro metropolis of New York and discovered that the aloofness from social problems that marked black religion in the South remained nearly as strong in the North. Shaken by memories of persecution and rejection, he soon conformed to this cautious mood and gradually began to prosper. His small coterie of disciples, some from the years spent evangelizing in the South, believed as before in their leader's divinity. Now, however, they kept this knowledge secret, at Divine's anxious injunction. Divine became known as a solid religious figure unlikely to disturb the tranquility of any community. When in 1919 he acquired property in a previously all-white suburb in Long Island called Sayville, it confirmed the success of his new, respectable image. It marked, as well, the submergence of Divine's volatile nature by a growing desire for acceptance and tranquility.

The conservatism of black religion in the early twentieth century had once led even the master of accommodation, Booker T. Washington, to warn that a "large element of the Negro church must be recalled from its apocalyptic vision back to the earth."[2] During the 1920s undercurrents of discontent permeated the ghettos and added new force to Washington's words. These stirrings included a heightened assertiveness by the NAACP in promoting black rights, the rising expectations of Negro veterans of the Great War "to make the world safe for democracy," a surge of mass enthusiasm for Marcus Garvey's movement for pan-African solidarity, and the cultural renaissance of the proud "New Negro." The era also witnessed the intensified urban migration of blacks from the rural South, many of whom were encountering severe problems of economic and emotional adjustment. All these developments sharpened the need for the Negro clergy to become more deeply involved in social issues. Yet in the absence of an overriding sense of crisis, most ministers — including the still withdrawn Father Divine — appeared content to lead mainly in the spiritual realm.

That transforming crisis came suddenly in 1929, from origins largely outside the ghetto's control. The Great Depression, by leaving the black working class desperate for relief and employment, crystallized a new militance among ghetto residents in demanding their rights. In this changing climate the Negro church at last faced concerted, community-wide pressure to contribute more vigorously to movements for social aid and reform.

For many clergymen, whose careers had always been chiefly devoted to spiritual pursuits, these growing obligations posed a difficult and painful adjustment. In the case of Father Divine, however, the crisis rekindled a latent sense of purpose and ambition, by providing the possibilities for reform leadership that he had once vainly sought decades earlier. The very impulses that had once resulted in his persecution now abruptly moved him from isolation to acclaim, as a symbol of the new progressive spirit in the Negro church.

To chart Divine's vicissitudes against the shifts in black religious attitudes is by no means to explain his rise in purely accidental or impersonal terms. The Depression era produced countless aspiring "Father Divine" types in the ghettos — ambitious cult figures with pretensions to mass leadership. Most of these languished in obscurity long after Father Divine had become the most widely discussed black preacher in America. It is also likely that a person of Divine's abilities, including an uncanny sense of opportunity, would have left his mark even in greatly varying circumstances. Yet the specific course of Divine's ministry and his sudden bolt into national prominence cannot be viewed apart from the ghettos' growing demands for a present-centered, socially active clergy.

Father Divine moved into the role of reformer through a transitional stage as philanthropist to poor and unemployed ghetto residents. As his modest communal movement based in Sayville continued to prosper during the Depression, Divine opened his home to all visitors, presenting free banquets and often finding jobs for his needy guests. Crowds came regularly from Harlem and Newark, venerating this mysterious provider as a heaven-sent deliverer. By the early thirties independent bands of disciples were forming throughout the ghettos and occasionally outside them. Even some whites joined these groups, out of a spiritual emptiness or admiration for Divine's progressive activity.

The mass conversions elicited a highly practical side to Divine's leadership. Relocating in Harlem, the heart of black social activity, he organized the far-flung groups of disciples — known collectively as the Peace Mission — into a tightly standardized network of religious cooperatives, dedicated to racial equality and highly responsive to his every command. Thus, even before fully entering the struggle for racial equality, Divine already had fashioned the largest, most cohesive movement in the northern ghettos.

Father Divine's reform activity over the next decade represented, to an extraordinary degree, the range of ideas and strategies among contemporary civil rights activists. Almost alone among these leaders, he had the mass membership, financial resources, and executive ability to implement, on a large scale, plans for individual betterment, desegregation, economic cooperation, and political action against discrimination. With the exception of Divine's inconsistent relationship with unions — which seemed to him prone to violence and coercion — he led or cooperated in virtually every major campaign for racial equality during the Depression.

The Peace Mission became particularly well known for its aggressive efforts to desegregate all aspects of American society. The movement itself was among the very few interracial religious bodies in the nation. In the mid-thirties Divine sought to expand it into the most exclusive northern neighborhoods. Using white disciples as secret emissaries to circumvent restrictive housing covenants, he acquired homes, hotels, and beachfronts for his integrated following in areas long regarded as unthinkable for blacks to inhabit. By the late 1930s the Peace Mission had acquired several dozen centers providing over 2,000 acres of choice property far from the city slums.

The call to form business cooperatives in the ghettos inspired some of the most diverse activists for black rights, including communist leaders, Urban League spokesmen, officials in the NAACP, and many clergymen. Father Divine's Peace Mission centers were by far the most successful of these cooperative ventures in both scope and profitability. Aided by Divine's careful supervision, disciples opened inexpensive restaurants, clothing stores, and numerous other trades, volunteering their labor and sharing all income. By the end of the Depression decade the Peace Mission had come to handle millions of dollars in business annually, accumulating savings reportedly in excess of $15 million. Moreover, the success of these interracial cooperatives belied the gloomy forebodings of W. E. B. Du Bois and certain other black leaders that only by accepting the harsh fact of segregation could blacks unite for economic progress.

The idea of resettling poor urban dwellers in rural areas was highly popular during the Depression, but federal efforts tended to slight poor blacks most in need of such programs. To help this overlooked element, Father Divine created in 1935 a "Promised Land" of rural cooperatives in Ulster County, New York. In sharp and deliberate contrast to the world of the sharecroppers, these colonies were interracial, debt-free, and located on excellent farmland. Within a few years the centers were thriving and even supplying Divine's urban cooperatives with agricultural products. It is indicative of Divine's organizing talent that his rural experiment, perhaps the most productive ever devised primarily for disadvantaged ghetto residents, was merely a sidelight among many other "utopian" programs that Divine successfully nurtured during this period.

Father Divine's increasing involvement in politics during the mid-thirties reflected the black community's growing spirit of optimism about the possibilities for reform during the Roosevelt presidency. The campaign against lynching, which engaged the vigorous efforts of many civil rights groups in this period, found Divine drafting model bills to send to congressmen, while his followers gathered 250,000 signatures on a petition to pass federal antilynching legislation. In this and all his political actions, Divine combined a faith in American democratic principles with a warning that the government strictly honor these principles or face massive resistance. "If the White House or the Capitol does not do right, it can be picketed!" he told his Harlem followers. "Every American citizen has a right and if he does not get it one way, he can protest such acts that may be deemed by him as unjust and unrighteous."[3]

Unfortunately for both Father Divine and the cause of racial equality, his influence and physical vigor waned sharply during the forties, just as the civil rights movement was gathering major force. Divine was already an aged man when he left Harlem in 1942, incensed by a growing pattern of government harassment and weary from a decade of unceasing reform crusades. He retired to an estate in Philadelphia, to preside in relative quiet over a few hundred devoted followers. By 1955 he was known to be seriously ill, and after 1963 he ceased to appear in public. The civil rights movement was then entering its period of greatest triumph, but Divine could only passively approve the freedom rides and marches for the cause he had once worked so vigorously to foster. He died in 1965, in his eighties, shortly after sending a warm message of congratulations to President Lyndon Johnson for giving a strong civil rights speech before Congress and the nation.

Among civil rights activists, Divine's passing did not go unmourned. Roy Wilkins, who first came to prominence in the NAACP during the 1930s, recalled Divine as having done "a lot of good" as a social leader who "held up an example to the Negro community of cooperative endeavor."[4] One of the younger generation of activists who acknowledged a debt to Divine was Leon Sullivan, a black pastor in Philadelphia who founded the nationally famous Opportunities Industrialization Center to train disadvantaged youth. Sullivan described Divine as "the forerunner . . . of much that we see in the practical aspects of religion today. While many people were yet talking about what religion could do about integration and self-determination and human dignity, he was practicing it."[5]

Yet today Father Divine's reform legacy is little known. The fact that the era of his greatest activity, the 1930s, witnessed neither the sustained protest nor the sweeping civil rights legislation of later decades only partly explains this neglect. A more serious stumbling block to recognizing his achievements is the tendency of most students of Father Divine to depict him chiefly as a cult leader. In particular, the phenomenon of Divine's apotheosis by black and white followers alike has absorbed the attention of numerous scholars and journalists, often to the exclusion of interest in his more mundane but progressive activity.

This focus on Divine has sadly distorted the character of his ministry, by permitting the term "cult" both to oversimplify his complex movement and to envenom appraisals of his reform efforts. One need not deny or minimize the importance of Divine's charismatic leadership in order to acknowledge his significance as an activist in the civil rights movement. Divine was one of those rare cult figures who derived his greatest sense of power and purpose from helping to shape society according to his ideas of justice. Rather than bask, immobile, in the adulation of his followers, he redirected their devotion outward, in support of the reform causes he valued: integration, equal rights, and economic cooperation. The Peace Mission "cult" thus became the indispensable and highly effective vehicle of Father Divine's struggle for racial justice.

Father Divine himself always linked his perceived heavenly mandate to his concern for the oppressed rather than simply to some unique spiritual gift. To a guest at the Peace Mission who publicly doubted his divine nature, the minister replied: "Because your god would not feed the people, I came and I am feeding them. Because your god kept such as you segregated and discriminated, I came and I am unifying all nations together. That is why I came, because I did not believe in your god."[6]

By word and deed, Father Divine was calling the Negro church back to earth. As he defined his driving religious mission to his followers in Harlem, "I shall not be discouraged until I emancipate all humanity."[7] It was a role that only a god could wholly fill, even as it reflected Divine's very human faith in the coming of "a new world of unity and dignity for all mankind."[8]

Notes to Introduction

1. Martin Luther King, Jr., *Where Do We Go from Here: Chaos or Community* (Boston: Beacon Press, 1968), p. 102.

2. Booker T. Washington, "The Religious Life of the Negro," *North American Review* 181 (July, 1905):22.

3. Sermon of Mar. 18, 1940, in *ND,* Mar. 21, 1940, p. 15.

4. *NYAN,* Sept. 18, 1965, p. 1.

5. William L. Banks, *The Black Church in the U.S.* (Chicago: Moody Bible Institute, 1972), p. 61.

6. Sermon of Oct. 27, 1937, in *ND,* Nov. 4, 1937, p. 14.

7. Sermon of Nov. 2, 1938, in *ND,* May 26, 1979, p. 3.

8. Father Divine to President Lyndon Johnson, telegram, Mar. 17, 1965, in *ND,* Mar. 27, 1965, p. 1.

Early Journeys

Origins

Father Divine shares with other Messiah-figures of history a past shrouded in mystery and a large responsibility for helping to weave that shroud. Like many aspiring saviors, he tried to inter the memory of early years that were too prosaic or too painful to befit a chosen messenger of the Lord. Divine shunned questions about even the simplest landmarks of his past, claiming that mundane records of dates and places were irrelevant to his spiritual mission.

On the rare occasions when Divine discussed his origins with reporters or, more typically, with trial judges, he was nebulous and at times hopelessly contradictory. His two varying accounts of his age mark his birth around 1877 and 1883 respectively. As if to enrich the confusion, he also routinely asserted that he married in 1882, which would push his birthdate back to the Civil War.[1] Taken collectively, these statements confirm only that Divine cared more to obscure his past than to clarify it.

The paucity of documentary evidence has not precluded a surprising number of "definitive" accounts tracing Father Divine's early life.[2] These locate his birthplace variously in Virginia, the Carolinas, Georgia, and islands off the southeastern United States. Most agree that a George Baker, born shortly after the Civil War in some part of the Deep South, was the man who later gained renown as "Father Divine." Although direct proof is lacking, the claim rests on a missing link between the lowly Baker and the exalted Divine known as "the Messenger," an itinerant evangelist during the early 1900s. The number of people identifying this preacher with either Baker or Divine is impressive, and therefore one can plausibly assume that Divine held these two earlier identities.

The question of Divine's origins takes a further twist with the claim by a woman named Elizabeth Maysfield, in 1936, that he was her son, christened Frederick Edwards some fifty years before in North Carolina.[3] She told reporters that she had seen Divine but once in fifteen years, when he visited her in Richmond while conducting a religious meeting. "He told me not to recognize him as son and that he would not recognize me as mother anymore," she recalled. This corresponds to Divine's well-known strictures against maintaining old family relationships. Maysfield charged that Divine had not helped her financially, though she had long been in need, and saw no reason why he would not give her money as he did for his followers. Father Divine's secretary curtly denied all. Divine himself made no direct reply. The story's credibility is marred by Maysfield's further claim that Divine deserted a wife and children in Baltimore ten years earlier; in 1926 his whereabouts were a matter of record, and by all accounts he had long since been leading a stable life. Yet the general outline of Maysfield's testimony accords with independent claims that Father Divine had lived in Baltimore for some years as George Baker, and that he had indeed deserted his family in the distant past.

Maysfield's agitated words, because they related to Father Divine, drew the inevitable front-page headlines in Harlem's leading journal. Then she quickly faded into oblivion as simply one more opportunist spinning tales in a bid to share Divine's new-found fame and wealth. She had long since been completely forgotten when, in 1960, Father Divine lay semicomatose in a hospital and gave as his first name — then assumed to be an alias — Frederick.

Despite the vagaries of his origins, one can learn much about Father Divine's formative years by exploring the influences common to black life in the Deep South. Under whatever name — Divine, Baker, Edwards, or perhaps another — the man who later called himself Father Divine responded to the poverty, racism, and evangelism that formed the heart of the black sharecropper's lot. His subsequent career, as viewed through his public deeds and private statements, reflects the profound impact that these three factors exerted on his values and character.

Father Divine often insisted that he came to spread a universal message, but his speech and manner clearly revealed a heritage peculiar to southern blacks after the Civil War. A lifetime of diligent self-education never erased a large repertoire of regional idioms and colloquialisms. Similarly, he conveyed many an abstruse spiritual message through earthy anecdotes that displayed a thorough familiarity with the smallest details of a sharecropper's existence. In one sermon against vice Father Divine was able to establish instant rapport with his southern-born listeners by recalling the way their parents felt at ease only with "toothbrushes" in their mouths; he drew knowing laughter as he distinguished these as instruments not for cleaning the teeth but for holding tobacco for chewing.[4] In all respects, from his particular evangelical style to his empathy for victims of discrimination, Divine carried with him the legacy of rural black America.

The southern tenant farming system into which Divine was born was a testament to the devastation wrought by the Civil War.[5] Farmers yielded to an endless cycle of debt and drudgery, in which they produced the same soil-depleting cash crops simply to meet interest payments on accumulating loans for feed, seed, and tools. The work routine from dawn to dusk spared few of any age or condition, while the chances for economic betterment by staying on the farm were so low as to drain one of hope, let alone ambition.

The "shelters" to which tenants returned after the rigors of the field fairly symbolized the poverty most farmers endured. The houses were generally unpainted shacks, leaking, and in acute disrepair. There was a complete lack of plumbing, and even outhouses were rare. The tenant's life at home was, in short, as primitive and hard as his labor in the cotton fields.

The tenant system also testified to the limits of Reconstruction in giving substantive meaning to the emancipation of black slaves. While destitution moved among all southern farming elements, it resided most conspicuously with the Negroes in each tenant class — cash tenants, renters, and the most numerous and abjectly insecure group of all, sharecroppers. Children suffered as grievously as adults in a system that made no exemptions from want. Arthur Raper's study of Negro tenant families in Georgia notes the universal lack of decent clothing among inhabitants in the Black Belt counties, in which "thousands of babies have only two or three dresses and a half-dozen napkins each, and most of these are made from feed and salt sacks."[6]

Malnutrition was common — and this in a region where all inhabitants labored to produce basic agricultural goods. Raper states that "one seventh of the families went a whole year without eating a chicken or an egg. A third of the families raised no meat, one-fourth no potatoes, two-fifths had no canned goods. The families who neither grow nor buy chickens are the same families who have least of other types of food."[7] Nor could these families turn to production for their own subsistence, for their indebtedness obliged them to grow cash crops almost exclusively.

Just how harsh a life Father Divine led as a youth in the Black Belt is a matter for speculation, but the conditions over which he waxed indignant in his later years hint strongly at past deprivations. It was probably not coincidence, for example, that the religion he preached featured the cardinal tenet that an individual should never place himself in debt, whether to purchase land or the smallest item of clothing. Divine also thought it disgraceful that people should suffer hunger in a land of great wealth. Although his religious code incorporated much ascetic conduct, a salient exception was in the area of nutrition. Far from limiting one's dining by fasts or by omitting certain foods from the diet, as Black Muslims and other sects prescribed, Divine encouraged his followers to eat freely and abundantly. Banquets became symbols of his movement; they were the center of religious services as well as the major social events of his ministry.

Father Divine's unrelenting denunciations of racial prejudice leave no doubt as to the feature of southern life that pierced his emotions most terribly. All Negroes contended with social degradation that was, in its way, as painful as their economic plight. Racism was virtually endemic to southern society, and the abolition of slavery merely led it into other channels of expression. By the turn of the century most southern states had developed extensive social prescriptions limiting black rights. These "Jim Crow" patterns were sanctioned by law as well as tradition and enforced rigidly by the dominant white population, often by extralegal means.

Racial segregation applied to all major public and private facilities. Because southern whites viewed segregation as a way of stigmatizing as well as isolating Negroes, all acts that might seem to confer a sense of racial equality and brotherhood were uniformly condemned. The taboo against interracial dining and drinking was for this reason especially well guarded, as sociologist Charles Johnson observes, for "eating together carries a strong suggestion of social intimacy which is universally banned. In fact, the question of interracial dining seldom arises because it is so thoroughly prohibited and severely punished by ostracism of the white and labeling of the Negro."[8] Father Divine's later insistence that black and white disciples mingle fully at his banquets suggests that he remembered all too well the humiliating segregationist codes of his native region.

When the races mixed in the South, it was according to carefully prescribed hierarchical rites. If Negroes ever had cause to enter white homes, they did so via the back door. A chance encounter between a Negro and a white required the Negro to tip his hat. The white was obliged only to refrain from reciprocating the courtesy. A white who dared treat a Negro openly as his equal might find himself stigmatized, if not endangered, almost as much as any Negro who was considered too arrogant toward whites.

While Negroes generally preserved enough perspective to realize that human force rather than cosmic will had placed them in inferior social positions, most resigned themselves to the indefinite perpetuation of their condition. "It don't make any difference how much money you have or how much education you have," one Negro in Mississippi confided to

Charles Johnson. The white man "won't look at you as his equal, and there is no use in you acting like you're his equal if you want to stay here."[9]

To ensure that blacks neither advanced in nor rebelled against the existing caste system, the white population sharply confined Negro educational opportunities. Schools were, of course, strictly segregated, in large part to curb black achievement. Separate buildings and teaching staffs were routine procedure, while Negro pupils and teachers were generally excluded from access to equipment used by the white children and white teaching staff. Moreover, many Negroes of high-school age did not go to school because their neighborhoods had only one school, which was naturally reserved for white children.[10]

Black schools in the Deep South received only a small fraction of the per capita funding given to white schools in the same region. White school officials often acknowledged the implications for black educational progress but responded by lowering the standards expected of the students. They reasoned, with avowed benevolence, that "since we give the colored people so little it seems a shame to require much of them."[11]

The most deadening aspect of this separate and unequal instruction was that black children never learned about other blacks who had transcended their environment and gained stature in the wider society. When Arthur Raper asked a child in Georgia's Black Belt named Booker T. Washington Williams about the Negro for whom he was named, he did not know. Nor did the three dozen other pupils in his all-black class. The teacher had heard the name — but could not place it. The same situation obtained with the mention of Robert Russa Moton, Paul Laurence Dunbar, James Weldon Johnson, W. E. B. Du Bois, Walter White, and other eminent Negroes. Raper concluded that the level of rural black education was so low, even compared with white rural schools, "as to leave one with the feeling that it is incorrect usage of language to write public education without quotation marks."[12]

Father Divine's youth was surely a study in frustration, if only for the fact that his creative and questioning mind could scarcely have found encouragement, let alone fulfillment, in the primitive Black Belt schools. Later, after he had reached fame as a religious leader, some ghetto dwellers who claimed to have known him in the South "reminisced" that he had early left school, in protest against its Jim Crow biases.[13] Whether or not true, it is consistent with all that is known of his behavior in every stage of his life. Even had he attended school, though, he would have learned little more than the bitterness of blocked ambition that inevitably overtook the "talented tenth" stranded in the Black Belt.

In the absence of opportunities for education, occupational advancement, or political participation, Divine — like the vast majority of south-

ern rural Negroes — poured his talent and energy into religion. Little of his
leadership ability surfaced in these early years. Rather, this was a stage
of quiet observation. His was an intensely impressionable nature that felt
wonderment at the pomp and exuberance of the black church service. He
took in the aura of piety, the passion of the worship, and above all the
preacher's art.[14]

Black preaching gave form to the emotionalism of the worship by root-
ing it in vivid biblical imagery. Addressing an audience of scant education and generally possessing only slightly more learning himself, the
preacher found alternative, often highly innovative ways to get his message across. Role identification became a high art among these preachers.
No character in the Scriptures, God included, was so remote as to be
beyond the ability of a first-rate preacher to act out. Urban middle-class
congregations, black as well as white, might scoff that such practices were
naive or even blasphemous, but a sermon that embraced the Bible with
such personal intensity could produce a powerful effect on its listeners.
Such use of dramatic license was, moreover, expected by the Black Belt
congregations, as Henry Mitchell notes: "The Black preacher who is so
'siddity' [sedate or overly proper] as to preach always in the third person
is clearly not Black culture — and not effective."[15]

Lacking the vocabulary and formal theological training to fashion complex commentaries, the black preacher often compensated by creating,
ex nihilo, new words to express unfamiliar concepts and convey the right
"sound" to his audiences.[16] A particularly creative preacher might turn
a meager vocabulary, equivalent to a few loaves and fishes, into a richly
textured feast of old, new, and modified words for an eager multitude
of parishioners. Such word invention did not please everyone. Black
ministers who had overcome all handicaps to gain a solid education in
letters and theology often found the ramblings of their less learned colleagues a deep embarrassment. Thus Daniel Payne, a distinguished Methodist pastor active in improving educational resources for blacks, lamented
one rural preacher's efforts at a sermon: "Brother Baker preached in his
usual vague and indefinite manner. This brother, I believe, is a good man
and means to do well, but he is one of the most unintelligible preachers
I have ever heard. He makes use of words which cannot be found in any
language under the sun."[17]

Certainly the lack of formal training was not, as so many ignorant
pastors defensively boasted, a sign that separated those with genuine grace
from the "unconverted" clergy tied to mere "book larnin'." Yet some un-
tutored preachers were truly gifted orators who developed a resourcefulness in conveying insights to a degree seldom demanded of men with a
conventional education. Such ministers found that within the informal

and intensely responsive black congregation, there existed ample ways to communicate a vivid understanding of moral principles, biblical narrative, and daily life.

An effective preacher did much more than inform; he induced or at least encouraged outcries of piety such as the old revivalists would have envied. A Black Belt service almost always ended in a crescendo of emotion. Worshipers — mostly women — flung themselves into the aisles, some shrieking, others "possessed" by the spirit in carefully stylized motions, and all bursting with hallelujahs proclaiming their faith in Jesus.[18]

While Father Divine later absorbed many new religious experiences, he always retained the basic style and technique of the incomparably inventive Black Belt preachers. He imbibed their informal and emotional approach to religion, their role playing and ability to speak of God unselfconsciously in the first person, their creation of new words in sermons, and their manipulation of an audience to "feel" the Lord's salvation. Most important, Divine felt a sense of the liberating power that the church held for even the most downtrodden of God's children. Although a web of pressures forced the Black Belt churches to confine that power to cathartic worship, it was a malleable force, waiting only for circumstances and leaders to turn it outward in social protest. Father Divine in these early years could not yet crystallize the full possibilities for turning religious values against Jim Crow and oppression generally. Yet he nursed indignation against injustice with the same fervor that he prayed for God's saving power, as he stood in the emotional shelter of the black church.

Heaven on Sundays, for a few brief hours, amid an endless purgatory of debt, dependence, and despair — this was the rural Negro's lot. Few, very few, individuals long retained initiative or independence under such a routine of grinding labor and racial subservience. Yet those who somehow resisted the debilitating effects of their environment often developed a strength of will no subsequent adversity could overcome. The youth who later called himself Father Divine was among these rare resilient individuals. He needed only to escape his immediate, static setting for his leadership qualities to emerge. When this happened, he galvanized whole southern communities and attracted both devotion and danger.

New Ventures

Father Divine left his home as a young man and assisted various itinerant preachers as he made his way north to relative freedom. The search for a new life through evangelism was common among ambitious Negroes, who had few other possibilities open to them. Chancellor Williams, in a fictional but penetrating account of Negro rural life and religion, describes the impact of monotonous tenant farm existence on a restless "cropper":

Nine children in a three-room shack that threatened to collapse at every heavy footstep. Grits for breakfast. Grits for lunch, when there was lunch. Grits and cabbage soup for dinner. . . . Brother Jackson had made good his escape from this maelstrom of poverty when he suddenly decided that God had "called" him to preach. More than that, God had directed him to carry the gospel from place to place as a traveling evangelist — safely away from Sister Jackson and the nine ragged children. Safely away from the collapsing shack and the eternity of hominy grits and cabbage soup. That was some years ago. Apparently God told him to keep on going. He had not been heard from since.[19]

Divine was just beginning to be heard from. His obscure origins began to clear around the time he moved north. He was then in his late teens or early twenties and his past evangelical missions were only dimly known. "But in 1899, beyond all question," St. Clair McKelway and A. J. Liebling observe in their fine study of his rise, "he was a man named George Baker and was earning an honest living in Baltimore, mostly by clipping hedges and mowing lawns." Divine much later confirmed the outlines of this chronology, recalling that "in the early days" he was residing in Baltimore, "from a personal point of view."[20]

The new arrival to Baltimore brought with him an old interest in religion. He taught Sunday school in the black Baptist church on Eden Street and, like others at the church's prayer meetings on Wednesday evenings, he sometimes rose to give informal sermons. He spoke about God's omnipresence, a formidable idea that he confronted with formidable words of his own devising: "God is not only personified and materialized. He is repersonified and rematerialized. He rematerializes and He rematerialates. He repersonificates and He repersonifitizes."[21] These speeches insouciantly trampled — and retrampled — linguistic niceties, yet they conveyed his deep conviction that the pious must seek God in all things, not simply in a remote "Heaven." Baker quickly gained favor with his fellow congregants, who shouted encouraging amens and "Brother, ain't it so!" throughout his messages.

Unlike some charismatic preachers, Baker projected a commanding aura that owed little to physical stature. His unusually broad shoulders and chest rested on an exceedingly diminutive frame, and he seemed to most observers scarcely five feet tall. Yet as an exhorter he displayed a compelling, lilting voice, an impressive command of the Bible, and an evident flair in improvising sermons. Add to this a gaze that could be at once beatific and hypnotic, and one can see a man who — even at this early stage of life—was able to enrapture audiences, while he shared his sense of God's awesome presence in the world.

In Baltimore Divine enjoyed—possibly for the first time—the security of a steady job and approving, even admiring neighbors. Yet this period of tranquility did not last long. He suddenly felt compelled to resume his evangelical travels, forsaking the stability only recently achieved. Some religious figures are known to have begun their ministry after some transfiguring experience; Divine (then Baker) had three, all within a brief period, and all relating to corruption of social or religious standards.

The first of these transforming episodes quickened Baker's revulsion toward moral decay in the churches. A sudden influx of beggars marched through the Negro quarter of Baltimore and sang mournful spirituals as they asked for money at each window. This seemed to Divine to be "blaspheming God." The beggars "were grafting after money on every side and they were trying to sell the body of God in my consideration—even the spirit thereof."[22]

The beggars' activity provoked Baker to reflect on the gimmickry of fund raising in the churches generally, and further strained his tolerance of existing conditions. He concluded that "speculation" was sanctioned

> all the way from the bishops of the churches down to the Sunday School teachers . . . taking a little child to the church and as soon as he entered the door a card was given him to beg. It was not according to the life and teachings of the Christ. Therefore, I said within myself, "I will go forth and prove to the people that the Gospel can be preached without money and without price!"[23]

The rise of Jim Crow laws around the turn of the century exerted a second and probably still greater challenge to Baker's values. These efforts to legalize the prejudice against Negroes drastically reduced their political and social rights in all the southern states. "That," the evangelist later recalled, "stirred me to the depths."[24]

Finally, the otherworldly sermons that issued from the black churches in Baltimore struck Baker as a perversion of human hopes. The object of religion, he believed, should be to keep people from sin, not from valuing their lives on earth. He concluded, "I will go forth and prove to the people—the world at large—that Christ died that we might live."[25]

The three convictions together—of the need for probity in the church, for racial tolerance, and for a present-centered religious faith—produced a sudden welling up of idealistic passion within George Baker. He knew he had to bring his truths to a wider audience at any personal cost. Yet, unlike such biblical prophets as Jeremiah and Jonah, who dreaded their perceived responsibilities, Baker found the prospect of a crusade for righteousness wholly exhilarating:

I jumped around like someone enthusiastically insane, saying, I will go South and prove to the world the Gospel can be preached without money and without price! . . . I also said, I will go South and break down the wall or partition if it cost my life; the wall or partition between the sect, the creed, and denominations of every sort, and also races, nationalities and colors, and let there be no division among them, for it is written, "Love ye one another!"[26]

Did George Baker in fact challenge the "partition" of color in the South? Details on his early life are sparse, but it is known that he once offended white authorities to the point of incurring a sentence of hard labor on a chain gang in Savannah. The exact circumstances of this episode remain a mystery, though several Harlem residents who claimed to have known Baker in Baltimore and in the South insisted that his arrest came at the close of the nineteenth century, while he was preaching under the name "the Son of Righteousness."[27] Given Baker's usually great respect for law, it is at least plausible that his punishment resulted from some breach of racial etiquette, such as preaching to interracial crowds or stirring black hopes for a better life on earth. Baker himself much later recalled, somewhat cryptically, that he had submitted his body as a human sacrifice on thirty-two occasions when the Jim Crow laws came out in the South.[28] Even if one diminishes this recollection by a factor of thirty-two, it suggests that his early missionizing activity may have been fraught with social conscience as well as spiritual consciousness.

Such challenge as Baker made to Jim Crow resulted in something of a standoff. The South continued to enforce its segregated social patterns. Much more surprisingly, Baker also continued living, despite the high risk of martyrdom through lynching or prolonged labor on a road gang. Some time in the early 1900s Baker returned to the simple pleasures of hedge cutting in Baltimore, at which vocation he remained quietly occupied for several years. Given his mercurial nature, though, it was only a matter of time before some new experience moved him again to challenge the complacency in his native region. This time revelation came in the form of two religious seekers. Their teachings brought Baker to a radically new understanding of divine power, human nature, and his own saving mission.

Baker encountered both of these self-ordained men of God in 1906. One was John Hickerson, who preferred the appellation "Reverend St. John Divine Bishop" and who had earlier affiliated with numerous religious cult movements. The other was a luckless preacher named Samuel Morris. He had a special talent for provoking congregations to expel him bodily from their church services, by attempting to enlighten them as to his divinity, at the most inopportune moments.

Morris was filled with an extra measure of the fundamentalist piety common in the rural South. He had moved to Allegheny City, Pennsylvania, at the time he discovered a key phrase in 1 Corinthians, third chapter. "Know ye not that ye are the temple of God, and that the spirit of God dwelleth in you?" Morris read, transfixed by the staggering import. Morris was God, the biblical text made abundantly plain. He set out for the Negro churches of Baltimore, where he determined to spring his theological surprise on the unsuspecting parishioners. In one church after another Morris went to the podium and, without warning, spread his arms wide and shouted, "I am the Father Eternal!" The congregants' reaction revealed that even fundamentalist literalism had its limits. Each time Morris reported the good news of his omnipotence, he would find himself suddenly in the street, never to return to that particular church. On one occasion he was helped to his feet by a lone believer, the young Baker, who invited him to his home in a boarding house run by a woman evangelist named Anna Snowden. Baker and Snowden became disciples of Morris, helped him obtain a job driving a wagon, and held several weekly prayer meetings for ten or twenty people.

Morris soon took to referring to himself as "Father Jehovia," while Baker, in keeping with his role as a harbinger for Morris, adopted the title "the Messenger." Morris himself explained the hierarchy thus implied: he was God in the Fathership degree, while his Messenger, Baker, held a similar status in the Sonship degree. For all this arrogation of divinity, the two caused little stir in Baltimore. Both men carried to extremes an established tradition among rural blacks—the intense identification with words of Scripture. Balancing their excess, however, they remained within a carefully confined circle of sympathizers while continuing to earn money in conventional ways and, in all other respects, leading lawful and conservative lives. They therefore escaped the unfriendly attention of both the government authorities and the residents at large.

What did Baker see in the work of Morris, whose extravagant claims had previously garnered only contempt from whole congregations? The young Baker was seeking a foundation for his belief in human worth regardless of race or social origin. Here now was Morris, announcing in the spiritual realm the end of artificial barriers and divisions among those yearning for God. One needed no special ritual, no exclusive institution, no external sign, for the Bible had explicitly stated that "the spirit of God dwelleth in you." For Baker, ardently pious and still at a highly impressionable age, this idea may have deepened both his belief in God's immanence and his sense of religion as an egalitarian force.

The influence of John Hickerson precipitated Baker's independent activity as "the Messenger." Hickerson was a veteran of religious movements like Pentecostal Holiness, Holy Rolling, Elder Robinson's Live Ever,

Die Never Church in Boston, and others. He, too, became a disciple of Morris but eventually objected to the latter's insistence on holding a higher status of divinity than that of his disciples. Morris may have assumed that the verse in 1 Corinthians had particular relevance to him as its "discoverer," but as Hickerson reasoned, every person contained equally the light of God within his soul. After Hickerson's democratization of divinity, the triumvirate's days together were numbered. In 1912 Baker and Hickerson each left Morris to preach on their own. Hickerson established the Church of the Living God in New York City, while Baker once more headed south, without disclosing his exact plans to anyone.[29]

"The Messenger" preached his way down to Georgia, reaching the town of Valdosta in 1914. There he exerted a magnetic effect on Negro churchgoers, especially the women, who started to desert their husbands and pastors for the sake of the Lord. He also apparently took Hickerson's teachings to heart, for he no longer confined himself to the "Sonship" degree of divinity. The Messenger was soon arrested as a troublemaker and the writ against him listed his identity as "John Doe, alias God."[30] This foreshadowed similar pretensions, on a far grander stage, two decades later; for the while, though, the Messenger was essentially reenacting the Passion of Samuel Morris in Baltimore's Negro churches.

While in the Valdosta jail the Messenger received a call from a writer on philosophy and metaphysics, J. R. Moseley. Moseley was visiting a professor in Valdosta when his curiosity was excited by rumors of a man claiming to be God. More intent to question than condemn — which made him a rare figure in Valdosta, among other towns — Moseley found himself engaged in animated discussion with the "bright-faced" prisoner. Moseley asked him if he was not denying his name and history and identity that he might make God all and in all. The prisoner replied, "You understand me better than anyone else." When Moseley offered his services, the prisoner explained that he did not accept money, but that he would be glad to have bread to share with his fellow inmates.[31]

The Messenger soon came to trial. His chief accusers were two Negro pastors resentful of his influence on their congregations. They asserted that the several dozen people who followed this intruding preacher believed him to be God and that he encouraged this belief. Therefore, the two pastors testified, the defendant was insane as well as a public nuisance. It appeared that this stranger in Valdosta would either be returned to jail or, worse, committed to an asylum. Instead he was saved by the first of many brilliant lawyers involved in his long career, a man named J. B. Copeland, who took the case as a favor to his friend J. R. Moseley.[32]

Copeland elicited testimony from each of the two pastors, one a Methodist, the other a Holy Roller, suggesting that anyone who believed in the creed of the other was clearly crazy. "Gentlemen," Copeland summarized to the jury, "the two principal witnesses against the defendant have testified that they considered each other to be of unsound mind, because of the same religious prejudice which is the basis of the present complaint." The jury members were much amused and moved to leniency, though the cases of wives who followed the Messenger while ignoring their families could not be altogether brushed aside. The jurors gave as their verdict that the young evangelist was indeed of "unsound mind," but not so much so as to be handed over to the Georgia State Sanitorium. The court accepted the jury's recommendation that he be turned loose on condition that he leave Georgia immediately.

Among the personal belongings returned to the reprieved man were a news clipping stating that he had served sixty days on a chain gang in Savannah and another clipping about the wreck of a car of prison inspectors. In the margin of this second article someone had written, "Be sure your sins will find you out."[33] This sentiment coincides with the preachings of Father Divine twenty years later, which spoke of retribution at work in every car crash and other misfortune.

Attorney Copeland talked with the Messenger just before his release and departure from Valdosta. "I remember," Copeland related, "that there was about the man an unmistakable quiet power that manifested itself to anyone who came in contact with him. He told me that he tried to do God's will and that he was not conscious of doing anything contrary to God's will, and that he thought that to the extent that he could identify himself with God, he was God."[34]

The newly freed defendant did not take long to attract further intolerance. His preaching offended some residents in another Georgia town and he was placed in a state mental institution. It may have been this otherwise unexplained incident, rather than the Valdosta trial, which Father Divine referred to during the 1930s: "many years ago, I was called in question among great ministers and bishops, etc., who desired to hold me for insanity."[35] He persuaded the warden there to write to J. R. Moseley, who vouched for the young preacher's good character and emotional health.[36] The Messenger was released a few days later, upon complying with the asylum's regulation that he first give a "human" name. He chose John, whether in reference to some long-discarded identity, a scriptural personage, or simply an ironical abbreviation of his legal appellation in Valdosta: "John Doe, alias God."

After stopping in Macon to pay a courtesy call upon his benefactor, Moseley, the Messenger at last journeyed north once more, in belated recognition that his future in Georgia and the South generally held little promise. On the way he gathered a few loyal disciples as he preached on street corners and occasionally in Negro churches. Around 1915 the Messenger arrived in New York City, then well toward becoming the center of Afro-American culture and religious life.

The spiritual and social world into which he entered was in the midst of a rapid transformation. An influx of southern black farmers into the northern cities was greatly adding to the populations of all the major ghettos. The migrants were people much like the Messenger, accustomed to stringent living standards and lacking in formal education. They were experienced in coping with a racist environment, but now hoped to escape its worst features by chancing the unknown rigors of the large urban centers.

The major northward push of the Negro population started around 1915 and continued at a high rate in succeeding years. A series of bad agricultural seasons, exacerbated by boll weevil plagues, heightened the pressures for migration. These people also were encouraged by the rising northern need for industrial workers when the world war drastically reduced European immigration.

These demographic changes brought a spectacular rise in the number of urban Negro churches, as the migrants relied heavily upon religion to help ease the transition to a foreign environment. New York City provides perhaps the most dramatic example of this trend. In 1865 the city contained only thirteen black churches, a number which slowly increased until the main period of migration, when it skyrocketed to approximately 200 by the 1920s.[37]

Many of the new churches were simple renovations of vacated storefronts, created by recent urban arrivals who found the ghetto's established churches too formal and socially aloof. Typically these churches featured highly emotional worship and close social ties similar to those the congregants had left behind in the rural South. Often they also emphasized some special point of doctrine (the importance of the Holy Ghost) or ritual (adult baptism) to impart a distinctive aura of holiness to their members.

The popularity of the storefront churches also stemmed from the fact that it was fairly simple to establish such an institution. In his classic novel of black lower-class religion, *Go Tell It on the Mountain,* James Baldwin depicts the genesis of a typical prayer house:

> It was a storefront church and had stood, for John's lifetime, on the corner of this sinful avenue. . . . The saints, arriving, had rented this abandoned store and taken out the fixtures; had painted the walls and built a pulpit, moved in a piano and camp chairs, and bought the biggest Bible they could find. They put white curtains in the show window, and painted across this window TEMPLE OF THE FIRE BAPTIZED. Then they were ready to do the Lord's work.[38]

These alternative religious movements tailored their spiritual message to the needs of the most disadvantaged ghetto residents. Seth Scheiner writes that their preachers told of "a personal God who looked upon the masses as His favored people. Holiness churches, in particular, maintain that they are the descendants of the ordinary people Jesus lived among, thereby giving their lower-class members a sense of importance in a society that told them they were nothing."[39] These groups substituted "spiritual upward mobility," as Norvel Glenn terms their otherworldly approach, for the upward occupational and economic mobility that seemed wholly beyond their reach.[40]

The formal qualifications of those who ministered to the storefront churches were often marginal. Thirty-eight percent of all urban black clergymen in 1926 had college or seminary degrees, less than half the ratio of urban white Protestant clergymen with comparable training.[41] Most of these certified ministers naturally chose to serve the larger, wealthier churches and leave the storefronts to ignorant preachers. Nevertheless, this seemed a scant drawback, if at all, to most storefront congregants, who found new opportunities in these churches for religious and social self-expression. Despite the plethora of exotic names and doctrines these sects propounded, considerations of theology were decidedly less important than the atmosphere of the service and the personal qualities of the church leader.

The personal factor was especially vital in the case of the black cults, in which the worship of storefront congregations centered on charismatic ministers. The cult leader typically presented himself as a unique surrogate for God and, as such, inspired frenzied displays of piety unmatched even by other storefront churches. His extraordinary authority also provided a sense of order and guidance for many uprooted people who found the impersonal environment of the city its most demoralizing quality.

Cults in the ghetto encompassed a wide range of religious faiths and forms, from Islam to Judaism, but the predominant type embraced evangelical Christianity as vital to the Afro-American cultural heritage. These cults sought to restore to black worship the emotional power that characterized religion in the Black Belt but had become attenuated in the ghetto's conventional churches. Most such cults minimized overt racial considerations in their quest for religious ecstasy. Several of the largest included some white members, a situation not unknown among black Pentecostal and Holiness movements that influenced Negro religion in the rural South.

There was considerable overlapping in church and cult membership, for even the faithful churchgoer might seek additional inspiration in the intense services of the cults. Miles Mark Fisher, a Baptist pastor in the 1930s, recalled: "[O]ne of my earliest Sunday school teachers was indeed a cult member but was buried as an outstanding [church] member, the superintendent of the primary department of the Sunday school of a Chicago church. I remember her demise several years ago and how the 'saints' virtually took charge of her body."[42] The cults deliberately exploited the opportunity to attract regular church members by holding their services on Sundays until long after Baptist and Methodist worship had ended. The cults also held meetings during the week when the churches had no services.

A student of the black cults, Joseph Washington, writes that they represented a yearning for black power among people who found no other recourses open to them.[43] His thesis might be extended further still, to note that this was not exclusively a racial phenomenon even among groups of entirely black membership. It is scarcely a coincidence that the cults were populated overwhelmingly by the poorest, least educated, and least socially accepted elements within ghetto society. These people craved black power, but also economic power, and most basically the power to command a measure of dignity among others of whatever race. The cults reflected, in short, a cry of the spirit against all forms of outward oppression and inward insecurity.

In 1915 the peripatetic Messenger was a decidedly minor cult figure. He presided over a handful of faithful adherents while standing aloof from the burning issues and major personalities of the day. Civil rights groups like the recently formed National Association for the Advancement of Colored People apparently failed to attract his notice, let alone commitment. Not even the appearance later in the decade of the charismatic West Indian Marcus Garvey, who trumpeted a dawn of black liberation and swept many ghetto dwellers into his movement, induced the Messenger to enlist in further crusades. He was a man clearly intent on a respite from the turbulence and danger that marked his past.

The Messenger's new-found prudence represented an accommodation not only with white racism but also with the conservative mainstream of Negro religious values. Even during the early 1900s some black churches in every major denomination favored a "Social Gospel" that closely linked religion with community action for reform. But most ghetto churches, hindered by a plenitude of financial weaknesses and a shortage of trained ministers, tended to avoid bold social initiatives. The rise of secular agencies for social uplift in the early twentieth century further spurred black clergymen to confine their own interests chiefly to otherworldly redemption.[44] A pastor who publicly challenged these priorities might risk censure and ostracism by his colleagues and possibly by his congregation as well.

The formidable difficulties facing ministers who pressed a combination of religion and social activism are evident in the career of Adam Clayton

Powell, Sr., a contemporary of the Messenger and perhaps the foremost black Baptist pastor in New York. Powell suffered the sharpest setback in his generally distinguished ministry when, in 1918, he unwittingly tested the force of conservative sentiment in the Negro church. As pastor of Harlem's large Abyssinian Baptist congregation, Powell had just helped secure a pledge by white Baptist leaders to donate a badly needed community house for his neighborhood. At the time he viewed this as one of the happiest achievements of his ministry, but when he and several associates buoyantly announced the news to a Baptist ministers' conference in Harlem, the reaction was far from anticipated:

> I expected that we would be canonized as saints, heroes and benefactors but, believe it or not, we were cannonaded. . . . After one brother had delivered a fifteen minute tirade against the community house idea, he asked, "What are a community house, anyway?" I answered, "A center where the people of a community can have their bodies, minds and souls improved." "That's what I thought," he said. "We don't want nothin' like that. We want a place where folks can git religion."

More than ninety of the approximately one hundred ministers at this meeting voted to reject the offer of the community center. Powell was so shaken by the reaction of his brethren in the ministry that "for eleven years I never made another effort to lead except in the Abyssinian parish."[45]

However discouraging these conservative influences were to Powell, they were vastly more intimidating to an anonymous and weary arrival to the ghetto like the Messenger. Lacking Powell's institutional base and reputation, he could hardly be more unyielding to the religious trends of the day. He therefore avoided public controversy on matters of race and suppressed his once great hopes of reforming society. The Messenger had already tilted against prejudice and injustice many times to his detriment. He now longed for the quiet joys of spiritual wisdom and serenity.

For the chastened evangelist, this was a period of creative withdrawal — a time to study the Afro-American evangelical world, with its dozens of creeds and exotic leaders. He took careful note of the varied preachers who arose and often as quickly disappeared after proclaiming a new variant of the "only truth." He learned what made some well-meaning and personally forceful ministers fail to sustain a following and how certain others, seemingly without special ability, continued to enjoy crowds of disciples. He came to understand, in brief, the technique as well as the theology behind successful religious leadership.

The Messenger surely found many negative lessons in the leadership of his old colleague John Hickerson.[46] The self-styled Reverend St. John Divine Bishop was in New York City, still preaching his doctrine of God-in-every-man. Hickerson was an enterprising theologian with a talent for exotic touches in costume and conduct. He also displayed a dynamic speaking style, which his tall, commanding presence made even more effective. Yet Hickerson had little notion of how to organize and maintain control over his congregation. The doctrine that each man contained the spirit of God was fine in theory, but in practice it led straight to anarchy. Many in Hickerson's flock, unbalanced by the heady notion of their own divinity, arrogantly accosted neighbors in other religious groups and denounced or even threatened them. Hickerson's pleas for restraint accomplished little. His nominal followers ignored his wishes because he was — as he had once told Samuel Morris — no more worthy or wise than anyone else, for all shared the infinite spirit. It was, in short, a sad case of each church member wanting to be a god and none a worshipper. The result was the steady deterioration of the congregation.

The Messenger learned from Hickerson's folly. He still talked of the divine spirit in universal terms but left no doubt as to who was first among angels. In order to guard his authority, still in its fledgling stages, he took care to keep his old colleague from unduly influencing his followers. McKelway and Liebling describe the Messenger's cautious approach to his renewed acquaintanceship with Hickerson:

> He was interested, as a member of the evangelistic guild, in what St. John Divine Bishop had done, and he sometimes invited his old friend to come to his flat around the corner, eat a meal, and talk about his organization. But he never brought his own disciples to St. John Divine Bishop's church. . . . He had grown rather secretive and did not talk much with St. John Divine Bishop about the Bible. He talked to him mostly about the financial side of the Church of the Living God.[47]

The Messenger soon after moved his flock to Brooklyn, perhaps to insulate it further from untoward outside influences. There the disciples led a secure, if simple, existence. They lived in one house and pooled their modest wages. Their ascetic religious conduct stretched their common funds considerably, for they abstained from liquor, tobacco, and most other pleasures beyond the freely shared ecstasies of religious communion. The Messenger held no job other than as spiritual leader, but he skillfully directed the economic organization of his commune. He obtained employment for many by placing and answering want ads. Those who had no jobs were assigned tasks in the common home, cooking or cleaning. A seamstress among the followers altered second-hand clothes at great savings for all in the movement. This simple life appeared wholly satisfying to persons whose primary concern was the bliss that the Messenger's spiritual tutelage brought them.[48]

By 1919 the Messenger was ready for yet another change or, rather, series of changes. First he purchased a new, spacious home in the all-white community of Sayville, Long Island. Racism, in a rare gesture to a bitter foe, enabled him to make this move when a townsman decided to spite a disagreeable neighbor by selling his home to a Negro buyer. He inserted the word "colored" in advertisements in various New York papers, and the Messenger sprang at the opportunity.[49]

A second change in his life was to formalize a partnership with a woman disciple named Pinninnah. While the evangelist had long advocated a chaste life, he found in Pinninnah a valuable assistant and loyal admirer, someone who affirmed his own sense of special purpose. Somewhat older than the Messenger and at least a head taller, she nevertheless played a relatively passive, subservient role in their relationship. By some accounts, Pinninnah was a veteran from the days spent evangelizing in the South; others held that she was a more recent follower from Newark.[50] In any case, by 1919 the Messenger and Pinninnah were commonly recognized as husband and wife. Moreover, her name appeared with his on the deed of sale for the Sayville residence. This signified the evangelist's public recognition of her importance in his career and also, perhaps, reflected her financial contribution to the purchase. Even with their combined savings, he could pay cash on only $700 of the $2,500 purchase price. It was one of the last times he entered into debt for any cause. On this occasion it was a wise investment in a future of middle-class security and respectability, far beyond the social horizons of his earliest years.

At this juncture "the Messenger," having apparently fulfilled his mission, disappeared in favor of a new symbolic identity. His signature on the deed of sale was "Major J. Devine," an incarnation that perhaps owed something to the popularity of military titles in the wake of the world war.[51] Shortly thereafter he discovered that his faulty orthography was interfering with the spiritual aspect of his desired image and changed his name from Devine to Divine. He also saw fit to call himself "Reverend," while receiving from his disciples the still more honorific title of "Father."

Ever on the move geographically and psychologically since his youth, this newcomer to the joys of suburban middle-class life was still seeking his niche; the rebirths as George Baker, the Messenger, and finally Reverend (or Father) Major J. Divine marked the main phases of his development. As George Baker, he lived as a common man, earning a respectable living and fitting comfortably within lower-middle-class Negro society. As the Messenger, he brought the wondrous tidings of God's presence in every man, until a succession of rebuffs returned him to an outwardly conservative tack. Growing in practical wisdom and religious insight, he prepared to assume two identities at once. To the outside world he was known only as a quiet, upright member of the community; to his inner circle of disciples, as the embodiment of the divine spirit. His reincarnation as Major J. Divine, combining the patriotic and the celestial, thus signified his new and quite successful dual life.

Sayville

The first decade of Divine's residence in Sayville marked a continuation, indeed a heightening, of his creative withdrawal from the bustling evangelical life of earlier years. The setbacks in Georgia had taken their toll, as he later implied in describing his new, wary view:

> I decided I did not desire to run in collision with the other versions of God, and other religions . . . so when I moved out on Long Island, I said, "I do not want anything out here in Sayville, but my own unadulterated mind and my own spirit, and my own life and my own unadulterated love," hence we remained out there, and I decided to give practical service to humanity. . . .[52]

This practical service still took the form chiefly of spiritual guidance — Divine at this stage in his career scarcely distinguished the two. Yet except for the instruction he gave to a few veteran disciples, Divine taught only indirectly, by distributing copies of religious writings that he had found of value. He effectively eliminated controversy over his preaching, for he let the various authors convey his basic spiritual beliefs while he remained in near anonymity.

Divine during this time particularly favored the writings of Robert Collier, Jiddu Krishnamurti, and other fashionable exponents of "New Thought."[53] His deep interest in these esoteric, often mystical volumes may have been partly a matter of insatiable curiosity about all matters religious — a heritage of his restless temperament and evangelical upbringing. Yet the popularity during the 1920s of writings that stressed individualism and positive thinking may also have done much to shape Divine's religious focus. From Bruce Barton's best-selling depiction of Jesus as a successful businessman in *The Man Nobody Knows* to Robert Collier's widely sampled advice for converting faith into prosperity, the religious temper of this age was intently earth-bound and optimistic. While Christian Science involved a rejection of materialism, many saw in it, as in New Thought, the key to success, health, and happiness on earth through contact with the divine spirit. Father Divine had every reason to find value in these tracts. In view of his own rise from sharecropper's origins to middle-class status through initiative and faith, the tenets of "practical religion" coincided perfectly with his experience. Divine never surrendered his evangelical religious style; within his home he and his followers regularly held emotional, stirring services that recalled their rural southern roots. Yet on this framework Divine was adding a theology of present-centered hope suited to the successful middle class and those who wished to join it.

In keeping with his desire to avoid offense, Divine became a model of suburban conservatism. McKelway and Liebling write that he kept his spacious, eight-room house immaculate at all times. "[Neighbors] used to see him doing odd jobs around his yard in his spare time, pruning the shrubbery, cutting the grass, and tidying up the places where the former owner had allowed rubbish to accumulate."[54] Those who often shared his residence appeared to be laudable, quiet people. They were Negroes who, like Divine, escaped any racial animus by maintaining a nearly invisible profile. They worked during the day and joined him at night or at least on Sundays for religious singing that kept an acceptable level and concluded early each evening.

With boundless initiative and an ingratiating manner, Divine obtained jobs for nearly all his followers as domestic servants for residents of Sayville and nearby suburbs. This greatly reduced the cost of commuting, which had been a considerable expense to the communal budget. Yet Divine continued to stress the value of thrift to his disciples. He set an austere example of frugality, for he was determined to sacrifice every luxury for the sake of future economic independence. In later years he recalled with obvious pride how he had taken pains to conserve funds in even the smallest actions, as in his travels between Sayville and New York: "I would not stop at a restaurant and get a luncheon for fifty or seventy-five cents, or for whatsoever I could have gotten one at that time; I would suck an orange . . . paving out the way for the comfort and convenience we are now enjoying."[55]

The parsimony which Divine and his followers displayed in their daily routines soon enabled them to pay off their debts and even to accumulate savings. He channeled part of this money into projects to accommodate and attract new disciples. He added extra wings to the Sayville home and began providing hearty banquets weekly, without charge and open to all. These repasts actually were quite inexpensive, but they built a reputation for Divine outside Sayville as a munificent religious leader who actually gave to followers rather than soliciting from them.

By the latter part of the decade the gatherings at Father Divine's home at 72 Macon Street gradually increased both in stature and numbers. Most of the new converts were also Negro domestic servants, but they worked for well-to-do residents and hotel managers of Suffolk and Nassau counties. Compared with earlier-recruited disciples, they were people "of some means, who earned sometimes as much as $100 a month, slept and ate in their employers' houses, and had bank accounts and insurance policies."[56] Most surrendered their wages and entire savings to the communal revenues.

Divine's reputation and personal magnetism were sufficiently great to attract occasional white converts to his growing communal movement. This was a rarity in American society, where religious activities were almost wholly segregated. The first white member of the movement joined in 1926,[57] and while only a few others entered over the next three years, their relative affluence and education made them especially valued disciples. They, in turn, were impressed by Divine's spiritual knowledge and demeanor, as well as by the idealism his other followers demonstrated — living chaste, upright lives and dedicated to the brotherhood of all mankind. The white converts mingled easily, even willingly, with the more numerous black adherents to Divine's movement, and proved as completely devoted to his leadership.

By the end of the decade, then, Divine's life formed a classic American success story, distinguished all the more by the handicap of his racial and social origins. Starting from a sharecropper's small plot of ground and equally small horizons, he had discovered opportunities for advancement and seized them all — northward migration, diligence at many vocations, self-education, and energetic preaching of a gospel thoroughly American in exalting individual worth. Divine culminated these strivings by grasping the chance for middle-class comfort and respectability in a neighborhood once barred to people of his color. He expanded his religious movement, careful never to upset the good will of his neighbors and confining his spiritual activities to the privacy of his home. Indeed, for ten years after purchasing his Sayville property, Divine appeared content simply to consolidate and enjoy his arrival into bourgeois society.

Yet one suspects that for an individual of Divine's volatile temperament and uncanny ability to rouse others, these halcyon days were not meant to last. He would eventually have sought a greater challenge for his energies, even had no sudden opportunity appeared for the purpose. As it happened, circumstance made the first overture, to which Divine responded with increasing vigor and imagination. The onset of the Great Depression in 1929 collapsed the ambitions of many Americans, but it made Divine's "practical religion" a widely desired commodity and spurred him to greater activity as preacher, philanthropist, and reformer. The period of creative withdrawal and consolidation gave way to a new phase of whirlwind evangelism and confrontation with the wider society. At the age of fifty Divine was still far from reaching the crest of his talents and achievements.

Notes to Chapter 1

1. Father Divine reportedly told Judge Lewis Smith in 1932, "I think I was born in Providence, R.I., and I think I am 55 years old." See *AA,* June 11, 1932, p. 1. St. Clair McKelway and A. J. Liebling, in "Who Is This King of Glory?" a three-part series in the *New Yorker* 12, pt. 1 (June 13, 1936):21, effectively cast doubt on the above quotation, however. They imply that a reporter inaccurately embellished Divine's words by failing to perceive his sense of irony. Divine had simply said, "Providence," referring not to a state in the Union but to a state of grace. A second quotation attributed to Father Divine and relating to his birth is in *SW,* Oct. 12, 1935, p. 9. It is the more reliable of the two statements because it appeared in a journal closely associated with Divine's ministry. To an interviewer who asked, "What is your age now, Father?" Divine replied: "I think they have the record around fifty-two. . . . They have it according to the records that were given from the legal transactions such as automobiles and such as that. That was necessary, years back, to give some reference humanly speaking, or from a legal standpoint. . . . We have spiritually and mentally in reality, no record."

2. The most ambitious efforts to trace Father Divine's earliest years are Robert Allerton Parker, *The Incredible Messiah: The Deification of Father Divine* (Boston: Little, Brown, 1937), pp. 78-107, and John Hoshor, *God in a Rolls-Royce: The Rise of Father Divine, Madman, Menace, or Messiah . . .* (New York: Hillman-Curl, 1936), pp. 30-34. The latter account contains several vivid and illuminating anecdotes not found in Parker's narrative, though these are of questionable reliability. On the period of Divine's young manhood, McKelway and Liebling, "Who Is This King of Glory?" pt. 1, pp. 21-28, offer an informal but penetrating account.

3. Maysfield's claims are reported in *NYAN,* Oct. 24, 1936, pp. 1, 7.

4. Sermon of June 16, 1935, in *SW,* June 22, 1935, p. 3.

5. Arthur F. Raper, *Preface to Peasantry: A Tale of Two Black Belt Counties* (Chapel Hill: University of North Carolina Press, 1936), offers a detailed and insightful depiction of this environment.

6. Ibid., p. 46.

7. Ibid., p. 53.

8. Charles S. Johnson, *Patterns of Negro Segregation* (New York: Harper and Bros., 1943), p. 143.

9. Ibid., p. 251.

10. Ibid., pp. 12, 19.

11. Raper, *Preface to Peasantry,* p. 313.

12. Ibid., pp. 334, 348.

13. Hoshor, *God in a Rolls-Royce,* p. 30.

14. Parker, *Incredible Messiah,* pp. 81-86, expands on this theme, detailing various alleged contacts that Father Divine, as a young man, had with Negroes claiming to be deliverers sent by the Lord. These leaders typically preached in fiery tones to the populace until suppressed by southern authorities.

15. Henry H. Mitchell, *Black Preaching* (Philadelphia: J. B. Lippincott, 1970), p. 169.

16. A revealing essay on the black preaching style, including ways of compensating for limits in formal education, is Hortense J. Spillers, "Martin Luther King and the Style of the Black Sermon," *Black Scholar* 3 (Sept., 1971):14-27. Spillers

emphasizes that even many educated black preachers retained much of the non-verbal technique honed by less learned rural pastors.

17. J. R. Coan, *Daniel Alexander Payne, Christian Educator* (Philadelphia: A.M.E. Book Concern, 1935), p. 60, cited by Harry V. Richardson, *Dark Salvation: The Story of Methodism as It Developed among Blacks in America* (New York: Doubleday, 1976), p. 181.

18. Raper, *Preface to Peasantry*, pp. 368-69, describes the emotional "arousements" overtaking a typical Black Belt service. For background on the role of worship in black communal life, see Harold A. Carter, *The Prayer Tradition of Black People* (Valley Forge, Pa.: Judson Press, 1976).

19. Chancellor Williams, *Have You Been to the River?* (New York: Exposition Press, 1952), p. 19.

20. McKelway and Liebling, "Who Is This King of Glory?" pt. 1, p. 21.

21. Sermon of Mar. 8, 1933, in *ND*, Dec. 9, 1978, p. 3.

22. Ibid.

23. Ibid.

24. Ibid.

25. Ibid.

26. Ibid.

27. Parker, *Incredible Messiah*, pp. 91-92.

28. Sermon of June 28, 1938, in *ND*, Mar. 8, 1980, p. 23.

29. The section on Samuel Morris and John Hickerson draws from material in McKelway and Liebling, "Who Is This King of Glory?" pt. 1, pp. 21-24.

30. Ibid., pp. 24-25.

31. J. R. Moseley, *Manifest Victory* (New York: Harper and Bros., 1941), pp. 106-7, relates the author's contact with the evangelist during the Valdosta trial. The quotation is on p. 107.

32. Ibid., p. 107.

33. McKelway and Liebling, "Who Is This King of Glory?" pt. 1, p. 25.

34. Ibid., pp. 25-26.

35. Sermon of Nov. 14, 1935, in *SW*, Nov. 23, 1935, p. 27.

36. Moseley, *Manifest Victory*, p. 107. Charles Samuel Braden, *These Also Believe: A Study of Modern American Cults and Minority Religious Movements* (New York: Macmillan, 1949), p. 8, relates that Moseley assured him, in correspondence, that the evangelist he encountered in Valdosta identified himself with God even at that early stage of his career. This is particularly notable because Moseley is the most reliable witness of those who claimed to know Divine both in the South and later in Harlem. Moseley, pp. 108-9, describes his meeting with the self-same evangelist two decades after the trial in Valdosta.

37. Seth M. Scheiner, "The Negro Church and the Northern City, 1890-1930," in *Seven on Black: Reflections on the Negro Experience in America*, ed. William G. Shade and Roy C. Herrenkohl (Philadelphia: J. B. Lippincott, 1969), p. 99. The number of black churches also increased rapidly in the nation as a whole. Benjamin E. Mays and Joseph W. Nicholson, *The Negro's Church* (New York: Institute of Social and Religious Research, 1933), p. 34, state that 189 of 609 urban churches examined by the authors originated between 1915 and 1930, as compared with only 16 of 185 rural churches studied (31 percent versus 9 percent). New York was thus in the forefront of a broad trend regarding the proliferation of black urban churches.

38. James Baldwin, *Go Tell It on the Mountain* (New York: Dial Press, 1963), p. 55.

39. Scheiner, "The Negro Church," p. 102.

40. Norvel Glenn, "Negro Religion and Negro Status in the United States," in *Religion, Culture and Society: A Reader in the Sociology of Religion,* ed. Louis Schneider (New York: John Wiley, 1964), p. 634.

41. See C. Luther Fry, *The U.S. Looks at Its Churches* (New York: Institute of Social and Religious Research, 1930), pp. 64, 66, and Scheiner, "The Negro Church," p. 107. See also the still lower estimates of formal training among Negro ministers in Mays and Nicholson, *The Negro's Church,* pp. 17, 41.

42. Miles Mark Fisher, "Organized Religion and the Cults," *Crisis* 44 (Jan. 1937):9.

43. Joseph Washington, *Black Sects and Cults: The Power Axis in an Ethnic Ethic* (New York: Doubleday, 1973), p. 13.

44. The decline of black urban churches as social institutions in the period 1890 to 1930 is insightfully and judiciously explored by Seth Scheiner, "The Negro Church," esp. pp. 98-109.

45. Adam Clayton Powell, Sr., *Against the Tide: An Autobiography* (New York: R. R. Smith, 1938), p. 209.

46. The section on Hickerson draws on material in McKelway and Liebling, "Who Is This King of Glory?" pt. 1, p. 26. Hickerson in later years looked enviously at his old associate's rise to fame. He complained that his contribution to Father Divine's career had been slighted: "I taught Divine all he knows about the God-within-man gospel. . . . I made that statement when I was staying at Divine's house in Baltimore, and Divine—he was only George Baker, a hedge-cutter, at that time, grabbed it and started out preaching that it had come to him from Heaven. It ain't right, if you know what I mean." Hickerson attributed his own discovery of the God-within-man idea not to Samuel Morris but to the Ethiopians, from whom he claimed descent. See *NYAN,* Nov. 23, 1932, p. 1.

47. McKelway and Liebling, "Who Is This King of Glory?" pt. 1, p. 26.

48. The financial organization of this fledgling commune is outlined in ibid., p. 28.

49. Ibid.

50. Ibid., states that Pinninnah was a resident of Newark; Banks, *The Black Church in the U.S.,* p. 59, describes her as a convert from the days at Valdosta. Father Divine himself frequently claimed to have married "Mother Divine" in 1882.

51. McKelway and Liebling, "Who Is This King of Glory?" pt. 1, p. 28.

52. Sermon of Feb. 19, 1935, in *SW,* Mar. 9, 1935, p. 3.

53. Divine's sermons reveal so much of the philosophy and phrasing of Robert Collier's writings that it is highly probable that he had read in detail at least some of these popular volumes. See, for example, Collier's *The Life Magnet,* 6 vols. (New York: Robert Collier, 1928); *The Book of Life,* 7 vols. (New York: Robert Collier, 1925); and *The Secret of Gold,* 2 vols. (New York: Robert Collier, 1927). It is not as clear that Father Divine read the works of Mary Baker Eddy, the founder of Christian Science, despite occasional parallels with her works in his own sermons. He may have gained much of his familiarity with her ideas through a popular contemporary book to which he often referred: Charles Ferguson, *The New Books of Revelations: The Inside Story of America's Astounding Religious Cults* (Garden City, N.Y.: Doubleday, Doran, 1929).

54. McKelway and Liebling, "Who Is This King of Glory?" pt. 2 (June 20, 1936), p. 22.

55. Sermon of Feb. 22, 1938, in *ND,* Mar. 3, 1938, p. 3.

56. McKelway and Liebling, "Who Is This King of Glory?" pt. 2, p. 22.

57. According to Hoshor, *God in a Rolls-Royce,* p. 38.

CHAPTER 2

The Rise of Father Divine

The Great Depression

The impact of the Depression on the nation's center of wealth and finance, New York City, was shattering. Over fifty breadlines operated there by 1930. Care for the homeless occupied the full resources of more than a dozen private organizations. Still the situation worsened, past the ability of public and private agencies to handle. Unemployed workers lost in wages some twenty times what they received in relief funds. Their chagrin at having to apply for this scant charity often seemed as devastating as their economic distress. As the months of hardship continued without respite or sign of recovery, the public mood in New York, as elsewhere in the nation, turned from bewilderment to intense frustration and, for many, despair.[1]

In nearby Sayville the undiminished prosperity and hospitality of the Reverend M. J. Divine began to assume a larger-than-life quality. The number of guests at his Sunday feasts multiplied, despite the limited accommodations, from dozens to hundreds. Six police officers regularly directed traffic near the home and kept people off the sidewalk so that pedestrians might pass. Most of these visitors came from Harlem and other ghetto areas in New York City and Newark, but white as well as black eagerly shared the "Father's" bounty.

The vocabulary of gossip about Divine changed as well—the old words "decent," "hospitable," "religious," seemed somehow inadequate to describe his beneficence amid the surrounding economic ruin. New accolades gained wide currency—the Father was "saintly," "holy," "miraculous." Could Jesus have done more in his time than this diminutive philanthropist was now accomplishing? Many pilgrims to 72 Macon Street thought not and looked upon their host as virtually a god in human form.

Divine's Sunday banquets offered a bright refuge from outside discouragements.[2] A sign at the entrance to his home specified "evangelical" rules of conduct to ensure that meetings maintained order and harmony. "Be on one accord, drive in slowly," the hand-painted greeting began, then: "Notice — Smoking — Intoxicating Liquors — Profane Language — Strictly Prohibited." Inside, hundreds sat or stood around a long table, ardently singing hymns and enjoying feasts that seemed to belie all the signs of a nationwide depression. As these satisfied guests departed, others took their places, a process that lasted from morning till night.

Observers marveled at the opulence of the meals, which impressed even for prosperous times. There were large silver consoles heaped with choice fruits found only in high-grade markets. Twelve coffee percolators were within easy reach of Father Divine, who poured it into cups that waitresses then served to the guests. Large roasts, chickens, and ducks all were of excellent quality and prepared in an obviously professional manner. The finest vegetables accompanied these dishes. It was a repast without end, for Divine was continually welcoming new guests and blessing new rounds of food and drink. When asked how many he served in a day, Divine promptly replied, "We feed as many as come. We serve from early morning until midnight." As to his recompense, he was equally emphatic: "We charge nothing. Anyone, man, woman or child, regardless of race, color or creed, can come here naked and we will clothe them, hungry and we will feed them."[3]

As startling as Father Divine's generosity was the thoroughly unexotic manner in which he presided over these gatherings. He displayed no religious relics or altars in the house, furnishing it instead in the manner of a typical suburban home owner. Neither did he don colorful, mysterious, or unconventional garments as one might have expected of a religious leader. Divine preferred a plain business suit of good quality but without ostentation.

Curiously, in view of Divine's instinct for the dramatic, he acted as if embarrassed by the sudden publicity. When a reporter asked him for a picture, he refused, with the explanation that he did not believe in advertising. Divine added that all the people the reporter had seen at his banquet had come through the advice of others whom he had helped.

Reports circulated among the crowds that the Father had wrought miraculous cures. This was apparently an important reason for many people to make the pilgrimage to his Sayville home. Yet Divine himself all but winced at the suggestion that he would personally cure people of their ailments. When a little woman shook hands with him, he quickly disabused her of any fantasies she harbored, saying, "My handclasp is that of companionship and so do not think that by shaking hands with me you can be healed."[4] The God that Father Divine embodied at this time was less a magician than a down-to-earth, conservative philanthropist.

The "Divine touch" did not lack technique. Although he assured all who inquired about his source of funds that "God will provide," he took practical steps to ensure that his store of manna endured. Observers who did not wholly succumb to his charisma reported that he used a tested routine for extending his supplies. Rather than serve all food at once, he had waitresses first bring out pitchers of water, tea, and other beverages while he poured coffee for the guests. All were encouraged to drink freely while talking and singing hymns. Only after much time had elapsed did the first solid food appear—mainly starches and perhaps some fruits and vegetables. By the time the meats arrived, visitors had pretty much filled up on the preceding, less expensive portions of the menu. The roasts passed back and forth impressively across the table, then were reclaimed fairly intact, to be frozen for future use.[5]

As Divine gained experience dealing with the crowds, the showman in him also blossomed. Playwright Owen Dodson recalled that he and his older brother often visited Divine's Sayville home and were struck by an apparent miracle—an endless supply of milk that poured from the spigot of a large dispenser on the table. Young Owen was much impressed, but his brother was more intrigued than awed. At meal's end he peeked surreptitiously under the extremely long tablecloth in search of a lower truth. He discovered that "the source of infinite supply" took the form of two small ghetto youths who pumped resolutely at an apparatus hidden beneath the table.[6] Of course, many would have considered it miracle enough to provide milk without limit or charge. But the minister, having already warmed to his image as divine father, was not taking any chances.

The expansive manner of "the Messenger" of earlier years could be seen re-emerging in full force, for Divine's growing flamboyance appeared linked to his renewed sense of mission. Just as he had once journeyed south intent on bringing God's truth at any cost, so he again felt a special, urgent call to redress the ills of a troubled society. Divine's vigor seemed undiminished despite the passage of a quarter-century, and it may be that his broadening responsibilities rejuvenated him.

The differences between Divine as young evangelist and as middle-aged minister were nonetheless substantial. Where once he had called vaguely for a new social order, with little idea how to attain the goal, now he worked with great effect to aid individual victims of poverty and to set a model of interracial harmony at his banquet tables.

The content of his preaching also matured greatly since his days as an itinerant exhorter. From an impressionable youth wrestling with a single striking concept of man's divinity, Divine had, over decades of reading, observing, and constant seeking, fashioned a theology that proclaimed equal rights for all people.

Divine explained to mostly black audiences that everyone contained the spirit of God, so that all were entitled to be treated with dignity, regardless of skin color. For the same reason of inner divinity, all were deserving of decent jobs and living conditions, no matter what their background. Divine was just beginning to work out the implications of this radical theological approach. Yet it was already clear that his antagonism to racial and economic injustice would never again be obscured by his deep interest in spiritual matters. Instead, as the Depression worsened, Divine highlighted his message of tolerance and aid to the poor, while reinforcing it with his religious ministry more prominently than ever before.

The Negro Church in Crisis

Father Divine might have remained in relative anonymity had he been among numerous other pastors energetically aiding unemployed ghetto residents. Instead, his ministry coincided with a crisis of social leadership in the Negro church, which the Depression mercilessly exposed to the mass of urban blacks. As economic conditions deteriorated, growing numbers of destitute people depended on their churches—the central community institutions—to provide economic relief. Yet during the early years of the Depression most ministers shifted only with reluctance from their largely otherworldly outlook. Divine's ministry to the needy therefore helped fill a crucial void in clerical activity and, in so doing, he rapidly became one of the ghetto's most influential religious figures.

The discordance between Father Divine's priorities and those of most black ministers during the early 1930s is evident from their respective sermons. While Divine frequently emphasized the need to save the masses from want, the typical black sermon of the early Depression years wholly ignored the theme of depression. Benjamin Mays and Joseph Nicholson discovered, for example, that of a hundred varied Negro sermons they studied in 1930, only six made any reference to the hardships wrought by economic collapse. Most of those allusions were incidental or blamed individual sins rather than larger, institutional failures. One minister explained the Depression with the hypothesis that "God is mad with the people." The minister charged that "one of the causes of this period of depression was that folks were so busy buying luxuries that they couldn't buy necessities." His sermon bypassed entirely the enormous possibilities for collective effort to aid the unemployed.[7]

Even among educated ministers, the weight of a long otherworldly religious tradition often was proof against the clamor for a socially concerned church. The Reverend Joseph Gomez, for example, wrote for the eminent Afro-American journal, the *Pittsburgh Courier,* but his comments even on the Depression could never quite keep from floating heavenward. In one sermon he described the intolerable economic conditions the masses faced, the "panic, stark and real," the "gripping overpowering fear" of destitute people watching their banks fail and their savings disappear. "Times such as these demand courageous leadership," he proclaimed, and called for "a new gospel of life." Yet this exhortation seems to have exhausted his social concerns, for his conclusion displayed a resigned, otherworldly tone markedly at odds with his earlier, fiery comments: "Times, such as these, demand Meditation and Prayer. 'Come ye yourselves apart into a desert place and rest awhile,' interprets the needs of our day. . . . Retreat to these quiet places of the soul and be prepared."[8]

This conservative orientation in the Negro church, compared with Father Divine's social activism, may be seen more concretely from a study of over 600 urban black churches in both North and South, conducted by Mays and Nicholson in the early 1930s.[9] At first glance their research suggests an impressive array of church projects, from missionary work to sponsorship of social, educational, and financial clubs. Closer inspection, though, reveals that in key areas of aid to ghetto residents, few congregations were active. Although nearly all the churches are listed as giving some relief to the poor, only eighteen provided food for the unemployed, or some 3 percent of the total. Two churches alone (0.3 percent) helped the unemployed find work. In short, those activities that Divine made a vital part of his ministry early in the Depression were still viewed by most black churches as peripheral to their main, spiritual mission.

Father Divine's resurgent activism, unlike his earlier periods of crusading zeal, came amid conditions that imparted a new respectability, even an urgency, to social action by black ministers. The eminent contemporary historian Carter Woodson unsparingly distilled the growing criticisms by educated blacks indignant at clerical conservatism during the economic emergency. "For lack of leadership," he wrote in 1931, "the Negro church has no program except that of 'saving souls' from hell when conditions against which the institution should fight are keeping the Negroes in hell." Woodson also explained the special frustration Negroes felt at the inadequacies of their church: "I appeal to the Negro church because it is the nearet thing to an institution developed by Negroes. They do not control anything else. . . . Negroes have given more to the church than to any other social agency. They are justified, therefore, in expecting more from it."[10]

The young, too, grew restless with a church that seemed preoccupied with the afterlife. A survey of Negro youth during the early 1930s showed an increasing orientation toward "a practical religion which might be applied to one's daily needs," marked by " 'service' or by an earnest effort 'to live cleanly, harmoniously and helpfully here on earth.' "[11] One seventeen-year-old Negro girl, the daughter of a sharecropper in Shelby County, Tennessee, expressed a view common to young blacks North and South:

> I think a preacher out here ought to preach today about things of today. He ought to give the people advice and help them out of their troubles by talking about things that happen today. I don't think a preacher ought to try to preach you into heaven. They had a funeral up at the church the other day, and the preacher tried to preach the body into heaven.[12]

The alienation of the young from the church evoked public jeremiads from conservative black leaders like educator Kelly Miller, who expressed bewilderment at the onset of an age that was "crassly irreligious." Miller lamented that the better-educated Negro youth were "turning away from the religion of their fathers and mothers. The pulpit and places of moral and spiritual authority are not being recruited from the cultured and college bred."[13]

Among lower-class blacks, cynicism and bitterness toward church leaders became pervasive during the Depression. Even regular churchgoers often described their pastors with words like "racketeering," "fake leaders," and "money-mad." One ghetto resident summed up the popular mood: "When the crash comes and you are not doing so well, they forget all about you."[14]

The social malaise in church leadership seeped even into the conduct of religious services, which increasingly divided the mass of poor blacks from a self-conscious elite. While the Depression accented lower-class desires for an emotionally expressive religion, numerous urban churches tended to favor a more formal, decorous service, in imitation of their white counterparts and as a display of bourgeois "refinement." William Pickens, a field agent for the NAACP, commented in 1931 on the orthodox churches' declining sensitivity to the majority of ghetto residents: "Is there not something wrong, something unfortunately missing, from a church whose ceremonies have lost their appeal to the child, to most of the young, to most of the normal and natural people, and which church has become an institution that appeals only to a very limited number of very 'proper' and very 'good' people?"[15]

The poor and the migrant answered this question, inarticulately but with telling effect, by flocking to cult movements that sought to make religion more responsive to mass needs. These groups succeeded in providing an atmosphere in which lower-class congregants could find acceptance and emotional release. Yet, with few exceptions, their social concerns remained largely inchoate, often limited to invocations of heavenly aid in daily life. Thus the cults essentially democratized the opportunities for spiritual escapism without resolving the basic social inadequacies of the Negro church.

Father Divine differed from most cult leaders in his social outlook as widely as he did from most orthodox ministers. It is true that he was an eager master in the realm of theater practiced by the cultists, offering uplifting sermons, stirring services, and an inspiring presence. Yet he also aided followers in tangible ways, while stressing that religion should chiefly promote justice and prosperity in this world. The history of the cults thus helps explain Divine's rise chiefly by underscoring how few black ministers, even those who courted lower-class favor, approached his efforts to make religion a force for social change.

A minority of cultists in the early thirties did combine evangelical magnetism with social concern, though to a more limited degree than Father Divine. Of these, easily the most famous was Solomon Elder Lightfoot Michaux,[16] who based his movement in the nation's capital. Like Divine and other similar mass leaders in the ghetto, including Rosa Horn in Harlem[17] and Lucy Smith in Chicago,[18] Michaux rose through preaching from a life of poverty in the South. He had long worked as a fishmonger in the black neighborhood of Newport News, Virginia, until suddenly feeling "reborn" and called to soul-saving while praying with his devout wife. His fiery sermons and services using gospel music soon came to the attention of CBS radio executives, and he became a "religious personality" mixing piety and brimstone for ever-larger audiences.

By the first years of the Depression, Michaux far more than Divine had become a world-class evangelist. Heralded as the "Happy Am I" preacher, after a hymn that featured in all his services, he sent God's word by radio to some 25 million people, including many in Europe and even to the unlikely site of South Africa. On Sundays he also personally exhorted capacity congregations, counting a sizable number of whites, at the 27,000-seat baseball stadium of the Washington Senators.

Michaux, like Divine, continued to profess a concern for the common man long after he had attained uncommon wealth and fame, and he did much to serve the lower classes in practical ways. He fed people at a free cafe, provided the needy with clothing, and kept four apartment houses for evicted members of his congregation. In 1932 Michaux also opened an employment agency, which reportedly obtained jobs for thousands.

Michaux's activities, matched on a smaller scale by Rosa Horn and Lucy Smith among others, demonstrated that cults, while appealing to the emotions, could also become vehicles for mass uplift. Yet there were sharp limits to their social vision. Compared with Father Divine, who increasingly viewed his ministry as the vanguard of a new social order, these leaders never evinced great interest in reform currents beyond their own admirable philanthropic endeavors. Almost no civil rights militancy accompanied their religious leadership; while they accepted both white and black disciples, they did not invest this policy with full meaning by emphasizing either a theological or a secular doctrine of racial equality. They were always, above all else, first-rate revivalists, and this spiritual calling rather than any social crusade dominated their words and deeds.

The abridged social concerns of an Elder Michaux or a Rosa Horn were still exceptional among black cultists in the Depression. These leaders were often little more than enterprising Bible toters who purveyed spiritual ecstasy in exchange for monetary expressions of piety by credulous followers. An example striking for his notoriety was Charles "Daddy Grace" Emmanuel, who conducted mass baptisms along the East Coast while systematically freeing all comers from the burden of their material possessions.

The self-annointed "Bishop" Grace, a tall man with flowing locks and a piercing look, built his United House of Prayer for All People into one of the largest and wealthiest of all the black cult movements.[19] His baptismal rituals and faith healings added a personal, charismatic touch to Christian worship, inspiring some white as well as black disciples. The bishop further enhanced his followers' morale and his own image of grandeur by conferring leadership titles on some 25 percent of the membership in his organization, thereby imparting a sense of upward mobility scarcely found in the wider community.

Yet whatever the intangible joys he afforded, Daddy Grace evinced no clear program to treat the deeper social and economic problems that corroded his followers' lives. Though his movement featured some business enterprises, a large proportion of these had slender value in the outside world: cult emblems and buttons and fanciful uniforms were typical products. Similarly, the bishop's gestures at philanthropy often had only symbolic value, such as the free banquet at the end of his annual convocations. Such largesse as Daddy Grace bestowed was, in any case, little more than a fig leaf for the relentless assaults he conducted on his followers' meager wealth. He routinely pressured them to buy specially blessed wonder products such as magical "Daddy Grace Soap" and "Daddy Grace Hair Pomade." He also pitted branches of his House of Prayer in frequent competitions to raise money for his private use, with winning collectors receiving such prizes as a seat near their leader at a banquet.

The efficacy of Daddy Grace's nearly continuous appeals for funds stemmed partly from his ability to intimidate his followers. He would inform them that he had given God a vacation, adding ominously, "If you sin against God, Grace can save you, but if you sin against Grace, God cannot save you."[20] Yet intimidation alone could not have induced his followers to part with their income so enthusiastically. Rather, his success as an evangelical predator despite his transparent greed remains an enduring tribute to human credulity. It recalls the words of veteran white evangelist A. A. Allen to the up-and-coming Marjoe: "Son, let me tell you something. Do you know how you can tell a revival meeting is over? Do you know when God is saying you can move on to the next town? When you can turn people on their head and shake them and no money falls out, then you know God's saying, 'Move on, Son.'"[21]

Although one historian of black cults views Daddy Grace as having "prostituted" the institution,[22] Grace seems to have differed from many other cultists chiefly in the scale of his rapine. Indeed, hundreds of lesser cult gods and prophets flourished in the ghetto, based on the same mass willingness to believe, and pay for the privilege, that Daddy Grace tapped so effectively. Perhaps the most numerous and flagrant manipulators were the spiritualists, who supplemented the Christian devotions of many urban workers by offering more direct ways to control divinity and thus destiny.

Like Daddy Grace, the spiritualists filled varied functions, however unconsciously, that reinforced the morale and social fabric of the urban poor. The presumed contact with the dead often was chiefly a context for using the magic — or insight — of the spiritualist for coping with daily problems, and using the atmosphere of the seance as an outlet similar to the worship in other congregations. The advertisements many spiritualists regularly placed in black journals attest to the wide range of services they provided, whose value was largely independent of the charisma or manipulative skills of any single practitioner. One recurrent message in the *Amsterdam News,* for example, asked, "Have you trouble with husband, wife, friend, job, loved one?" If so, then "Prof. Ben Bay" would resolve the situation. Another advertisement, for the "Truth Institute," listed such a diversity of services as to suggest that recreation and socializing were functions as integral to the sessions as purely spiritual aid. The institute provided astrology classes, "message services," and, on Saturday nights, a "Spiritual Club," featuring mediums, messages, and refreshments.[23]

Yet for all their diversions, the spiritualists met the problems of ghetto dwellers in ways that were severely limited, largely escapist, and often fraudulent. A large proportion relied almost exclusively on preplanned illusions in interpreting heavenly will and conveying a sense of contact with the spirit world. In this form the black cult converted almost all social needs and grievances into a realm of fantasy, to be painted by the leader as carefully as he could discern the wishes of his clients. Ira Reid offers a vivid portrait of one such exercise in shamanship, in a study aptly entitled "Let Us Prey!"

Half of the time the messages were wrong, most of the time they were so general they could be applied to anyone, and the rest of the time they were so jumbled nobody could understand them. The whole thing was a farce yet one old man sat in the meeting, paid the medium his two dollars—that he evidently needed very badly for himself—and listened with tears in his eyes to the message from a dead relative. The medium failed to mention just which relative it was.[24]

With their intensely personal leadership and focus on ethereal realms, the spiritualists accentuated both the strengths and weaknesses of the black cultists, who collectively provided an array of circuses but scant bread for the masses. Few cult leaders commanded the resources, the administrative skills, and the motivation required to run both spiritual and philanthropic or reform enterprises. Nor did they need to in order to maintain a following. So long as they could provide what the conventional churches did not—a sense of respect for lower-class members and their religious traditions—these alternative preachers were assured a regular constituency.

It is a measure of the weaknesses within the regular denominations that the sects and cults came to outnumber the conventional churches in Harlem, making it problematic as to which were "established" and which "marginal."[25] Seth Scheiner notes that storefronts in the mid-twenties "comprised 39 percent of the Negro churches in New York City"; by 1930, 75 percent of Harlem's churches were storefronts.[26]

In addition to outright desertions to the sects and cults, a sharp increase in cases of overlapping church and cult membership also struck the churches a devastating blow. The churchgoer who also worshiped in a cult was likely to divide his modest donations between the two rather than devote them all to the church. During the Depression this—together with declining membership rolls—happened often enough to bankrupt a church or cripple all its activities but for a weekly service.[27]

In desperation the churches in the thirties looked for ways to win back adherents from the flourishing cult leaders. Some appealed more vigorously to the spiritual predilections of the proletariat. The grand master of this strategy was the Reverend G. Wilson Becton, who until his mysterious slaying in 1933 was among the most wealthy and famous pastors of the ghettos.[28] A college graduate, Becton nevertheless freed himself of any intellectual constraints in his approach to church worship. His "World's Gospel Feast Party," a traveling musical troupe, provided an array of entertainment in the orthodox churches that often surpassed the cults in sheer emotionalism. Soon local churches were copying his example, adding their own musicians and gospel singers on a permanent basis.

The problem with these clerical efforts to imitate the cults was that they responded incompletely to the deeper causes of declining church membership and prestige. No matter how the churches modified their services, the cult leaders would always find new ways to capitalize on the class antagonisms and proletarian frustrations within ghetto society. A religious institution that hoped to answer fully the needs of lower-class blacks would have to confront the poverty and racism that undermined their lives at every turn. The Negro church, in short, could expect to regain mass loyalties and the respect of other community leaders only by restoring its own long-dormant sense of social mission.

Edgar Rouzeau, a contemporary black writer on the ghetto's religious trends, viewed the Depression as marking a turning point in clerical attitudes. "With church attendance dropping off at an alarming rate," Rouzeau wrote, "progressive ministers turned from the milk-and-honey and hell-and-damnation brand of religion and began to take an interest in the struggles of the masses for bread and butter."[29]

It is perhaps fitting that the Reverend Adam Clayton Powell, Sr., should have led the resurgent struggle against clerical conservatism. Emerging from more than a decade of relative quiescence, Powell challenged his fellow ministers in December, 1930, to either aid the unemployed or else resign as unfit to lead their congregations. He was careful to express confidence that the churches would meet his challenge, but a sense of both urgency and indignation pervaded his words.[30]

A vehement reaction by church conservatives followed. One minister wrote to Powell that it was doubtful "whether the church should actively engage in making medicine, serving soups and juggling jobs and the like."[31] Other respondents wasted no time on substantive discussion but launched immediately into personal invective. The Baltimore Baptist ministers' conference sharply censured Powell for arrogant behavior.[32] In Newark a committee of 250 black Baptist ministers warned Powell in an open letter, "Let not your ambition for a cheap notoriety spoil your real worth."[33]

This time, unlike in 1918, Powell was not so easily isolated or discouraged. Realizing that the balance of forces within the black clergy was fast changing, he dispatched his own open letter, in which he told the Newark committee that those "preachers who are fighting me instead of feeding the people, will be a shameful memory in a few years. . . ." Powell's memoirs later in the decade revealed that time had not healed the wounds from this clerical battle. He looked back at his adversaries as relics from another era who "seemingly thought that it was their duty and my duty to feed hungry people on ideals in order that they might physically starve to death and go to heaven quickly for milk and honey, long white robes and golden slippers."[34]

Other eminent ministers increasingly borrowed Powell's cudgel to administer attacks on clerics unconcerned with the here-and-now. Their sharp defenses of "social Christianity" helped strengthen the resolve of lesser-known liberal pastors who faced reproval by colleagues in the clergy. This was especially important for a rising leader like Father Divine, whose status as a cult figure already imparted considerable controversy to his ministry. While he offended many conventional ministers as heretical, the sharpest attacks came chiefly from conservatives. These clergymen often seemed to include among Divine's alleged blasphemies his rejection of the idea that a church was primarily a guardian of souls. When their diatribes gained attention in the black press, Divine, instead of withdrawing once more into anonymity, was fully ready for a vigorous dialogue with his accusers.

Bishop R. C. Lawson of the Refuge Church of Christ in Harlem was especially active among the clerical opponents of Father Divine. By no means the most conservative of clergymen, he nevertheless saw the church mainly as a source of otherworldly salvation and viewed Divine simply as a demagogue subverting orthodox faith. In January, 1932, he publicly excoriated Divine at a conference of predominantly Methodist Negro ministers in Salem, New Jersey. Lawson fleetingly conceded that he did not object to Divine's charitable work, then went on to leave no stone uncast in his attempts to discredit the prophet of Sayville as corrupt, blasphemous, a false preacher, and an Antichrist of the modern era. His remarks drew enthusiastic applause, with no dissent recorded.[35]

Father Divine's prompt rebuttal of Lawson's charges entered fully into the spirit of invective that frequently characterized debates between ministers in the ghetto. While assuring a reporter that "I hold no ill feeling toward the bishop," he expressed disdain for the "jealous" carping of a man who "does not fully understand that which he is supposed to preach."[36] Divine also approved a still more piquant public statement by disciple Priscilla Paul, who referred to Lawson's "Refuse Church of Christ" and suggested that the bishop "practices everything else but Jesus."[37]

Amid the personal barbs of Priscilla Paul's writings, Divine also offered the first major defense of his present-centered religion, as opposed to a concern for future salvation. Paul argued that Father Divine, far from being a "sham" as Lawson alleged, was providing real beds, rooms, clothing, and "the best of food to eat and an abundance of it." Father Divine did not even take a collection for his services, despite Lawson's "uncalled

for lie" that rich disciples gave Divine money. "But if it were true," Paul
wrote,

> which one would be justified in his work, Father Divine in taking
> money from wealthy people, ones who were able to give, and using
> it for a good purpose, a good cause like he does, or Bishop Lawson
> preaching death as the gospel of Christ, heaven above the sky, hell
> below the ground, nothing that man can reach in his life, yet charging
> for that. . . . Which one is justified?[38]

The debate with Bishop Lawson marked a new stage of confidence and
prestige for Father Divine, though no clear-cut victor emerged from this
clash of personalities and values. Their confrontation was, in this regard,
a small enactment of the wider struggle occurring within the Negro church
throughout the Depression era. The vigorous revival of a reform ethic in
the church by no means signaled a final triumph over the forces of otherworldly religion. Throughout the Depression ministers chiefly involved
in programs for social uplift remained a minority within the Negro church
and could not hope to displace altogether its emphasis on individual salvation. Yet neither could the conservative ministers any longer rebuke the
reformers with impunity, for the social pressures favoring a more active
clergy had become too strong to ignore.

Pulled by two sharply opposed perspectives, black religious leaders in
the thirties groped for a new synthesis that would maintain the old emotional style of worship while bringing "Heaven" within closer reach of
people's daily lives. It was a difficult merger of values that was never fully
achieved. Nevertheless, a growing number of pastors, of whom Father
Divine was an outstanding example, were discovering the radical possibilities of a religion that embraced a people's social as well as spiritual
needs.

The Trial

Father Divine's burgeoning influence fully restored his utopian mood, particularly his commitment to "break down the partition" between black and
white. As his social radicalism resurfaced, however, so did the racial intolerance he had encountered in the past. The precipitating factor was the
influx of Sunday visitors into Sayville, for their sheer numbers created
inconveniences for other residents and their singing kept some people
awake. Yet had this been the extent of the problem, it is likely that the
residents and the ever pragmatic minister would have reached an amicable
accord. Instead, the presence of so many blacks triggered long-dormant
racist sentiments, as residents expressed fears that their town was becoming a Negro haven. Divine's wealth and prominence exacerbated the situa-

tion, for the fact that a Negro held such influence, however benevolent, was in itself a "provocation" to less affluent white townsmen.

The first skirmishes took place covertly. Suffolk County's district attorney commissioned an undercover investigation of Divine's finances and morals. Two attractive women from Harlem pretended to join the following and, in the most flamboyant traditions of espionage, used every means from eavesdropping to attempted seduction to find the mystery of his wealth.

All in vain, the female investigators reported to Suffolk officials. Divine was incorruptible. He fed them, sheltered them, treated them kindly in all ways, and asked nothing in return. He was also oblivious, one of the women added, to the hints of sexual availability she had cast his way. The fact that the agents were themselves awed by the movement and perhaps influenced by other Negroes from Harlem might have affected their report, but in any case this and subsequent investigations disclosed no irregularities in Divine's ministry.[39]

The failure to find evidence of wrongdoing was not sufficient to shield Divine from "justice." In the first direct step by Sayville residents to drive Divine out of their town, neighbors complained to police late one Sunday night in November, 1931, stating that the chanting and shouting by his followers was disturbing the peace. The atmosphere oozed hostility on either side.

The followers apparently resisted the intrusion of their privacy, as authorities attempted to disrupt one of their meetings. The outnumbered and fearful town officials massively reacted by summoning five deputy sheriffs, half a dozen state troopers, and eventually firemen carrying hoses, doubtless anticipating a pitched battle. The assistant district attorney, Joseph Arata, crashed through the back door in either a brazen display of courage or a subtle re-election bid, only to be sent into bliss by a roundhouse blow from a follower at the gates calling himself St. Peter. A riot call sounded, authorities deputized additional villagers, and firemen readied their hoses and threatened to "let them have it" unless they surrendered.

Arata, revived and now inclined to take a diplomat's approach to the situation, called out Father Divine and advised him to quiet his disciples. Divine promised to surrender his entire congregation to the police. He and eighty followers then voluntarily left in orderly fashion for three buses that carted them off to the town hall to answer for their excessively loud praying.

"If singing the praises of God is disorderly conduct, then I plead guilty," declared one of the followers arrested with Father Divine. Although fifty-five disciples paid the fine of $5 assessed each of them by a local court, twenty-five—including Father Divine himself—contested the charge.[40]

Already one could see a pattern of martyrdom forming around the black prophet of Sayville. His fellow townsmen not only denied him honor in his own county but now mobilized their legal resources to purge what they considered a menace to their security and peace of mind.

To ensure that the larger point of their previous actions did not escape Divine's notice, some 1,000 Sayville residents gathered in the town high school to protest his presence in the community. Spokesmen took pains to deny that racial feeling motivated their actions, itself a suggestion of what people in Sayville were concerned about. Their conduct belied their assurances on several counts. Citizens had initiated the meeting only after discovering that Julia Arias, a white woman and former governess to the children of a Republican state leader, was part of Father Divine's movement. She had disappeared three weeks earlier and resurfaced, to the consternation of Sayville's samaritans, at 72 Macon Street. Authorities committed her to the state asylum for treatment of symptoms diagnosed as religious paranoia.[41]

The mass meeting gave evidence of racism in more direct ways. Officials entertained suggestions for banning Divine's following that focused alternately on Divine in particular and Negroes in general. Some suggested that they would be content with a permanent injunction against Divine and his disciples, but at least one person proposed a zoning ordinance restricting Negroes to certain quarters within the village limits. Leading citizens stressed their concern that property values in this resort town were depreciating because of Divine's congregation and urged, in "the best interests of this community that Divine take steps to plant his cult where it can prosper unhampered by the limits of a residential section."[42]

Participants generally concurred with the subcommittee member who acknowledged that there was no complaint against the moral character of Father Divine or his followers. The question, rather, had gone beyond minor complaints and concerned the crisis of having a "Harlem colony" in Sayville. On this ground, unless Divine agreed to a rapid withdrawal from Sayville, the planned indictments against him and some two dozen disciples would go forward the following week.[43]

Father Divine himself entertained no doubts that racism was at the root of his ordeal. He later recalled that from the time he moved onto Macon Street, certain prejudiced people had sought any pretext to oppose his residence in the community: "They said my car disturbed them when I would start it up. They said many different things were disturbances, and I said to them, 'Yes, my success and my prosperity disturb you.' "[44]

The minister was not alone in tracing Sayville's actions to prejudice. What began as a local disturbance suddenly became a *cause célèbre* for

Afro-Americans when James C. Thomas, former assistant district attorney under Thomas E. Dewey, offered his services on behalf of Father Divine. The influential lawyer issued a ringing libertarian challenge to the black community:

> To allow an incident of this nature to go unchallenged is to weaken the foundations of democracy in the United States and to single out the Negro group as one not entitled to full enjoyment of every right, privilege and immunity guaranteed by the Constitution. Such a situation is the concern of every Negro man, woman and child in the United States, for if it is permitted to go unnoticed, who can say but that tomorrow these and other constitutional rights and privileges will not be denied to each of us?[45]

This statement had a powerful effect on Negro public opinion. For example, Harlem's leading journal, the *Amsterdam News,* had formerly reported the controversy in a neutral tone. After Thomas entered the case, however, it focused on his resentment of "the insistent and unreasonable demands" of the Sayville townsmen in the face of Father Divine's generous concessions, and referred to Divine as the "harassed" leader.[46]

Black opinion that racism created the furor over Divine's ministry became stronger as he began to seek alternative sites for his congregation, only to be rebuffed by hostile white home owners. When he visited a Massapequa, Long Island, estate not far from his home, the respectable East End Civic Association sponsored a rally to consider how to thwart Divine's possible plans to purchase the property. The fact that once more all opponents were whites, acting despite the absence of any action more provocative than Divine's looking at a home, strengthened the conviction of ghetto residents that the minister was being victimized by a racist conspiracy.[47]

The renewed prospect of martyrdom, after a decade and a half of relative tranquility, hastened Father Divine's passage from spiritual to social leader. A series of rallies in New York City crested in late December, 1931, when Divine spoke at Harlem's Rockland Palace. The throng of disciples, admirers, and curious seekers surpassed all expectations. Between 5,000 and 10,000 people pressed tightly against each other in a hall whose seating capacity was barely 5,000. An observer reported that not since the appearance of Marcus Garvey had Harlem witnessed "so spontaneous a mass demonstration and such religious fervor as has greeted the appearance of the Rev. Major J. Divine. . . ."[48]

The character of the crowd suggests that Divine was striving toward the goal of an integrated following but had only partially achieved it at this time. Of the fifty followers honored by places on the main platform, some twenty-five were white, thus giving the tone of a fully integrated meeting. In the auditorium, though, "there were only a scattered few whites lost in a sea of dark faces."[49]

Divine was content mainly to introduce other speakers and lead hymns, but there was no doubt whose day it was. His entrance with Pinninnah—by then known as Mother Divine—brought a prolonged ovation a reporter characterized as "hysterical."[50] Divine at last addressed his cheering thousands. He told of defying twenty-two lynch mobs, including that of Sayville residents attempting to make him leave his home. Then, leaping acrobatically, he told of the power of God made manifest through him, so that he might convey blessings to all mankind. One has only to recall Divine's earlier avoidance of "collisions" with other religious groups and his extreme reluctance even to propound theories under his own name, to judge the powerful impact his new-found acclaim had on his perspectives:

> I am a free gift to mankind. Of the plenty and abundance which I have I give to you freely. I ask of you only faith. I take from you nothing. I take your sorrows and give you joy. I take your sickness and give you health. I take your poverty and give you peace and prosperity, for I am the spirit of success and health.
>
> None who has faith in me need suffer from depression. No depression has descended upon the kingdom of God. It is a state of consciousness of which we may all be free. I have limitless blessings to bestow upon mankind, spiritual, mental, material and social. All that is necessary is the understanding of the spirit of the consciousness of the presence of God. I have healing for you all. It is not necessary to contact me personally. It is necessary to be spiritually attuned to this consciousness of the presence of God made manifest through me.[51]

In short, God's blessings were available to all, but Father Divine had shown himself uniquely able to draw upon and express the divine bounty. In keeping with the spirit of his address, no collection disrupted this meeting—or any others Divine later held.

Rallies, speeches, and celebrations continued to punctuate the long wait between Divine's arrest and his trial for disturbing the peace. Often the gatherings verged on pandemonium, only barely contained by police and the minister's own insistence on law-abiding conduct. In February, 1932, 1,200 persons crowded Rush Memorial African Methodist Episcopal Church in Harlem, while police of five uptown precincts dispersed 1,000 others who tried to force their way inside for a glimpse of Divine. It required the frantic efforts of New York police for half an hour simply to enable Father Divine to negotiate a path from his car to the packed church.[52] Divine was by now far more than a religious leader; he had been transformed, albeit willingly, into a symbol of Negro hopes and resentment against racial injustice. Thus, as his legal status became ever more precarious, his popularity in the ghettos continued to climb.

The case of "Sayville v. Divine" came to court in May, 1932. A glance at the charges confirms that race prejudice lay behind much of the hostility toward Divine and his followers. The bill of particulars included among its accusations that the defendant "conducted so-called religious services, at which services colored and white people did congregate and mingle together in large numbers. . . ."[53] In this way, indeed, Father Divine was resolutely disturbing the peace.

The trial recalls elements of Divine's earlier evangelical career. As at Valdosta, he was not involved in criminal activity, yet seemed naturally to polarize an entire community against him. Once more he was arraigned on the vaguest possible charge, for want of a more convenient means of quashing his ministry. This time James Thomas ably assumed the role that attorney J. B. Copeland had filled in 1914. The jurors, too, proved as lenient as their indulgent counterparts from the Valdosta trial. Unfortunately for Divine, a major change in scenario resulted when the trial site was moved to Mineola, in Nassau County. Thomas had requested this as a precaution against a racist atmosphere, only to discover that the presiding justice was the most implacable racist in the courtroom.

Lewis J. Smith could have served as the prototype of the oft-maligned, stern, humorless judge. A composite of defendants' nightmares, he earned a reputation for handing down maximum sentences and was known as the "dry judge" for his particular severity toward those who violated prohibition. In his private life Smith was a Presbyterian of puritanical bent whose notion of religion was a world apart from the rollicking prayer sessions and cult-like worship of Divine's following.

The trial descended into travesty from the moment Justice Smith saw and took an instant dislike to Father Divine. The prosecution produced twelve of the minister's neighbors "who claimed with varying displays of emotional involvement that there was loud shouting and singing at 72 Macon Street and that they had often heard followers give praise to Father Divine as people normally give praise in a church."[54] Smith then began actively to assist the prosecution, apparently feeling that the witnesses' displays of religious prejudice were obscuring the proper issue at hand — the dangers of racial mixing.

Judge Smith intimidated one follower, Agnes Hunt, into abandoning her color-blind view of humanity when he insisted on probing the racial composition of Divine's congregation:

Smith: [Is the following] white and colored?

Hunt: I don't recognize color.
Smith: I beg pardon?
Hunt: I only recognize one color.
Smith: I didn't ask you what color you recognized! I asked you, white
        and colored?
Hunt: As you express it, yes.[55]

Smith could not conceive of a worthy motive that might have led white
persons, particularly women, to join Father Divine's following. There was
the case of Helen Faust, a secretary to Father Divine who had spent two
years at Boston University and one year at business school. In answer to
Smith's skeptical probing of her finances, she explained, "I don't receive
a salary, your honor. I live and board there and get whatever clothes I
need. I'm working for the cause." The puzzled judge asked what cause
and tensed at the enthusiastic response: "God's cause, Father Divine's
cause. Peace and the brotherhood of man." Smith afterward had the girl
privately interrogated by the district attorney to determine if she were under
age, in which case he would know his legal duty.[56] Other followers received
similarly cynical questioning by Smith, who seemed more intent than the
prosecutor on discrediting Divine. Attorney Thomas continually objected
to Smith's high-handed manner, but the justice predictably overruled him
each time. To the justice, the defendant was in some way evil and dangerous, and this warranted suspension of the most elementary judicial safe-
guards.

The jury quickly agreed that Father Divine was guilty of being a public
nuisance. It also recommended leniency toward the defendant, but Judge
Smith would entertain none of this misguided kindness. First, he made
several efforts to coerce Divine into revealing the source of his wealth.
But the defendant, who seemed to be reliving the Passion with his calm,
dignified demeanor and laconic, cryptic replies, disclosed nothing of substance. The exasperated judge had Divine languish two weeks in jail before sentencing him. Then he censured Divine in a manner less suited to
an inquest than an inquisition:

> I find that the defendant is not an ordained minister. I am informed
> that his name is George Baker and not Divine. . . . I am informed
> as to his income that he obtains work for people who come to his
> place and uses their wages, and that as to others who come under
> his spell, that they are induced to transfer property to him.
>
> I have information that this man is not a moral man but immoral.
> I believe that he is not a useful member of society but a menace to
> society.[57]

Smith then added for good measure that Divine had even deceived his
own lawyer into believing him. It was a mock trial to the end.

Having found Divine, in effect, guilty of "menace," Smith disregarded the pleas for leniency and gave the maximum sentence of one year in jail and a $500 fine. The defendant accepted this with a quiet dignity that impressed many in the courtroom. Yet it was a time that tested his faith in God's will and his own mission, and the tensions showed. A reporter for the *Baltimore Afro-American* watched the authorities lead Divine off to jail, as his disciples called out to him, "Peace, brother!" Divine "looked at them with a mingled expression of confidence and wounded despair, and passed on."[58]

Few of Divine's partisans were as restrained as their leader. Some, who earlier had warned Judge Smith against giving Father Divine even a single day in jail, now loudly predicted that Smith, for daring to oppose the power of God Almighty, would die. The *Amsterdam News* asserted, more rationally but with equal resentment:

> [T]he principal charge against him [Divine] seems to have been his color, and Mr. Justice Smith is not deceiving us about it. The man was not on trial for unlawfully taking the wages of people or of inducing them to transfer their property to him; neither was he on trial on charges of immoral conduct. Therefore, unsupported information to that effect, no matter what Justice Smith may think about it, should have no weight against him. If Mr. Justice Smith is so sure Divine is guilty of all these crimes, why not put him on trial for them? Prosecution and persecution are different.[59]

At this critical juncture Judge Smith exhibited an unaccustomed flair for the dramatic. In an act perhaps more influential than any in his long and active career, he changed the course of cult history when, three days after sentencing Divine, he suddenly keeled over, dead. He was fifty-six and had been in apparent excellent health during the evening preceding his death. One suspects that the trial had taken its toll on his physical and emotional well-being; to many who had watched Father Divine's career in awe, there seemed more direct causes for Smith's abrupt end.

Father Divine himself revealed an exceedingly elastic sense of opportunity when informed of Smith's sudden demise. Previously, despite his impeccable demeanor and assurances of his willingness to stay in jail, Divine had seemed to visitors somewhat subdued and apprehensive. Now, however, he was again in full command. Controlling whatever emotion he may have experienced on hearing of Smith's death, Divine paused a moment and then said sadly, "I hated to do it."[60]

The minister was soon after released from prison on bail, and his exit bore the same benevolent hauteur as marked his entry and brief stay. A reporter characterized him as "nattily dressed in a blue serge suit, blue shirt and blue tie, and his hair was trimmed and his face freshly shaved. He thanked the warden for the many courtesies extended him . . . and told the sheriff that, even in the face of persecution and execution, he was prepared to 'do the same thing over again.' . . . Inmates of the prison sang and shouted as Divine waved his farewell. 'You are taking away a good man,' one of them told Attorney Thomas."[61]

The trial had done nothing to diminish Divine's sense of indignation—and irony—at the racism and hypocrisy in American society. En route by car to New York City to meet his assembled followers, he noted a newspaper clipping on the sentencing of the Scottsboro boys, nine Alabama youths convicted of rape after a blatantly racist trial. Divine commented to a fellow passenger that New York, which had sentenced a man to jail for feeding the hungry and clothing the naked, "had nothing on Alabama."[62]

Divine first stopped on a small mission of peace before meeting his throng of admirers. At Smithtown, Long Island, he visited a woman whose imprisoned husband had lamented to Divine that she had not communicated with him in months. Divine obtained a promise from the woman to call her husband immediately. Then he drove on to New York, emerging to the hosannas of thousands of screaming followers. That scene recurred several times in the next week, most blaringly at a "monster rally" at Rockland Palace, which by now Divine could seemingly pack at will. There, caught up in the spirit of his own apotheosis, he escalated his claims of providential powers:

> You may not have seen my flesh for a few weeks but I was with you just the same. I am just as operative in the mind as in the body. There were many who thought I had gone some place but I'm glad to say I did not go anywhere. . . . I held the key to that jail all the time I was in it and was with you every time you met. They can prosecute me or persecute me or even send me to the electric chair but they can never keep me from you or stop me from doing good.[63]

Attorney Thomas meanwhile continued his skillful efforts to ensure that Divine remained free "in the body" as much as in the mind. He cited judicial prejudice against his client as the basis for a new court ruling. On January 9, 1933, the Appellate Division of the New York State Supreme Court unanimously agreed that the trial had in fact been marred by gross prejudice by the presiding judge, and overturned the verdict. More than a year later a Suffolk County justice heard the case on appeal, voided the convictions, and ordered the trial court to refund the fines levied in 1931 against Divine and seventy-eight co-defendants. Divine's triumph was complete.[64]

The trial and its aftermath had been all a messianic figure could wish for. This episode marked Divine's passion, crucifixion, and resurrection all in one. He had been seized and censured by the forces of racism, his ministry apparently ended, only to resurface miraculously with the demise of the chief Pharisee and his own return to the adoring multitudes.

Soon after his release from jail Father Divine relocated in Harlem, the heart of his burgeoning following. He explained his departure from Sayville in predictably magnanimous terms, observing that he would not stay where he was unwelcome. Yet even had residents reconsidered their sentiments toward him, he would probably have found some other reason for announcing his change of venue, for Sayville could no longer provide a setting large enough for the deeds of its newly famous pastor.

As word of Divine's brush with martyrdom spread, clusters of converts formed in widely scattered locales. They adopted the cooperative economic system of his original band of disciples and dedicated themselves to his will. These centers became known collectively as the "Peace Mission," a possible allusion to Divine's teachings on inner bliss and on interracial harmony. This informal christening served chiefly to confirm that the minister now led a full-fledged social movement; its ideals were still developing but its numbers and fervor were fast making its leader a figure of national renown.

The trial was also crucial in Divine's career for its effect on the inner man. Unlike some of history's religious mystics who, in desperate circumstances, wondered if Providence had not after all forsaken them, Divine had adhered to his sense of mission both in the courtroom and in prison. Now, having wrestled with his supreme test of faith, he experienced a feeling of overwhelming vindication. Doubts dissolved, and the distinction between the Messenger and the Author Himself blurred yet again. The experience crystallized Divine's self-image as a special executor of the Lord's will. Fittingly, his first act upon release on bail was to greet James Thomas with cries of "Peace!" and declare to him, "I am returning to my fold with new vigor and a firmer grip upon the teachings of the Almighty."[65] Father Divine's messianic ministry had begun in earnest.

Notes to Chapter 2

1. These figures are drawn largely from Albert U. Romasco, *The Poverty of Abundance: Hoover, the Nation, the Depression* (New York: Oxford University Press, 1965), pp. 150, 154.

2. The description of Father Divine's hospitality in Sayville is drawn primarily from Bing Bart, "Sayville Religious Teaching Draws Big Crowds," *Island News— Suffolk's Pictorial Newsmagazine*, Oct. 1, 1931, reprinted in *ND*, June 15, 1974, pp. 18-19.

3. Ibid., p. 19.

4. Ibid.

5. McKelway and Liebling, "Who Is This King of Glory?" pt. 2, p. 28; interview with Owen Dodson, in New York, June 28, 1977.

6. Interview with Owen Dodson.

7. Mays and Nicholson, *The Negro's Church*, p. 86.

8. "Times Such as These," *PC*, Feb. 4, 1933, sec. 2, p. 10. Joseph Gomez was minister of St. Paul A.M.E. Church, St. Louis.

9. Mays and Nicholson, *The Negro's Church*, pp. 122-23.

10. Carter Woodson, "Church Disunion Forces Preachers into Politics," *NYAN*, Sept. 16, 1931, p. 9.

11. Charles H. Wesley, "The Religious Attitudes of Negro Youth—A Preliminary Study of Opinion in an Urban and a Rural Community," *Journal of Negro History* 21 (Dec., 1936):376-93. The quotation is on p. 386.

12. Charles Johnson, "Youth and the Church," in *The Black Church in America*, ed. Hart M. Nelsen, Raytha L. Yokley, and Anne K. Nelsen (New York: Basic Books, 1971), p. 97.

13. Kelly Miller, "An Open Letter" to the Reverend L. K. Williams, president of the National Baptist Convention, Chicago, in *NYAN*, July 23, 1930, editorial page.

14. St. Clair Drake and Horace R. Cayton, *Black Metropolis: A Study of Negro Life in a Northern City*, 2d ed., 2 vols. (New York: Harper and Row, 1962), 2:420.

15. "A Holiness Church Service," *NYAN*, July 15, 1931, p. 8.

16. Material on Michaux is drawn chiefly from accounts in major black journals; of especial value is Edgar Rouzeau, " 'Happy Am I' Preacher Is Ex-Virginia Fisherman," *AA*, Oct. 6, 1934, p. 5.

17. Rosa Horn's evangelical career is reviewed by H. Norton Browne in "You Pray for Me . . . ," *AA*, Oct. 20, 1934, p. 5.

18. For an examination of Lucy Smith's ministry, see Drake and Cayton, *Black Metropolis*, 2:643-45 (text quotations are on pp. 644-45), and Washington, *Black Sects and Cults*, pp. 65-67.

19. A comprehensive treatment of Daddy Grace's ministry and movement is provided by Albert N. Whiting, "The United House of Prayer for All People: A Case Study of a Charismatic Sect" (Ph.D. thesis, American University, 1952); see also Whiting, "From Saint to Shuttler—An Analysis of Sectarian Types," *Quarterly Review of Higher Education among Negroes* 23 (Oct., 1955):133-40, distilling aspects of his larger work. There is also a brief but penetrating analysis of Daddy Grace's movement in Arthur Huff Fauset, *Black Gods of the Metropolis: Negro Religious Cults of the Urban North* (1944; reprinted Philadelphia: University of Pennsylvania Press, 1971), esp. pp. 22-30.

20. Fauset, *Black Gods*, p. 26.

21. Jack Morris, *The Preachers* (New York: St. Martin's Press, 1973), p. 1.

22. Washington, *Black Sects and Cults*, p. 127.

23. Both ads are found in *NYAN*, May 10, 1933, p. 7, among other issues.

24. Ira De A. Reid, "Let Us Prey!" *Opportunity* 4 (Sept., 1926):276-77.

25. Fisher, "Organized Religion and the Cults," pp. 9 ff, treats the changing status of sects and cults in the ghettos.

26. Scheiner, "The Negro Church," pp. 100-101.

27. Fisher, "Organized Religion and the Cults," p. 9.

28. On Becton's career, see the three-part report by Edgar Rouzeau, "Becton and the Consecrated Dime," in *NYAN*, May 31, 1933, pp. 1, 3; June 7, 1933, pp. 1, 14; June 14, 1933, pp. 2, 14; and Miles Mark Fisher, "Negroes Get Religion," *Opportunity* 14 (May, 1936):150.

29. Edgar Rouzeau, "Bread and Butter Program Adds to Power of Church," *PC,* Oct. 29, 1938, p. 12.

30. *NYAN,* Dec. 17, 1930, pp. 2, 11.

31. Powell, *Against the Tide,* p. 230.

32. *AA,* Dec. 27, 1930, p. 12; and see *AA,* Jan. 3, 1931, p. 5, for similar reaction by Reverend G. H. Sims, president of the New York State Colored Baptist State Convention.

33. *PC,* Jan. 24, 1931, sec. 2, p. 6.

34. Powell, *Against the Tide,* pp. 240-42.

35. *Age,* Jan. 30, 1932, pp. 1, 5.

36. Ibid., Feb. 6, 1932, pp. 1, 7.

37. Ibid., Feb. 20, 1932, p. 1.

38. Ibid.

39. Parker, *Incredible Messiah,* pp. 11-12; Hoshor, *God in a Rolls-Royce,* pp. 58-64; Sara Harris, with assistance of Harriet Crittendon, *Father Divine* (New York: Collier Books, 1971), pp. 29-30; and McKelway and Liebling, "Who Is This King of Glory?" pt. 2, p. 28, each give varying accounts of the investigators' experience. McKelway and Liebling claim that the investigators were already followers of Father Divine and thus the inquiry was foredoomed. The authors do not cite any evidence for this suspicion, however, and they are alone in making this claim. In any case, independent investigators, including Eugene Del Mar, a nationally renowned philosopher, and journalist Millard Bloomer reached similarly favorable verdicts regarding Divine's ministry.

40. The account of the disturbance is drawn chiefly from *NYAN,* Nov. 18, 1931, p. 2. The quotation of Father Divine's disciple is in Parker, *Incredible Messiah,* p. 17. Also see *Age,* Nov. 21, 1931, p. 1.

41. *NYAN,* Nov. 25, 1931, p. 2.

42. Ibid.; and *Age,* Nov. 28, 1931, p. 1.

43. *Age,* Dec. 5, 1931, p. 10.

44. Sermon of Dec. 25, 1936, in *SW,* Jan. 2, 1937, pp. 6-7.

45. *NYAN,* Dec. 2, 1931, p. 2.

46. Ibid.

47. Ibid., Dec. 16, 1931, p. 11.

48. Ibid., Dec. 23, 1931, p. 1; see also *Age,* Dec. 26, 1931, p. 1.

49. *NYAN,* Dec. 23, 1931, p. 1.

50. Ibid.

51. Ibid., p. 11.

52. Ibid., Feb. 3, 1932, p. 3.

53. Harris, *Father Divine,* p. 34.

54. Ibid.

55. Based on ibid., pp. 37-38.

56. Hoshor, *God in a Rolls-Royce,* p. 80; Harris, *Father Divine,* p. 38.

57. *NYAN,* June 8, 1932, p. 8.

58. *AA,* June 11, 1932, p. 2.

59. "A 'Colored' Sentence," *NYAN,* June 8, 1932, p. 8.

60. Hoshor, *God in a Rolls-Royce,* p. 85; but Parker, *Incredible Messiah,* p. 28, maintains that Divine remained silent.

61. *NYAN,* June 29, 1932, p. 2.

62. Ibid.

63. Harris, *Father Divine,* p. 43; see variant quotation in *NYAN,* June 29, 1932, p. 1.

64. For information on Thomas's determined defense efforts, see *NYAN,* June 8, 1932, p. 3; Nov. 23, 1932, p. 2. The State Supreme Court ruling of Jan. 9, 1933, is detailed in ibid., Jan. 11, 1933, pp. 1, 15. The little-known but important decision voiding the convictions is covered in ibid., Mar. 17, 1934, p. 2. It was this decision that guaranteed Father Divine's freedom from prison or further harassment regarding the charge of disturbing the peace in Sayville.

65. *AA,* July 2, 1932, p. 2.

CHAPTER 3

The Peace Mission

Membership

The Peace Mission was a melting pot of the discontented. Its membership represented every social background, economic level, and racial group in the nation. These people also displayed as unpredictable a variety of personality traits as "any group of similar size chosen at random,"[1] to the discouragement of two visiting psychologists at the Harlem missions. Yet amid this diversity of circumstance and temperament, followers shared the powerful unifying belief that only Father Divine could fill some vital lack in each of their lives.

Father Divine himself suggested that he was a social and spiritual physician.[2] To critics who charged that his movement bred emotional instability and dependence, he insisted that, on the contrary, he was engaged in a healing ministry to the weak: "Remember, this movement in itself, it is as a hospital. . . . Those who come to me are sick and afflicted. . . . They are seeking some information; they are seeking some help and some aid; they are seeking some deliverance from certain conditions, if it is only mentally, if it is only theoretically, they are seeking something. . . ."[3] As a general diagnosis of his disciples' general state, Father Divine's appraisal left little to fault. However much their specific needs and ailments may have differed, the multitudes who followed Father Divine were nearly all, on some level, people in crisis.

Lower-class ghetto dwellers formed a substantial majority of the Peace Mission's membership during the Depression. In New York and New Jersey, states which contained the heart of Father Divine's support, the following was 85 to 90 percent black. In states farther west the proportion of blacks in the movement often dropped sharply, but almost never below a third of the disciples in any Peace Mission center.

Father Divine attracted ghetto residents in part because he seemed the ultimate role model for many poor, uneducated blacks seeking evidence that they could improve their lot. Divine was one of them—a dark-skinned evangelical preacher, with an earthy humor, colloquial speech, and an accent unmistakably from the Black Belt. Yet he was also a man—or deity—of almost incomprehensible powers, planning deals involving millions of dollars, distributing charity with funds from unknown sources, and challenging white authority with a boldness and success that surely was miraculous. Marcus Garvey had once stirred crowds in Harlem with the prophecy, "A black God is coming. Be ready when he cometh."[4] Now thousands in the ghettos, including many former adherents of Garvey himself, professed to see that prophecy fulfilled in the person of Father Divine.

The testimony of a woman reborn as Beautiful Faith reflects the willingness of many ghetto residents to deify Father Divine in order to erase old images of racial and class inferiority. "Father gave me my first chance to be somebody," she declared. "All my life I didn't amount to nothing—just cooking and cleaning for the white folks. But since I come to know Father is God, I'm important. I'm a dietician in God's kitchen."[5]

Others found the proof of "Father's" deity in his restoration of their livelihoods, which hard times and prejudice had placed in jeopardy. A secretary in the movement, June Peace, recalled that during the Depression the refusal of whites to employ her was an embittering experience, but Father Divine quickly provided her with a job and "loved all the bitterness away."[6] Another veteran disciple, Mr. Patrick, long a chauffeur for Father Divine, confided that he was once unable to obtain work in his native Newark. "But Father Divine gave me a job, he solved my problem. He can solve all your problems."[7]

Although Father Divine helped solve, or at least ease, the problems of racism and poverty, this cannot fully explain the devotion he enjoyed. Only a small proportion of lower-class blacks—almost certainly less than 5 percent—was active in the Peace Mission. Conversely, some of Divine's disciples were whites for whom discrimination and hunger were merely disquieting abstractions. In seeking the causes for Divine's loyal following, therefore, one must explore a range of social and psychological pressures, often but not always underscored by the hardships of ghetto life.

Women formed between three-quarters and nine-tenths of all Peace Mission members, an imbalance evident among both white and black disciples. The predominance of female members was equally true of cults led by such rivals of Father Divine as Daddy Grace, Elder Michaux, and Rosa Horn. It suggests that the inferior status of women in the wider society was a contributing cause of conversion to these unconventional religious movements. The Peace Mission was typical of the cult groups in treating women as equal with men in prayer, at the banquet table, and in running the "kingdom extensions."

Women were highly visible in the upper and middle echelons of the Peace Mission organization. The chief administrator for Father Divine and his most honored disciple during the mid-thirties was a black woman named Faithful Mary. She enjoyed the rare privilege of speaking on Divine's behalf to distant Peace Mission branches; alone of all the followers, she held numerous properties of the movement exclusively in her own name. Divine's secretaries — positions that often involved administrative responsibility — were mostly women. So, too, were the majority of cashiers and supervisors in the various Peace Mission branches.

The elderly were also prominent among both white and black Peace Mission members, reflecting another source of discontent in the wider society. During the Depression the special hardships that fell on the aged sparked a political movement several million strong, which worked for a dignified pension plan and contributed to the passage of Social Security. The process of aging in American society also created psychological insecurities, particularly severe among women undergoing midlife changes. For those unable to cope with such strains, a religious movement that welcomed, cared for, and respected people regardless of age or gender had a potent appeal.

An observer of several Harlem missions estimated that over half the women there were middle-aged or beyond, compared with a more normal age distribution among the men. This observer thought that "[o]n the whole, they were a sad-looking, weary and disconsolate group. My guess is that most of them were single or widowed or divorced and were economically and socially insecure at this very important period of their lives."[8]

Others who found social adjustment difficult were also relatively likely to join cult movements like the Peace Mission. West Indian immigrants, among other newcomers to the ghettos, were strongly represented among Father Divine's followers. The West Indians, generally from the darker-skinned and least affluent strata of their native societies, brought with them a widespread interest in cults, which the strains of migration intensified. In addition to undergoing a major change of setting, these immigrants proved largely immiscible with native Afro-Americans for reasons of cultural differences and economic competition. Trapped in the ghettos by racism and isolated even within ghetto society, many West Indians were susceptible to appeals by cults that provided full acceptance and emotional release through religion. Father Divine extended a special welcome to foreigners as part of his crusade for universal brotherhood, thus making his Peace Mission a particularly inviting haven for these otherwise alienated people.

Southern migrants also flocked to the Peace Mission. Scorned by long-settled ghetto residents as unrefined and ignorant, they found solace and communion as followers of Father Divine. The fact that Divine himself was obviously of southern origin added measurably to their feelings of belonging.

Many southern migrants faced an additional, sometimes overwhelming problem of adjustment that cult leaders were quite willing to handle: the difficulty of making independent decisions. Freedom was desirable in the abstract, but after decades of enforced servility the sudden transition to the impersonal world of the city—and in the harshest of social and economic circumstances— was often traumatic. In particular, former sharecroppers had long been conditioned by a "plantation tradition," as Charles Johnson describes it, involving the "almost complete dependence upon the immediate landowner for guidance and control in virtually all those phases of life which are related to the moving world outside."[9]

Father Divine provided a personal authority figure to fill the void in these migrants' lives, and he did so with a benevolence they had scarcely if ever known in the South. "Sing Happy," a septuagenarian who became a follower during the thirties for reasons of health, employment, and above all security, put it best: "Father Divine takes care of everything."[10]

The search for acceptance brought to the Peace Mission some people who had affluence and social standing yet felt unappreciated by their peers or families. Their conversion often appeared as an act of social rebellion, however vaguely focused, and perhaps a bid for attention. This seems to have characterized the actions of young whites of middle-class background, who deserted their parents for the communal life of the Peace Mission. For example, Josephine Welch, daughter of a municipal judge in New Brunswick, caused considerable commotion by joining a Peace Mission center in 1936. Of her filial ties to the anxious magistrate, she conceded only, "Yes, Father [Divine], I was supposed to be his daughter."[11]

The range of social maladjustment reached its most exalted level with the case of an alleged French countess, Roberte de Quelen of the Chateau Historique de Surville, Montereau, France. The countess claimed to be in flight from "the sobriety of imperialism" and took refuge among the friendly Americans of the Peace Mission. The relaxed atmosphere of the Harlem centers pleased her, as did the lack of formalized hierarchy—the royal presence of Father Divine notwithstanding. Above all, the countess enjoyed being near Divine and listening to his inspirational sermons. "I don't speak very well English," she proved to an enthusiastic audience on one occasion, "but I can say I love this place and I love you all."[12] For her the Peace Mission upheld the French Revolution's ideals of Liberty, Equality, and Fraternity, and went one step better, with Security.

A history of illness, often clearly related to emotional pressures, was another spur to conversion affecting individuals of widely varying social and economic backgrounds. Like the members of numerous cults and Holiness sects across the country, followers of Father Divine believed that their leader could promote "spiritual healing" of any physical disability. The alleged miracles might even occur far from Father Divine's presence, as in the case of a crippled woman who heard someone call the name of Father Divine, meditated fiercely on it, and suddenly felt able to walk. In her reborn state "Redeemed Love" persuaded the other members of her family to join her in serving the Father.[13]

Father Divine himself denied that he personally cured anyone, though these demurrals sounded ever more lightly as his career progressed. He did state that perfect faith would ensure perfect health, regardless of his efforts. To those in need of a more human, tangible object of faith, however, his protestations appeared simply as signs of divine modesty.

In the rodent-infested and overcrowded ghettos, where disease and demoralization bred together, the importance of faith healing to a cult leader's prestige was understandably great. Charismatic cultists such as Daddy Grace and Rosa Horn regularly staged healing sessions, in which many ghetto residents — and sometimes whites as well — claimed to be cured of crippling conditions. Father Divine employed no such demonstrations, whether of special rituals, exhortations, or "laying on of hands." Yet he received testimonies of miraculous cures, as fervent as any in the cults given to faith-healing practices.

The most arresting testimonies to Divine's wonders came from a woman named Viola Wilson, reborn as Faithful Mary.[14] For years she had been an emaciated wastrel in Newark, to all appearances tubercular and without hope of cure. Upon contacting Father Divine in 1934, Faithful Mary inexplicably blossomed into a glowing, vigorous woman of nearly 200 pounds, beaming good health to all she met. Equally to the point, she beamed verbally as well as physically, declaring that Father Divine had cured her of tuberculosis, heart trouble, and a long litany of other anatomical ailments.[15] To the many ghetto residents who knew of her former gaunt and repellent appearance, the newly radiant Faithful Mary became a special symbol of Father Divine's saving power.

Lower-class blacks were not alone in seeking the reinvigorating influence of a forceful religious personality. Ellee Lovelace, for example, was a Negro attorney whose severe arthritis had compelled him to retire and who soon after became a disciple of Father Divine in Sayville. Lovelace claimed to experience a profound sense of well-being in Divine's presence and, within months of becoming a convert, felt wholly rejuvenated; he later acted as Divine's counsel.[16] White followers seemed equally convinced that Father Divine could dispel their infirmities. The minister's Duesenburg was an expensive testament to this belief. It was a gift from an elderly white disciple from California who wore braces on her legs until suddenly feeling cured by Father Divine's spirit.[17]

The nature of the diseases and healings that followers experienced must, for the most part, remain speculative. In a large proportion of the testimonies, however, the close interweaving of physical maladies with social and emotional problems is striking. Followers who in one breath described terrible pains or digestive difficulties might in the next breath recall an adulterous past or feelings of emptiness. In restoring dignity and meaning to their lives, therefore, Father Divine possibly cured them more effectively than any physician's treatment.

Many converts may best be designated as inveterate religious seekers. For them, the attempt to find answers to all problems through spiritual solace was an established way of life. While their search for higher light certainly did not, in itself, mark them as ill adjusted, their lives often disclosed a pattern of extreme credulity and frantic peregrinations from one ultimate religious truth to another. Their searchings were also generally marked by ever-increasing despair. One woman formerly of Jewish faith told a gathering of Peace Mission members: "I have wandered long, many years, and through many states, always searching for the truth. I have studied metaphysics about twenty-two years. I went from one course to another and spent thousands of dollars in contacting teachers until much disappointed and disillusioned. I never was contented. . . ."[18] This woman, according to her further testimony, was "at my extremity" when she prayed all night that a change would come and she would contact someone or something to lead her to truth. The next day a friend told her about Father Divine's teachings and she soon became a devoted follower.[19]

That confession, with details varied, characterized the behavior of numerous other converts to Divine's movement. Brother Lynn spent over fifteen years studying Christian Science, five years with the Rosicrucian Brotherhood, several years with the Temple of Living Thought, and several with the Spiritualist movement, before finding fulfillment with Divine's Peace Mission.[20] Arthur Carter, an elderly gentleman, recalled that decades earlier in Harlem he sought vainly for religious truth among the conventional Christian denominations. Like many others who later joined the Peace Mission, he turned to Christian Science, whose tenets on the spiritual nature of reality were closely akin to Father Divine's philosophy. This still left Carter dissatisfied, however. Only on hearing Father Divine preach and watching him at work did Carter find the answer to his quest. Asked to explain what about the minister's philosophy appealed most to him, he emphasized Divine's ideas of following Jesus. But did not other clergymen preach this as well? Yes, some, he admitted — but Father Divine exemplified this as no one else.[21]

The diversity of religious groups contributing members to Father Divine's Peace Mission was extraordinary. Journalist Hubert Kelley observed in 1936 that some followers, "only a few years ago, were proclaiming the glad tidings that Jiddu Krishnamurti, a young Hindu, was the Messiah. I have met scores of others who until recently were worshiping under the smile of Aimee Semple McPherson. All manner of cultists are bolting to Father Divine's national movement toward God-in-the-flesh and Heaven-on-earth."[22]

With the great majority of converts, one senses a terrible desperation, whether from material or purely emotional lacks. Some followers, however, had been able and respected members of society before joining the Peace Mission communes. Most, though not all, of these were white and of middle-class backgrounds. They tended to be well educated and skilled in such vocations as business management, printing, stenography, and journalism that were of value in building up the Peace Mission organization. Their testimonies reveal no chronic agonies beyond a vague malaise, a sense that somehow they might be deriving still more from life.

The discontents these privileged followers experienced were of a decidedly rarefied nature. There is the typical case of Miss "Orol Freedom," who presided over many Peace Mission meetings to discuss civil rights and other political issues. Buoyant yet proper, with a diction that betrayed aristocratic New England origins, Orol Freedom was once a conventional wife and mother, as well as active in social and civic affairs. Yet she sought a more fulfilling religious dimension to her life. Born an Episcopalian, she converted to Christian Science, then drifted away from organized religion altogether until contacting Father Divine. This experience transformed and enriched her life in some way she could not fully describe. She claimed to realize that "Father is the only reality" and in this belief achieved a previously unknown state of happiness.[23]

John Maynard Mathews was another who found his life productive and secure yet spiritually unrewarding. Mathews operated an auto agency in Boston for seven years before joining the Peace Mission. A student at three colleges and inclined toward religious reflection, he wished to make a fuller commitment to a spiritual life. Upon becoming convinced of Father Divine's teachings, he sold his automobile business, gave his wealth to the Peace Mission, and entered Divine's service. Soft-spoken, dignified, and meticulous, Mathews—now taking the name "John Lamb"—quickly became one of Father Divine's most valuable aids. He transcribed all of Divine's messages in shorthand, helped administer the network of kingdom extensions, and defended his leader's ideals to outsiders with notable calm and clarity.[24]

Others came to Father Divine from a lifetime of professional work in religion. Unlike many for whom the Peace Mission was a last resort for the solution of paralyzing problems, these were productive people highly esteemed by society. Eugene Del Mar, featured in most *Who's Who*

volumes during the thirties for his contributions to philosophy, first con-
tacted the Peace Mission as an investigator commissioned by Suffolk
County in 1931. Del Mar reported in glowing detail that Divine was incorruptible and a wise religious teacher. Though not strictly a disciple, he
maintained a warm acquaintance with Divine for years after.[25]

The career of London-born Walter Lanyon provides a still more striking example of a respected philosopher who revered Father Divine as a
spiritual master. Lanyon published a series of books on religion in which
he stressed the workings of a divine spirit in every person. Praising Father
Divine as the inspiration for his ideas, Lanyon dedicated his volume *The
Eyes of the Blind* to Divine in 1941. Lanyon became something of the
Peace Mission's Saint Paul, in Chancellor Williams's apt phrase; he elo-
quently preached Father Divine's message throughout Europe and helped
create branches of the movement abroad.[26]

In an era when young men felt encouraged to reshape society, the Peace
Mission's cooperative system and its stand for racial equality drew more
than a few idealists into its ranks. Some were aspiring utopian architects
who saw the Peace Mission as a golden forum for promulgating visions
for a better world. The editors of the Los Angeles *Spoken Word,* a journal affiliated with the Peace Mission, exemplified this point of view. While
they dutifully reprinted every syllable of Father Divine's sermons and off-
hand comments, they also produced economic polemic far more strident
and uncompromising than most of his expressed attitudes. Father Divine
usually condemned only the abuses of capitalism but praised Ford, Carnegie, and other "enlightened" entrepreneurs. The editors of the *Spoken
Word,* however, appraised the American economic order with almost
unremitting hostility. They looked to the day when "millions of Peace restaurants" and other cooperative shops "will speedily take the government
out of the hands of the Morgans, Mellons," and other capitalist mag-
nates.[27]

Affluent, educated blacks with an interest in civil rights also were to
be found among Divine's disciples. Arthur Madison was a successful attorney who had studied at Columbia University before earning his law degree
at the University of Wisconsin. He recalled that his teachers at Columbia,
including John Dewey and Edward Thorndike, were "wonderful," but they
could not compare with Father Divine, whose spiritual and social messages had changed his life. Madison's continued marriage and modest reservations regarding the minister's deity made his status as a disciple somewhat suspect. Yet he donated his legal services free to the Peace Mission
and became one of Divine's closest counselors.[28] More briefly, the attorney
James Thomas also referred to Father Divine as his spiritual guide. Although Thomas at first agreed to defend Father Divine in Mineola only

out of a concern for civil rights, he also briefly developed a personal interest in the Peace Mission. At one pretrial rally Thomas intently thanked Father Divine for sending him blessings through "mental contact."[29]

Middle- and lower-middle-class blacks also were present in the Peace Mission. While many of them were racked by illness, obvious emotional problems, or some social crisis, others seemed brimming with good health and high morale. Priscilla Paul, a disciple from the days in Sayville, provides a classic illustration.[30] Observers at Father Divine's banquets frequently commented on Priscilla's earthy, humorous nature, sharp intelligence, and congeniality with both men and women. She composed hymns for the banquet gatherings and peppered her testimonies with bantering remarks. A creative dress designer and businesswoman of some ambition, she was far from the stereotype of the poor ghetto dweller coming to the Peace Mission for aid.

The presence of the Peace Mission's John Lambs, Walter Lanyons, Arthur Madisons, and Priscilla Pauls dictates a caution in generalizing about the personalities and motives of followers. Unless their veneration of Father Divine is taken as conclusive *prima facie* evidence of emotional ill health, they appear to have been at least as stable, competent, and mature as most people outside the movement. Their devotion to Father Divine and his teachings does not, of course, negate the fact that most followers did come to Father Divine desperate for some kind of help. Yet it suggests that one cannot ascribe every case of conversion simply to material deprivation or acute anxiety. It also reflects the fact that the Peace Mission possessed a vital communal life, a spiritual commitment, and a strong social vision—it was never merely a passive haven for the weak.

Whether people approached Father Divine for sustenance, spiritual truth, social leadership, healing, or shelter from any of dozens of personal troubles, they soon left behind the signs of their former identity. They adopted a rigorous code of discipline; acquired in many cases a new, "spiritual" name to symbolize their religious rebirth; and learned to live for "the cause" and, more specifically, for Father Divine.

The followers also left behind all inherited social and cultural barriers. White and black, West Indian and native American, rural southern migrant and long-settled Harlem resident all coexisted easily in the Peace Mission, in sublime disregard of the hostilities permeating the larger society. Even old theological disputes died away, as one-time Christian Scientists, Rosicrucians, Baptists, Methodists, Holiness church members, spiritualists, and others long given to an exclusive religious certainty or denomination renounced all past feelings of disdain and rancor toward each other.

The transformation was, in Father Divine's famous words, "truly wonderful," though troubled observers noted that the disappearance of these conflicting fanaticisms related to the ascendance of a new, unifying fanaticism. The sharpest differences of origin and interest receded into insignificance before the unshakable belief that Father Divine perfectly embodied the divine spirit. Therefore, what might have been a series of intractable factions arguing over religion, politics, economics, social priorities, and cultural traditions merged instead into a strikingly homogeneous instrument for the pleasure of one, deified man.

Scope

The kingdom of heaven as represented by Father Divine was, if not infinite, at least immeasurable to the world at large. Estimates of Divine's following during the thirties varied sharply with each observer's biases about the Peace Mission's nature and appeal. Father Divine himself kept no records of either the membership or the finances of his movement. One biographer, John Hoshor, put the figure at 2 million disciples in 1936.[31] Robert A. Parker, a more careful scholar, thought this exaggerated but hesitated to say by how much.[32] *Time* reported the widely accepted figure of 50,000 followers in 1937.[33] St. Clair McKelway and A. J. Liebling offered the lowest estimate of a few thousand followers in 1936,[34] while Divine less modestly acknowledged 22 million as the most accurate approximation of his support.[35]

A major problem in attempting to solve the riddle of the movement's numerical strength, aside from the absence of official records, is the task of defining who was a true member of the Peace Mission. Father Divine liked to think — in the best evangelical tradition — that members joined in their souls rather than through such mundane means as donations, membership rites, or even attendance at his sermons. "I want you to always keep in mind," he boasted, "you are at liberty to come or go as you will, we take no names and we do not have roll call — not after the similitude of men. The call that you will get is that call within!"[36]

The above difficulties are compounded because the largest single category of followers appears to have been that of the nominal member who often came to the banquets and perhaps to some services yet did not become a full convert to the movement. It is obviously impossible to say how devoted such people were to Father Divine personally or in how many ways their behavior conformed to Divine's teachings.

One can discount the most far-reaching claims with fair certitude. A. J. Liebling notes that if Hoshor's estimate of 2 million were correct, it would have remarkable implications. Since the movement was about 10 percent white, "certainly not more than 15 per cent," he reasoned, and since the movement scarcely touched the South, where the majority of blacks lived during the 1930s, then by Hoshor's estimate about 75 percent of Negroes in the North would be Divinites. "This," Liebling rightly concluded, "is manifestly absurd."[37] Yet Liebling's analysis is itself vulnerable, because it somewhat undervalues the number of white members. His figure of 10 to 15 percent seems to have been derived by concentrating on the northeastern United States. Outside that region, however, the proportion of white followers increased greatly and at times constituted a substantial majority of the membership.

Some have tried to calculate the hard core of Father Divine's following based on the number of registered voters with "spiritual names." It was a reasonable proposition that anyone on the voting rolls calling himself "Happy Lamb" or "Faithful Love" had assumed that name as a symbol of spiritual rebirth after joining the Peace Mission. On this basis Divine's strength in New York City was never much more than 1,000 followers. Since over 10 percent of all the Peace Mission centers were in New York City and since Father Divine focused his leadership there, one could place the number of his strongest supporters at about 10,000 as an upper limit.

The method of extrapolating from registration figures has its difficulties, however. First, not all followers took a spiritual name; this seemed to be a matter of individual choice, and even some of the most devoted Peace Mission members preferred to keep their old names. A related problem in calculating membership figures from voting lists is that Tammany-appointed registration officials frequently harassed people with spiritual names, whether from prejudice or from fear that the disciples would vote in a bloc against their faction. As a result, a disproportionate number of followers who succeeded in registering were those who had retained their old names. This, in turn, precludes more than a partial identification of the movement's voting members.

A further weakness in the use of voting lists is that it marks only one, narrow definition of what constituted a supporter of Father Divine. It excludes the thousands more who shared his hospitality and at times — during the trial in Mineola, for example — rallied to his defense, without being consistently committed to the movement. It also excludes many people, particularly in the ghettos, who did not attend Divine's banquets or subscribe to his theology yet admired his leadership as a champion of racial equality. When these "fellow travelers" are included, the estimate of 50,000 supporters becomes plausible.

Popular lore and dozens of self-proclaimed apostles carried word of Father Divine's Peace Mission throughout the United States and to several foreign nations during the 1930s. The number of Peace Mission branches multiplied in the early years of the decade to a peak of around 150 to 160, a figure sustained through the early forties.

Even during the Peace Mission's peak years, many centers changed location frequently. This perhaps indicates a rapid turnover of membership;

more likely, economic difficulties in establishing permanent centers, and the opposition of outsiders to such residences, determined the shifts. Father Divine's own considerable mobility and his interest in creating new, more advantageously situated branches heightened this tendency to relocate often.

Other demographic features of the Peace Mission movement remained fairly stable during the thirties. Its organization centered in New York, a testament to the importance of Harlem and neighboring black districts as a source of recruitment. In 1936, while the Peace Mission was at the height of its popularity and influence, an official directory listed over 150 branches with addresses, of which more than a quarter were located in New York state. Seventeen were in New York City alone, with most others in rural areas upstate.[38] Among businesses that advertised in the major Peace Mission journal, a substantial majority were based in New York City.[39]

About a third of all American branches of the movement were located west of the Mississippi, and of these the great majority were in California. The state was even then unrivaled as a greenhouse for religious and political experiments among the middle class, and the Peace Mission there took on much of the local coloring. Its membership was perhaps 70 percent white, nearly reversing the ratio of race mixing common in the northeastern centers. A substantial number of followers were educated and well-to-do, though marked by many of the same emotional problems that characterized their eastern counterparts. They were also highly political, reflecting California's widespread enthusiasm for utopian crusades, such as Upton Sinclair's democratic socialist plan to end poverty in California and Francis Townsend's single-minded drive for an old-age pension panacea. The Californian members of the Peace Mission absorbed much of this vaguely left-wing and antiplutocratic rhetoric, and at a similarly naive level. They also staunchly supported the Peace Mission's central principle of racial equality, again less from experience or the observation of ghetto conditions than from an abstract desire for social justice. The California centers thus differed in tone if not substance from the eastern Peace Missions. While the ghetto-based centers in New York and New Jersey chiefly represented a rising of the urban proletariat, the Californian-dominated western branches revealed the reform impulses of a socially restive white middle class.

Father Divine's authority ebbed sharply south of the Mason-Dixon line. The Peace Mission listed only twelve centers in the former Confederate states in 1940, or about 7 percent of the total. The reasons include the obviously fatal tenets of racial integration and equality, plus the fact that Father Divine did not often venture south in the thirties, whether because of bitter past experiences or preoccupations in Harlem. It is questionable whether any of the centers in the South except for those in Florida were interracial, which might have led to their rapid suppression. The centers were certainly unobtrusive. If any Peace Mission members there ever demonstrated on behalf of social reform, let alone integration, no record of such an act of courage exists. Father Divine implicitly conceded that any popular movement for racial equality in his native region would have to wait upon the struggles of a later generation.

Over two dozen Peace Mission centers operated outside the United States during the thirties, mainly in Canada, Western Europe, and Australia. Most were led by English-speaking men or women who had visited Father Divine or read his sermons and felt called to proselytize in their native countries. Members were recruited largely from the urban working classes, the same social and economic elements that formed the core support for other sects and cults in those nations. Except for the veneration accorded to Father Divine, the Peace Mission centers in foreign lands blurred with the numerous other puritanical religious groups of the day.

The foreign missions nominally upheld Father Divine's principles of racial integration and equal rights. Yet the conditions that gave rise to these principles — specifically the existence of a submerged racial caste — were remote from the experience of the nearly all-white membership. These centers focused instead on the Peace Mission's spiritual and pacifist aspects, to the neglect of that reforming spirit that marked the branches under Father Divine's personal direction.

However much the foreign branches deviated from the practices of the main Peace Mission centers in America, they nevertheless greatly enhanced Father Divine's prestige. The fact that Divine could attract groups of white men and women far more concerned with finding God than eliminating Jim Crow laws only confirmed the universality of the minister's religious appeal. The distant locations of these groups contributed to the credibility of Father Divine's claims of a vast following extending to all points of the globe.

The scope of Father Divine's influence, indeed, ranged unaccountably far. Disciples at his Mount Olympus at 20 West 115th Street in Harlem liked to regale visitors with a postcard on display at their center. It was sent from China and addressed: "God — Harlem — U.S.A." This was ample identification for postal authorities to deliver the card without delay to the Reverend M. J. Divine.[40]

Organization

Peace Mission members frequently boasted that theirs was a religion without formal organization, membership, or ritual. One key aide claimed that Father Divine allowed but had no need for organizations to carry on his work.[41] Such statements carried strong conviction and in turn helped the disciples project an aura of unmatched spontaneity to the outside world; yet the reality was quite different. The Peace Mission may have offered aspects of freedom previously unknown to many of its members. Nevertheless, its strictures were as imposing and comprehensive as those of any established church.

In theory, followers of Father Divine were those who felt an inner call. Those who operated the "kingdom extensions," or branches, might well have added that, while many were called, few were chosen. Any person caught smoking or drinking liquor on Peace Mission premises was summarily discharged, even if these acts occurred in the "privacy" of the person's room. Swearing, unless the offender quickly made amends, was punishable by the same means. Cohabitation was, of course, the ultimate disgrace for a professed disciple, and doors to all residences were notably devoid of locks. Despite what many observers fancied about the uninhibited followers of Father Divine, these converts in fact adhered to a regimen of remarkable self-discipline in matters of personal morality.

Although Father Divine did not formally require disciples to live in Peace Mission communal centers, most chose to do so on a permanent basis. In the large cities of the East and Far West, more Peace Mission accommodations served as all-purpose centers with dormitories, assembly halls, kitchens, and dining rooms. A special "studio" was almost always set apart for Father Divine, no matter how remote the chance that he would ever avail himself of this architectural tithe.

The majority of the kingdom extensions generally functioned in the humbler portions of a city. In San Francisco disciples renovated a modest brick building in the notorious Barbary Coast district. Seattle's Peace Mission conducted its evangelical affairs in the equally discouraging haunt known as Skid Road. Peace Missions in the Northeast operated chiefly among the poorest streets of ghetto neighborhoods.

The aged cluster of seven Peace Mission dwellings on 126th Street between Lenox and Seventh avenues in Harlem revealed the exceedingly modest nature of Father Divine's urban paradise. The largest of these four-story edifices was already in a state of advanced old age when the Peace Mission declared it a heaven and converted it into a residence for perhaps 100 disciples. Visitors described it in terms generally reserved for haunts in gothic tales. Some of the imitation-marble stairways were cordoned off because they were too rotten to be safely used. Those who wished to go to rooms on the upper floors were obliged to use a front flight of steps on one floor, a side flight on another, and a back flight on the next. Plumbers refused to undertake major repairs on the rust-eaten pipes for fear that the whole system might soon collapse. The interior of the building was damp and some walls contained mold.[42] The rooms themselves, however, were kept "scrupulously clean," a visitor observed, and "like the kitchens in 'Heaven,' comply with the health regulations."[43]

The pride of the Divinite firmament was a three-story edifice at 20 West 115th Street in Harlem. Father Divine gave more sermons here than at any other kingdom extension; the building's red "tapestry" brick facade and imposing arched entrance imparted a sense of grandeur amid the surrounding signs of poverty. In earlier times the building had served as the meeting place for a white fraternal order, but it was abandoned when blacks entered Harlem in great numbers during the early 1900s. Lena Brinson, a former fried-chicken vendor, leased the building while Father Divine preached in Sayville and offered it gratis as a place of worship for his Harlem-based disciples. Later, when Divine moved to New York, this became a frequent residence, and in late 1933 he made it his official headquarters. Typically, he refrained from placing it in his own name, instead having Miss Brinson retain nominal control of the property.[44]

The functional division of the grounds at 20 West 115th Street seemed consciously to parallel the hierarchy within the movement. Deep below street level a banquet hall accommodated several hundred followers who mingled without discernible barriers of race or rank. The main floor provided a large assembly room where Father Divine and selected disciples or visitors could address the multitudes. Upper floors served as dormitories for the members, but with separate office space for key administrators and secretaries. A "studio" room further distinguished the top floor, forming "a sort of penthouse structure on the roof."[45] There, seated behind a desk bordered by two stuffed doves, Father Divine could often be found, flanked by secretaries, working well into dawn.

Those who saw only the philanthropic aspect of the movement wondered at Divine's seemingly "infinite supply" of wealth. Yet the Peace Mission operated on a sound business basis; its revenues from donations, rents, and dining charges were ample to meet its low per-capita expenditures. The core following known as "Angels," who donated their wages or labor to the movement, in return received food, shelter, and clothing but otherwise entailed a minimal financial burden. While they could not be said to lack for emotional release, their recreation centered almost entirely on communal celebrations of a most inexpensive nature.

While Father Divine preached in Sayville, the great majority of his disciples became "Angels," pooling all property. As his reputation grew, however, he attracted a host of fellow travelers whose loyalty to him often was considerable but stopped short of a readiness to part with all their wealth. St. Clair McKelway and A. J. Liebling point out that Father Divine lacked the time to proselytize these individuals with the thoroughness of former years, but he valued such personal and financial commitment as they were prepared to make. He therefore created a new class of followers, the Children, who observed his teachings and paid to live in the Peace Mission residences but retained their private property. "Angels are still created every now and then," McKelway and Liebling wrote in 1936, "but save in exceptional cases, and in cases of well-to-do whites, they must first be Children for a while."[46]

The kingdom extensions on 126th Street in Harlem exemplified the pattern of profit that characterized Peace Missions throughout the country. The main building of the seven leased for $300 a month, the other six brownstone houses for $75 each. "Angels" living rent-free predominated in the main building, but some 300 "Children" paid $1 to $2 a week to live in the brownstones, providing annual revenues upward of $15,000. A conservative estimate, then, would place net revenues for the seven buildings at over $6,000 annually, exclusive of the money contributed by the "Angels."[47]

The growth of Peace Mission businesses further ensured the prosperity of the movement. Most involved retailing of goods and services requiring small initial capital investment. The very low cost of living for these entrepreneurs enabled them to charge prices considerably less than market value and, as a result, these businesses thrived beyond all expectation. They were particularly plentiful in Harlem, where clusters of "Peace!" signs identified grocers, barbers, shoe shiners, and others as followers of Father Divine. Even in areas remote from lower-class black neighborhoods, the pace of sales for Peace Mission businesses was generally brisk.

Father Divine took a keener interest in this realm of Caesar than he cared publicly to admit. He encouraged new business ventures, supervised the practices of Peace Mission hotels and dining services, and took careful, daily inventory of transactions in many centers. If a branch was not meeting expenses, Divine either redirected the members to a new site or replaced its administrator, always with an "Angel" of high reliability. Some cashiers who left the movement later claimed that Divine scrutinized their records thoroughly and questioned them sharply about the slightest apparent inconsistency. The cashiers, in brief, had to be absolutely trustworthy but were never absolutely trusted.

Whether or not administrators turned over money directly to Father Divine or simply accounted for its whereabouts, there is little question that he ultimately controlled the uses to which it was put. "My true followers consult with me before any venture,"[48] he occasionally boasted when not feeling too acutely the pressure of the law or the Internal Revenue Service. This is not to deny the generosity of his financial leadership, for literally thousands were indebted to low Peace Mission prices for their ability to survive during the Depression. It is clear, however, that Father Divine's kingdom was very much of this world.

As the Peace Mission spread and diversified, specialization among the membership became imperative. During the early thirties the movement developed a class of administrators to supervise the kingdom extensions, disseminate information, provide legal counsel, and attend to Father Divine's personal needs. This rapidly expanding bureaucracy enabled a successful transition from a modest commune to a corporate network spanning the globe and managing millions of dollars in personal and real property.

In addition to the many cashiers, bookkeepers, and general managers of the kingdom extensions, Father Divine relied on a corps of about twelve personal secretaries. Most were of middle-class background, with some college education and training in stenography. The ablest often assumed major administrative responsibilities, but all helped preserve the Father's words for publication in journals connected with the movement. Father Divine seldom went anywhere without an escort of these scribal amanuenses, who could often be seen, in a cluster, recording his every utterance. As a god, Father Divine could by definition speak no trivial ideas, so these secretaries were at constant readiness lest, on rising from a nap, he should spring forward with a gem of cosmic wisdom.

Journalists among the Peace Mission members became as valuable, in their way, as Divine's secretaries. The movement needed to standardize its message as it spread far beyond the confines of a single building, city, and country. The inclusion of news about the Peace Mission by a few sympathetic journals provided only a makeshift solution. Some of these journals, like the *New York News,* a black weekly not to be confused with the city's huge-selling *Daily News,* quickly folded. Others, like the *New York Age,* another black weekly, were far more prestigious and commercially successful but less constant in their sympathies for Divine. The *Age's* impressionable religion reporter, Clifford Smith, initially covered Father Divine's activities in Sayville much as Matthew and Mark recorded the ministry of Jesus, but Smith found Divine increasingly inaccessible to him and grew both disillusioned and embittered. Within a short while new and more skeptical journalists had taken his place, leaving the Peace Mission once more in search of a dependable news organ.

Of several journalistic ventures operated by Peace Mission disciples, the *Spoken Word* was the first to achieve widespread and sustained acceptance as the courier for Father Divine's message.[49] It began operations in Los Angeles in October, 1934, reprinting Divine's sermons as fast as it received transcripts from the East. It also featured directories of the Peace Mission centers, announcements of upcoming activities, and editorials on their leader's achievements in refashioning society.

The *Spoken Word* inspired creation of a similar journal in New York, the *New Day*. Its proximity to the main Peace Mission centers aided it in reporting Father Divine's sermons quickly and in obtaining advertisements from firms seeking patronage by the membership. During the thirties many major department stores in New York responded to the Peace Mission's energetic solicitors by placing ads regularly in the *New Day*. Consequently, the *New Day* thrived long after the *Spoken Word* went bankrupt in 1937. The infusion of new editorial talent from the defunct Los Angeles journal also assured the *New Day* of quality writing within its self-imposed limits as a journal less concerned with objectivity than hagiography.

Father Divine and the *New Day*'s editors maintained that this journal, like the *Spoken Word* on which it was modeled, was an independent paper. This was true in that its financial operations depended for revenues chiefly on businesses outside the Peace Mission movement. Moreover, Father Divine apparently did not censor the *New Day*'s columns, beyond proofing his own printed comments. Yet the editors all were dedicated disciples of Father Divine. They also enjoyed his strong endorsement, without which there would scarcely have been a readership for their paper. For all practical purposes, then, the *New Day* was from its inception an organ of the Peace Mission movement.

It is a sign of the Peace Mission's growing bureaucracy that a number of Father Divine's key advisers were among the least committed to him personally. These were his lawyers, about half a dozen during the 1930s. Except for Arthur Madison, the lawyers tended to have a wide range of professional interests aside from representing the Peace Mission. They also gave little sign in court of being disciples of Father Divine. Counselors such as Kevie Frankel and Abraham Unger instead appeared to be "keen-witted, sophisticated, and even cynical champions of civil liberties. . . ."[50]

The responsibilities of the lawyers proliferated in rough proportion to the growth of Peace Mission branches and activities. They advised on purchases of property, on ways to foil suits by townspeople hostile to neighboring Peace Missions, and on how to curb liability for various financial claims against the movement. The lawyers also provided shrewd general counsel on running this staggeringly complex and far-flung organization. Never did these aides become powers behind the throne, yet as a group the Peace Mission lawyers were indispensable to the smooth and efficient running of the Divine kingdom.

The egalitarian ideal of the Peace Mission receded somewhat before the practical needs for special skills and contributions. "Angels," whose financial commitment was vital to the Peace Mission, were considered a higher order of disciples than "Children," who formed perhaps 75 percent of the following. Among "Angels" themselves, distinctions of status were evident between the mass of unskilled seraphs and those who served as cashiers, supervisors, journalists, secretaries, and lawyers. The latter two groups met often with Father Divine and not uncommonly held places of honor near him at the banquet table. Some followers who performed special services were also rewarded, if they so desired, with superior living quarters. The personal chauffeur of a leading administrator in the movement occupied a choice room in his hotel, and his bed was covered with a pink satin spread. Others in that hotel slept four to a cubicle and without any decorative frills.[51]

The tangible benefits to officials in the Peace Mission were nevertheless modest in most cases. Distinctions between "Angels" and "Children" were based on degrees of sacrifice rather than privilege; anyone who was so determined could become an "Angel" simply by living communally without reservation. No special uniforms, medals, certificates, or rank distinguished any of the special functionaries in the movement, nor were these officials given a great deal of authority over other disciples. They were required to follow fairly strict guidelines, and if they failed to do so were likely to be replaced. The monetary rewards to officials in this communal movement were likewise negligible. For the most part they lived in as plain and disciplined a way as the rest of the membership, and with only those perquisites that related to the performance of their specific duties.

The sole potentially troublesome inequality was the disproportion of white disciples holding positions of responsibility, a situation that obtained in Harlem as well as California. No direct prejudice was involved; on the contrary, it was a policy of awarding positions based solely on education and professional certification that naturally favored the largely white middle-class element in the movement. The followers themselves, far from appearing discontented, seemed to regard the Peace Mission as fully dedicated in practice and theory to promoting racial equality. This is partly because, in comparison with the larger society, the Peace Mission did provide ample opportunity for advancement to blacks as well as whites. It achieved this, moreover, without apparent regard for filling any kind of racial quota. Thus nearly all Father Divine's secretaries during the thirties were white, as were most of the lawyers. Whites also contributed greatly to the quality of the Peace Mission publications. On the other hand, "Faithful Mary," a poor black woman with a police record, became Father Divine's closest disciple and served as personal envoy to the new California missions in 1934, where she received much credit for their rapid success.

"Mother Divine," the minister's wife "in the spirit" and highly honored in the movement, was also black. So was Divine's attorney, Arthur Madison, who may well have been his single most trusted aide. Clearly, the high representation of whites in leadership roles did not reflect a deeper intent to establish or regulate any racial hierarchy.

The spirit of the movement was perfectly captured by Ross Humble, a prominent follower who gave up a lucrative practice as a psychologist in California to serve the Peace Mission without compensation. When asked about his racial status, he objected to being classified as white, reiterated his devotion to the principles of Father Divine, and reminded the interviewer that none of Divine's followers was ever distinguished by "complexion."[52]

Ultimately the Peace Mission's greatest insurance against rigid divisions among the membership was less its idealism than the fact that it already had a two-tiered and impassable hierarchy of surpassing import. On the top level Father Divine stood in splendid isolation, hailed as the embodiment of God on earth and plotting every move behind the Peace Mission's growth and policies. The Peace Mission's following, from the most exalted counselors to the thousands of anonymous votaries who cheered at the mention of Father Divine's name, occupied the infinitely wide bottom rung of this simple hierarchy. They acknowledged "Father" as sole authority of the Peace Mission, shaped their lives around his wishes, and based their self-esteem on his continued favor.

Given the chasm between the Peace Mission following and the deified image of Father Divine, differences in stature and influence among individual disciples quickly faded into insignificance. Divine had so constructed his movement as to reduce all others in it to a virtual equality of humble, devoted service. Outsiders might doubt his claims to divinity, yet there is little question that, within the realm of the Peace Mission, Father Divine truly reigned supreme.

The Banquet

The banquet table was the center of communal activity in every Peace Mission branch. There hundreds gathered to praise Father Divine as befitted an all-providing benefactor, while enjoying repasts of a scope to awe many a doubting Thomas outside the movement. The sharing of elaborate and well-prepared meals had, of course, a special meaning in an age of widespread privation. The banquets also represented a timeless aspect of religious life: the search for God through human fellowship and devotion to a common spiritual leader.

The praise sessions at these banquets, as Raymond Jones observed, were "scenes of confusion, unconstrained emotional release, frenzied handclapping, yelling back and forth, dancing, hustle and bustle of young and old. . . ."[53] The tumult came in waves that reached deafening crescendos and never completely subsided. Individual members enjoyed the fullest cathartic expression in an atmosphere of group encouragement: "A seventeen year old girl went swirling around the room with her eyes clamped shut, careening into tables and breaking chairs and smashing china and tumbling to the floor with a crash that must have been heard in Times Square. Her sisters pulled her to her feet and sent her whirling on."[54] There was not a single, concerted display of feeling so much as a host of highly personal performances all more or less oblivious of each other. At one typical Harlem gathering in 1933, the commotion seemed quite random as well as physically taxing and possibly dangerous to some participants:

Four young tots merrily skipped about at the height of the capers . . . one woman rolled gleefully on the hard floor for ten minutes, and a man rushed crazily around the hall four times, miraculously managing not to strike his head on two large wooden pillars supporting the balcony. The manner in which he and several others, who did their ocean-waving in the hall escaped harm, led one to believe that perhaps, after all, Father Divine was looking after his flock.[55]

A sermon or even appearance by Father Divine at any banquet was an emotional catalyst of frightening power. Although many banquet halls, despite fanciful legends to the contrary, were often only half-filled, any Peace Mission center at which Divine was rumored to appear would invariably be packed to overflowing. He rarely entered at the beginning of the festivities but preferred to let the assembled followers work themselves into a frenzy of anticipation. Then, sometimes after hours of this deliberate tantalizing, he briskly strode into the meeting hall, receiving a thunderous ovation. Surges of yearning took the form of shouts, whistles, clapping, leaping, even fainting. Some held aloft their homemade signs of "unevenly spaced black and gold and silver letters, [stating] that Father Divine and the Deity are one. Fanatic devotion, rather than professional skill, has gone into the making of these verbal ikons."[56]

Invariably the acclamations continued unabated for minutes after Father Divine had made his way to the far end of a U-shaped central table. All the while the "Father's" doe-shaped eyes looked out with kindness, approval, and a certain wistfulness at these people who came to him for meaning. To many, who had been slipping in the most basic struggle for subsistence, this would take the form of meals and shelter in his care, when no government or private relief agencies reached them. To others, spiritual searchers or refugees from some personal tragedy, the Father's benevolent gaze and words were the meaning their lives required. To all, this was a Peace Mission in its literal sense, a haven from a world that desperate souls had found unfulfilling and sometimes shattering.

Much to the dismay of the multitudes, Father Divine usually declined to speak at length so soon after his appearance in the banquet hall. Instead, he limited himself for the moment to a few simple rituals, which nevertheless had a powerful emotional impact on those present. He stood before the crowds like a beacon serenely radiating authority as he waited patiently, almost humbly, for the shouted praise and devotion to subside. He then welcomed all to share his bounty, perhaps adding a few words to assure outsiders—special guests, hungry passers-by, those who were simply curious—that they, too, should feel at home. Thousands pressed forward for a closer look at the human god as he prepared to bless the first courses of food, in a very effective ritual of communion:

> Every dish on which food is placed passes at least once through his [Father Divine's] hands. When a platter of meat is to be sent around, Father Divine places the serving utensil upon the platter with his own hands. He places the ladle in the tureen of soup, he cuts the first slice of cake, pours the first glass of water, introduces the serving spoon into each container of ice cream. He is thus part of every activity of the feast.[57]

Each guest served himself as large a portion of every item as he wanted and passed the dish on to his neighbor. All knew that the very poor need never pay for this food, while the affluent were likely to donate amply to cover the cost. The act of personal sharing was moving in itself, but the cumulative effect of the sheer number and diversity of dishes gave the ritual a true grandeur. Over fifty courses, and on some occasions as many as 200, were featured at these banquets. Of the many descriptions of these seemingly limitless feasts, the most captivating is given by Charles Braden, a student of religion who visited frequently with Father Divine. Although this account is from an experience in 1945, it accords in all essentials with records of Peace Mission hospitality in earlier years as well:

> Eleven different cooked vegetables passed in quick succession: steamed rice, green beans, green peas, boiled cabbage, sweet corn, succotash, stewed tomatoes, lima beans, greens, and carrots. I, not knowing what to expect, had begun by taking a little bit of everything but soon saw that this was not wise and became more selective. Then came platters of meat. It will be recalled that this experience was still in wartime and rationing had not yet been lifted. First came three or four cold cuts, including baked ham. Then appeared the hot, freshly cooked meats: roast beef, beef curry, meat loaf, fried chicken, roast duck, roast turkey, beef steak, each heaped high on the platters

which were passed around the festive board. Then came salads: fruit salad containing Persian melon, cantaloup, alligator pears, and lettuce, and sliced tomato salad. Next came bread: hot corn bread, hot rolls, white bread, brown bread, rye bread, raisin bread, and for good measure, crackers, accompanied by a good serving of butter. There was cranberry sauce for the roast turkey, apple sauce for the duck, and jams and jellies in profusion. The drinks consisted of iced tea, iced coffee, and iced water. I was assured that I could have hot coffee if I wanted it. Dessert consisted of two kinds of cake, one of them with fruit and whipped cream. On another like occasion, great heaping bowls of ice cream of two or three flavors were circulated around the table. Along with all of this went sweet pickles, mixed pickles, ripe olives, green olives, and all the condiments that would ordinarily be served on such an occasion. The average number of different dishes served at these banquets is around fifty-five.[58]

The tale of Jesus feeding the multitudes scarcely seemed more miraculous to Peace Mission members than their own awesome feasts, huge enough to have converted every Pharisee in Galilee, or to convince thousands in the nation's most frightful slums that Father Divine was truly God on earth.

The continuous passing of plates and bowls, far from pacifying the crowd, often signaled a resurgence of motion and music. It also stimulated individuals to make vivid confessions of sin to Father Divine while shouting his superhuman virtues and thanking him for protection against illness, aging, and death. The spontaneity of these exercises is open to some doubts. Robert Parker writes, for example, that the specific cures Divine had supposedly wrought "were enumerated with all the thoroughgoing detail of a station announcer bellowing out the route of a departing train. The assemblage endures this cataloguing with the polite indifference of a miscellaneous gathering in a waiting room."[59] Even the mass shouting often appeared prompted by certain key leaders. Another observer noted that in the middle of the hysterical singing and praising, "the object of all this adulation kept on eating and apparently paying no attention whatever to what the various people were saying."[60] It suggests that, for some, at least, individual ecstasies had been reduced to a form of worship in its own way as rigid and conventional as the established Negro church services, although somewhat more audible. In this, as in his "monster" rallies, Father Divine could to a great extent program and manipulate "spontaneity," even as his banquets and accompanying hosannas could elicit ecstasy with Pavlovian precision.

To perceive the force of habit and custom among the members of the Peace Mission is not, however, to deny the genuine quality of their sentiments, particularly among those who testified. Within the stylized conventions they unconsciously obeyed, they bared their lives and souls in a way that few churches encouraged.

The testimonies revealed an infinite variety of detail, though certain general patterns marked most of these recountings. Some told of miraculous healings, others of character reformation that included renunciation of crime, liquor, adultery, and all sexual relations. A few narratives related incidents of deep spiritual searching followed by sudden and unshakable conviction. All testimonies, however diverse in subject matter and language, were united by the apparent desire of all speakers to express gratitude and loyalty to Father Divine, symbol of their regenerated lives.

A selection of testimonies from a Peace Mission banquet, held in Baltimore shortly before the Mineola trial, may suggest their nature more concretely. They alternated with singing, clapping, and stamping, which rocked the banquet hall and made some visitors uneasy for the fate of the balcony supports. The followers were oblivious to the trembling walls, however, as they cheered on each disciple rising to tell his story of personal redemption.

The first speaker, a buxom woman with a pronounced foreign accent, typified many others in describing her earlier life in the most unflattering terms, then telling of a sudden, total change in her behavior through Father Divine's influence:

> I used to get drunk so much I was ashamed of myself. My husband didn't want me to drink because I would fight him. I had a sweetheart, and I used to be with him as much as my husband. Then Father Divine came into my life. The only person in the world I am scared of is Father Divine, because you know he is the true and living God. When he gets in you, you are independent, you don't need nothing.[61]

During one part of the banquet service a woman in the left section of the building went into violent contortions, but the testimonies continued without pause at this not uncommon occurrence. Another woman, slim and also speaking with a foreign accent, combined elements of faith healing and ascetic reformation in her story of deliverance:

> I want to tell the people of Baltimore what my Father did for me. I had a sinful body and a wicked soul. I had weak lungs, bad kidneys, and a nervous breakdown. For three years I had been getting worser and worser. When he came into my life I realized he was God and was made whole. Now, I have no heart trouble, no lung trouble, and no nerve trouble. I was a great adulteress, never without a boy friend or a husband. I don't need these now as Father Divine gives me everything I want.[62]

Speakers commonly referred to Father Divine as one would talk of a conscience. A woman given to mystic visions claimed that Father Divine "certainly worked on me. . . . He is the only God who has kept me from playing cards, from being an adulteress."[63] Another woman spoke in similar terms, describing him as the one influence that could restrain her from evil: "I am going to tell you what my God has done for me. He has saved me from sin and shame. I used to do every wrong thing. I was first class at everything. I had two husbands and nobody could clean me up. Father Divine came and saved me. Father Divine is God."[64]

A big, powerfully built man on the platform spoke at length in a husky voice. He alluded to the large proportion of former criminals in the hall: "You've never seen an audience like this at any convention or conference unless they had to have policemen. Freely you come and freely you are seated. Now, ain't that wonderful?" Cries of "Yes, yes!" greeted his remarks. The man then told how "Father" turned him from a life of debauchery:

> I bought [whiskey] by the gallon and sold it by the half pint. I drank a whole lot, too. I drank so much the man wondered what I was doing with all the whiskey I got. When Father Divine came, he told me to get all sin out of my life and walk in his steps. He looks like a man but I never hears of any man who can put the spirit in you. He didn't tell me but I went home and threw out the three decks of cards I had, and the checker boards. I didn't throw out the little bit of liquor I had left, but just drank it up. I dumped out everything else, too; the last thing I dumped out was my girl friend. The desire I had to do these things diminished away from me. I have no desire to do these things now.[65]

This convert hinted at a facet of Father Divine's appeal as important as his preaching in winning over these veteran criminals and derelicts to a moral life. "Here we have God with us, walking and talking just like us. Isn't that wonderful?" he exclaimed. Shouts of joy met his insight into the mystery of Father Divine's hold over these people.[66] For all were indeed searching for a god and guide they could comprehend and even, on these exhilarating occasions, personally address.

In a movement that so highly valued emotional expression, testimony was one of many ways that followers could release their feelings. Another was the musical artistry of a new generation of psalmists, whose often implicit object of devotion was Father Divine. Typical of the many paeans to "Father" is the following:

> I want to love you, Father,
> A little bit more each day,
> I want to love you, Father,
> In all I do and say,
> I want to love you, Father

For the wondrous works you do,
For I know you're God Almighty
And I've given this heart to you.[67]

A student of these compositions writes, "The music is so lively and rhythmical, although not exactly jazz, that one feels that one must join the foot tapping, clapping, and dancing which often accompanies the songs. The chanting is mostly by women and is entirely individual and unrehearsed."[68]

Singing absorbed most of the long hours at the banquets, rising and ebbing again but never quite ending. Guy Johnson observed: "Someone would start a song, others would take it up gradually, and finally most of the people would join in and sing lustily. Most of the songs had strong rhythms and were accompanied by hand clapping, foot patting, swaying, and sometimes by a sort of shuffling dance." There was a definite cycle to the emotional level of the participants, according to Johnson: "They would sing heartily, almost hysterically, for a while, then there would be a lull during which there was either no singing or only half-hearted singing with many of the people seeming to be almost asleep, and then the tension would mount again and rise to another climax of singing, hand clapping, etc."[69]

Johnson writes that the lyrics and delivery of these songs often revealed a sensual longing for "beautiful Father Divine":

[M]any of the singers, especially the women, accompanied their songs by looks and gestures of adoration, flirtation, surrender, ecstasy, etc. They would look at the large photograph of Father Divine, throw kisses, smack their lips, make gestures of embrace, and make such exclamations as "Father, you are so sweet," "Father, I love you so," "Sweet Father," "Father, I know you belong to me" . . . . The words of the songs are interesting from this same point of view. . . . "I got a right to this body of God." "He's so beautiful." "Father, I know that you are real." "I know that I am His and He is mine."[70]

The degree of originality and meaning in the full range of Peace Mission songs is a matter of some dispute. Edwin Buehrer, writing in the *Christian Century,* deprecated the musical outpourings as "a sentimental hash of obsolescent Protestant theology, revival hymns and familiar Broadway jazz hits."[71] Yet Guy Johnson, immersed in the study of Afro-American culture, concluded from his study of the Peace Mission that the songs at times demonstrated considerable inspiration and that their origins might shed light on the development of old Negro spirituals. Although the tunes were mostly from popular songs, a few resembled the African "shout songs" that characterized antebellum black worship. Most songs seemed

fairly well set in advance, but some, in Johnson's view, were improvisa-
tions from the testimony of followers. A man recounting how Father
Divine helped him bear his burdens

> became very emotional and spoke in a sort of rhythmic sing-song
> fashion. He finally started something which became a song. Swing-
> ing his body and patting his feet, he said, "He is making us like our
> Savior in this world, in this world." After he had repeated this several
> times other people began to take up the refrain line . . . and shortly
> they were singing rather heartily to a tune which was very similar to
> "She'll Be Coming 'Round the Mountain When She Comes."

The followers themselves insisted that the songs were created on the spot
and that the reason they were not printed was that, in the words of a
woman follower, "They are outpourings of the spirit." Johnson more
cautiously concluded that these meetings were "a perfect laboratory" for
the study of how spirituals originated.[72]

The lyrics of some songs also suggest affinities in purpose with the antebellum spirituals, even though, as Johnson maintained, the specific verses
differed. The following chant, for example, comes from the Peace Mission repertoire but might as well have originated with a slave entreating
his divine father for rescue from earthly cares:

> Just give me sweet Father Divine,
> Just give me sweet Father Divine,
> You may have all the world,
> With the pleasures it gives;
> But give me sweet Father Divine.[73]

Another song declared still more simply:

> Father Divine is all I need, all I need, all I
>   need;
> Father Divine is all I need, all I need, all I
>   need.[74]

In effect, the followers turned the spiritual of antebellum days to a new
religious direction, centered on a human deliverer now but still seeking
heavenly solace from a lifetime of trouble.

The common surrender to Father Divine overwhelmed the considerable
disparities of social and economic background, as well as racial origin,
among the banquet assembly. A student of Negro cults, Arthur Huff
Fauset, highlights this in an account of several Columbia University students who attended a nearby Peace Mission service in Rockland Palace.
The students were clearly anticipating with relish a display of "African
fetish or Haitian voodoo worship." They were quickly disconcerted by
an elderly white man who declared to them, "Peace, everyone! I know

that you may not believe this, but many of us who are in this place will never lose the bodies we now have. . . . This is heaven on earth." Then he led followers in a song, "My Father's love shines more and more." At this point the students' cultural and racial stereotypes began to dissolve amid a rush of confusing images:

A white woman who had been playing castanets . . . suddenly leaped to her feet and began dancing back and forth across the front of the hall.

The white cornetist, who for a while played in the manner of Louis Armstrong, was so profoundly affected that he had to cease playing, and he joined lustily in the singing, shaking his head and his entire body in rhythm with the song. Presumably playing the cornet interfered with the execution of the body movements he was desirous of performing.

Then another white woman circled conspicuously in pinwheel fashion all over the front of the hall, while a very heavy-set middle-aged man, whom I later identified as a Jew, ran about the same place clasping his hands rhythmically, singing loudly and gaily, and contorting his face and body. . . . And finally, one of the Columbia University students, too overcome to remember where she was or what she was doing, began to sing freely and to tap the floor with her feet.[75]

The extremes of ardent behavior at these banquets occurred mainly among certain women followers but still cut across racial and class lines. Apart from their sensual singing, these followers greeted each appearance by Father Divine in a manner more prurient than pious. Guy Johnson recalled a banquet in which one woman spent a whole evening "either making soft, cooing, sounds or letting out hysterical shrieks. On two or three occasions when Father Divine happened to glance in her general direction she gave out a loud shriek, held her hands in the air, trembled all over, then made a whirling movement and collapsed in the arms of women standing around her."[76] Some of these women, black as well as white, appeared to experience sexual orgasms during their frenzied behavior at the banquets.[77]

This suggestive behavior by a minority of the women followers reflected the unreserved love that disciples felt for Father Divine but did not typify its expression. Notwithstanding the commotion and fervor at these banquets, they were largely puritanical affairs. The Peace Mission's tenet of chastity was upheld by the separate seating of the sexes and the fact that men and women never danced together. Even the most ardent overtures by female followers to Father Divine seemed a sublimation of sexual impulses rather than a prelude to further gratification. As for the great majority of both male and female disciples at the banquets, emotions reigned free but the prevalent spirit was one of Agape rather than Eros.

No banquet service could be considered complete without a message from Father Divine. At most gatherings, of necessity, a secretary read aloud from a reprinted sermon that the minister had given at some other function. But when Father Divine himself attended a banquet, the anticipation of hearing him speak precipitated outpourings of feeling which, by the third and fourth hours of festivities, exceeded all previous demonstrations of emotion.

Divine was a master at addressing crowds, an observation that momentarily united his most sympathetic listeners and bitter critics. Quick of mind and movement, he uncannily timed each banquet sermon to coincide with the crest of popular clamor for his message. Then he rose "like a cat," in the words of one visitor, who compared Divine's instinct for an audience to the ringside skills of his contemporary, the ghetto-born national hero Joe Louis. The crowds cheered and Divine paused, "waiting, his eyes down and his arms hanging limp; the instant the last cheer has died, completely died, he comes alive, shoots out clipped words that fly like bullets."[78]

Followers were rapt but not entirely silenced, which contributed to Divine's easy rapport with these people. In the manner of a southern black preacher, he encouraged shouted responses from the assemblage. He drew laughter with entertaining anecdotes and evoked affirmations at homilies on injustices that touched many followers personally. To bring his listeners into still fuller contact and create common denominators of empathy, he punctuated his vision frequently with the phrase he made famous: "Peace! It is truly wonderful!"

Individual sermons branched into tirades against race prejudice, calls for moral conduct, and discourses on the unity of being. Yet all were messages of present-centered hope for mankind generally and, most of all, for the discouraged and downtrodden with him that night. Father Divine told his listeners that all of them had unlimited potential for good, that they could lead upstanding and prosperous lives without waiting for the consolations of a future heavenly world. He described a society already coming, when all men and women could view themselves as free and equal, as partakers of the one, infinite spirit that created them.

Whether Divine preached twenty minutes or two hours, one could observe his followers intent to catch each inflection in their leader's speech. When he concluded with a modest, "I thank you. Peace!" the tightly massed disciples responded with a roar of approval that to discomfited outsiders seemed never to end. Yet the service and festivities often churned on gaily, featuring further testimonies, singing, dancing, and shouted praise without constraint or let-up. This ritual would be repeated with equal vigor and enthusiasm the next day or perhaps in a matter of hours, that same evening.

Ecstasy reigned among the poor, the racially outcast, and the troubled in spirit, so long as the good Father remained to inspire them. Twice a day, every day, the banquets broke through the monotony in their lives to bring them what they knew with deepest conviction was the kingdom of Heaven on earth.

Notes to Chapter 3

1. Hadley Cantril and Muzafer Sherif, "The Kingdom of Father Divine," *Journal of Abnormal Psychology* 33 (Apr., 1938):153.

2. See, for example, Father Divine's sermon of Apr. 2, 1935, in *ND,* Oct. 20, 1979, p. 9, in which he stated that he was not "an M.D. diagnoser, but I could be classed as a D.D. diagnoser."

3. Sermon of Jan. 10, 1938, in *ND,* July 22, 1978, p. 20.

4. Quote is in Hoshor, *God in a Rolls-Royce,* p. 89.

5. Ollie Stewart, "Harlem God in His Heaven," *Scribner's Commentator* 8 (June, 1940):26.

6. Testimony at banquet, in Tarrytown, N.Y., July 4, 1977.

7. Interview with Mr. Patrick, in Woodmont, Pa., July 4, 1977.

8. Guy B. Johnson, "Notes on Behavior at a Religious Service at the Father Divine Peace Mission," p. 12, Appendix D to "The Church and the Race Problem in the United States: A Research Memorandum," prepared in 1940 by Guion G. Johnson and Guy B. Johnson, with the assistance of E. Nelson Palmer, for the Carnegie-Myrdal study of the Negro in America, in the Schomburg Collection of the New York Public Library.

9. Charles S. Johnson, *The Shadow of the Plantation* (Chicago: University of Chicago Press, 1934), p. 3; see also William M. Tuttle, Jr.'s, development of this idea in *Race Riot: Chicago in the Red Summer of 1919* (New York: Atheneum, 1970), p. 96.

10. Related by Fauset in *Black Gods,* p. 54.

11. *SW,* May 9, 1936, p. 13.

12. Ibid., Jan. 19, 1937, p. 18.

13. Fauset, *Black Gods,* pp. 77-78.

14. Claude McKay describes Faithful Mary's role in the Peace Mission movement, in "Father Divine's Rebel Angel," *American Mercury* 51 (Feb., 1940):73-80.

15. See, for example, Faithful Mary's testimony at a Peace Mission banquet in Los Angeles in 1934, in *SW,* Nov. 3, 1934, p. 6.

16. Parker, *Incredible Messiah,* pp. 13-14.

17. Fauset, *Black Gods,* p. 53.

18. *SW,* Mar. 23, 1937, p. 18.

19. Ibid., p. 19.

20. *ND,* July 9, 1936, p. 13.

21. Interview with Arthur Carter, in Newark, July 1, 1977.

22. Hubert Kelley, "Heaven Incorporated," *American Magazine* 121 (Jan., 1936):108.

23. Jack Alexander, "All Father's Chillun Got Heavens," *Saturday Evening Post* 212 (Nov. 18, 1939):70.

24. On the career of John Maynard Mathews, see Hoshor, *God in a Rolls-Royce,* pp. 78-80, 161-64, and Alexander, "All Father's Chillun," p. 70.

25. The report by Eugene Del Mar to the Suffolk district attorney, Nov. 23, 1931, is reprinted in *SW,* June 22, 1937, pp. 14-15.

26. Williams, *Have You Been to the River?,* p. 217. Williams claims that Lanyon rather than Father Divine was the inspired thinker. Lanyon certainly was an elegant stylist, but his ideas seem closely patterned after Divine's; indeed, the bulk of Lanyon's work appeared in the early forties, nearly a decade after Divine had already gained international renown.

27. "Father Divine's Economic Empire," *SW,* Oct. 12, 1935, p. 24.

28. Parker, *Incredible Messiah,* p. 61; see also McKelway and Liebling, "Who Is This King of Glory?" pt. 3 (June 27, 1936), p. 22.

29. *Age,* Dec. 26, 1931, p. 5. Thomas and Divine later parted ways in a dispute over the costs of Thomas's defense, as reported in *NYAN,* Feb. 8, 1933, p. 1.

30. Parker, *Incredible Messiah,* pp. 165-67, details Priscilla Paul's role in the Peace Mission.

31. Hoshor, *God in a Rolls-Royce,* p. 139.

32. Parker, *Incredible Messiah,* p. 134.

33. "Messiah's Troubles," *Time* 29 (May 3, 1937):61.

34. McKelway and Liebling, "Who Is This King of Glory?" pt. 3, p. 28.

35. See preamble of the Peace Mission's "Righteous Government Platform," reprinted in numerous issues of both *SW* and *ND,* beginning with *SW,* Jan. 14, 1936, pp. 7-16.

36. Sermon of Sept. 3, 1933, in *ND,* Sept. 28, 1974, p. 13.

37. A. J. Liebling, "The Rise of Father Divine," review of *God in a Rolls-Royce* by John Hoshor, in *Saturday Review* 14 (Oct. 3, 1936):11.

38. *ND,* July 16, 1936, p. 16.

39. See, for example, the classified directory of advertisers in *ND,* July 4, 1940, pp. 109-12.

40. Parker, *Incredible Messiah,* p. 154.

41. Arthur Madison, testimony at Peace Mission banquet, New York, Feb. 24, 1935, in *SW,* Mar. 16, 1935, p. 15.

42. McKelway and Liebling, "Who Is This King of Glory?" pt. 3, p. 23, is the source for information on the Faithful Mary extension "heavens."

43. Kelley, "Heaven Incorporated," p. 106. A more critical view of sanitary conditions in the Peace Mission "heavens" is given by Raymond J. Jones, *A Comparative Study of Religious Cult Behavior among Negroes with Special Reference to Emotional Group Conditioning Factors* (Washington, D.C.: Howard University Press, 1939), p. 120.

44. McKelway and Liebling, "Who Is This King of Glory?" pt. 3, p. 26; Parker, *Incredible Messiah,* p. 109.

45. Parker, *Incredible Messiah,* pp. 108-9.

46. McKelway and Liebling, "Who Is This King of Glory?" pt. 3, p. 25.

47. These figures are based on information in ibid., p. 24.

48. Office talk, Nov. 7, 1940, in *ND,* Feb. 17, 1979, p. 7.

49. For information on other journals associated with the Peace Mission, see Stephen Zwick, "The Father Divine Peace Mission Movement" (Senior thesis, Princeton University, 1971), p. 132, and *NYAN,* July 6, 1932, p. 1.

50. Parker, *Incredible Messiah,* p. 263.

51. Kelley, "Heaven Incorporated," p. 106.

52. *NYAN,* Mar. 9, 1935, p. 2.
53. Jones, *Comparative Study,* p. 117.
54. Frank S. Mead, "God in Harlem," *Christian Century* 53 (Aug. 26, 1936): 1133-34.
55. E. W. Baker, "Witnesses Here Testify How Father Divine Helped Them to Depart from Varied Ways of Wickedness," *AA,* Apr. 15, 1933, p. 5.
56. Parker, *Incredible Messiah,* p. 110.
57. Fauset, *Black Gods,* p. 57.
58. Braden, *These Also Believe,* pp. 3-4. Similar accounts of banquet meals are found in Parker, *Incredible Messiah,* p. 6, Hoshor, *God in a Rolls-Royce,* p. 134, and Harris, *Father Divine,* p. 356, among many other sources.
59. Parker, *Incredible Messiah,* p. 113.
60. Edwin T. Buehrer, "Harlem's God," *Christian Century* 52 (Dec. 11, 1935): 1591.
61. *AA,* Apr. 1, 1932, p. 1.
62. Ibid., p. 4.
63. Ibid.
64. Ibid.
65. Ibid.
66. Ibid.
67. Kenneth E. Burnham, *God Comes to America: Father Divine and the Peace Mission Movement* (Boston: Lambeth Press, 1979), p. 130.
68. Ibid., p. 128.
69. Johnson, "Notes on Behavior," pp. 3-4.
70. Ibid., p. 4.
71. Buehrer, "Harlem's God," p. 1593.
72. Johnson, "Notes on Behavior," pp. 5-7.
73. *SW,* Nov. 17, 1934, p. 13.
74. Ibid.
75. Fauset, *Black Gods,* pp. 104-5.
76. Johnson, "Notes on Behavior," p. 9.
77. Ibid.; and see Harris, *Father Divine,* pp. 117-18.
78. Mead, "God in Harlem," p. 1134.

Father Divine addresses a banquet gathering at the Rockland Palace in Harlem.

Father Divine with his personal secretary, John Lamb.

atured are attorney James Thomas, seated at far left, and Pinninnah, Father Divine's
fe, at the minister's right.

Serving disciples at a banquet.

Peace Mission banquet in Philadelphia. The integrated seating pattern characterized
such assemblies.

A Peace Mission parade.

Father Divine emerges from the twelve-passenger Balank airplane he often traveled in during the early 1930s.

Father Divine inspects the camera used to film a "March of Time" movie about him.

CHAPTER 4

Reform from Within

Father Divine's personal experience had convinced him that oppressed people had to take the first steps toward their own emancipation. His life offered a striking demonstration that through pride, independence, ambition, and hard work one could overcome the twin obstacles of prejudice and poverty. He therefore sought to instill these qualities in his disciples, in the hope that they would rise from the slums and, through their example as model citizens, help defuse the racism simmering in the country.

Independence

Father Divine wished to see his followers independent in both spirit and economic means. He sternly warned them never to rely on state or private aid if they were able to work instead. He appealed to their often dormant pride, explaining that "there is more respect for a person who can respect himself independently than that person who is dependent on charity."[1]

Peace Mission members refused federal welfare benefits because Father Divine objected to a law requiring that those seeking public works jobs — of which he approved — first apply for unemployment relief. Divine complained to Secretary of the Interior Harold Ickes and WPA administrator Harry Hopkins that the law, by diminishing the work ethic, "lowers the standard of a person for the present, and for his future generation." His disciples conscientiously sought and merited government jobs, but would not "go on the welfares as beggars and as incompetent and unreliable people."[2]

One could achieve full independence only through fair dealing, Father Divine cautioned. "Honesty" became a watchword of the Peace Mission movement, as Divine added baroque flourishes to Benjamin Franklin's aphorisms on the subject. He harangued audiences to prove their devotion to him by paying their bills.[3] He forbade credit purchases as immoral, an understandable perspective for one who had known the sharecropper's world of entangling debts. And he warned his followers, many of whom had once been criminals, that there was no such thing as a small or harmless theft: "He who would steal an apple, would steal an elephant, if he could get him in his pocket, and get away with it, and he who would steal an egg would steal an ox, if he could get away with it."[4]

With his usual thoroughness Father Divine extended his campaign for honesty to every conceivable financial situation. He anathematized chain letters, which were supposed to bring ten cents to whomever's name was included in the list. That, Divine warned, was to fall into the weakness of mortal mind, which "is always trying to think up some material way of speculating and gambling, trying to do something for luck, getting something for nothing."[5]

Stock investments came in for similar condemnation as unwarranted speculation. When a businessman offered Father Divine and his followers shares in a new company, Divine conceded that enterprise should be commended. Still, there was a difference between selling merchandise, which "does not involve a gamble to win" but rather provides goods that are "tangible, practical and real, being useful at the time of the sale," and selling shares in a corporation, "especially an unorganized and undeveloped enterprise where it would be impossible for one to know definitely whether their investment would be safe, practical and profitable."[6]

Divine set an exacting example of financial rectitude for his disciples. He returned all outside contributions to the movement, usually with a note "explaining" that God provided for his needs.[7] He refused offers of $10,000 for speaking engagements, on the grounds that it was wrong to charge for spreading the word of God.[8] Unlike many other cult leaders, he denounced attempts to sell buttons and other items with his endorsement, calling it racketeering.[9] Finally, his insistence that disciples spurn all welfare unrelated to employment indirectly cost his movement an enormous fortune. One municipal official estimated in 1939 that Divine's forbearance had saved New York City alone over $2 million in welfare funds during the Depression.[10]

Disciples literally matched their leader's honesty to the last dime. They deluged stores with monetary atonements for thefts committed in earlier, less pure states of being. Restitution was generally accompanied by written testimonies like the following from a disciple in California:

> Inclosed you will find a money order for $3.00. This amount I am returning to you because 16 years ago, I worked for your firm, Store No. 5, and while there, I took candy & Icecream, and ate it while on the job, and no doubt some small change, and I knew in my heart

I was stealing, as it was not mine. Am sure the $3.00 will cover what I took. To be honest, I had no intentions of ever paying for these things, but since Father Divine, God Almighty has entered into my heart, not only mine but also 22 million of us, He has absolutely changed our minds and bodies.[11]

Virtually no misappropriated item was too small to warrant the most agonizing soul-searching, nor could time heal these wounds. One disciple, for example, astonished the superintendent of the Central of Georgia Railway in Macon by writing, "I wish to confess over forty years or more ago I rode the train from Andersonville, Ga., to Americus, Ga., without paying the fare. Since I have come in contact with Father Divine, he has caused me to confess and pay the same. Enclosed find 66¢ for the two rides."[12] That same week, a woman, who had perhaps recovered from the theft of two stuffed toy mules ten years before, received a letter from a former maid, Sallie Jones, who understated, "No doubt you'll be a bit surprised to hear from me. . . . I am sending you $2.50 to pay for a pair of mules of yours that was taken from Mrs. Cunningham's apartment."[13]

Even religious groups that disdained or feared Father Divine as a vexatious rival benefited from the new code of honor his disciples observed. A clerk for the Messiah Baptist Church in Yonkers, for example, gaped at a $300 donation by a man who had just left the church for the Peace Mission. The donor wished to make up "unpaid membership dues covering an 11 year period."[14]

The honesty of Father Divine's followers was a most effective advertisement for the movement. Outsiders may not have been converted by the return of a 75-cent debt, but they were frequently impressed, even overwhelmed, by the constructive impact Divine was making. A real estate agent named Fred Dickens expressed the feeling of many grateful entrepreneurs upon receiving payment for a bill long since given up as lost: "Then, I began to take Father Divine seriously."[15]

Personal reform required discipline as well as good intentions, and Father Divine made the avoidance of liquor and drugs a cardinal tenet of his movement. This had especial relevance to followers from the ghettos, for crimes related to alcoholism and drug addiction afflicted lower-class black life severely. The Peace Mission centers proscribed all such "indulgences" and expelled anyone caught drinking or involved in a similar breach of self-restraint.

When possible, Father Divine based his injunctions against vices on some biblical support. He cited the abstention of the Nazarites from liquor, quoting Numbers 6:3: "He shall separate himself from wine and strong drink." In general, though, Divine stood on practical health grounds: liquor and drugs were debilitating. They could "overbalance your mind," especially the widespread use of cocaine, which worked "to ruin the lives of humanity generally."[16] As ever, nothing if not thorough, Divine included cigarettes in his list of banned vices, this too receiving strict enforcement at Peace Mission centers.

The Peace Mission and the Law

The stress on independence, honesty, and self-discipline all contributed to a dramatic lowering of the crime rate wherever new Peace Missions established themselves. A municipal court judge in Los Angeles noted that in a district with several recently created Peace Mission centers the number of arrests declined by 2,600 in one year.[17] Jonah Goldstein, a respected progressive magistrate in New York City, frequently visited the main Harlem Peace Mission to thank Father Divine for his civic accomplishments. "I have a fair camera eye for my customers in court," Goldstein addressed one banquet crowd, "[but] I see none of my customers in court here. . . ."[18] Captain John A. Brady of the Fourth Precinct in Newark believed that "the practice of this religion has had a restraining effect on a group which heretofore had been regarded as a very undesirable and, in some cases, lawless element."[19] Of "Faithful Mary," once a prostitute, alcoholic, and derelict in Newark before becoming an exemplar of virtue as an aide to Father Divine, Brady said, "I want to thank Father for taking Public Enemy Number 1 and making her one of my best friends!"[20]

The reform of this criminal element by the Peace Mission parallels the work of numerous sects and cults, such as the Black Muslims, which offered people a sense of purpose and community. The Peace Mission, in addition, provided jobs to many who formerly had been unable to obtain respectable employment. Those who discussed their reformation tended to speak in more general terms of "Father's will," suggesting that the force of his personality was perhaps the strongest salutary factor in their lives. The testimony of a thirty-eight-year-old black woman, who renounced a life of crime upon joining the Peace Mission, is typical in its focus on Father Divine as a savior from sin:

> I ran a "red-light" house and a gambling house at 82 E. Kinney Street, 188 McWhorten St. and 12 Garden Street [Newark]. I have a police record in Westfield, N.J. . . . "Father" Divine brought me out of sin and shame.
>
> I do not drink liquor, tell any lies, nor run any bad houses. "Father" Divine is cleaning up the town of bad people. Sometimes I would be on the floor drunk and my husband drunk on the bed and no-good people lying around. "Father" Divine has cleaned us up and made us respectable.[21]

Some Peace Mission members contributed more actively to this reduction in crime. Not yet having negotiated the full passage from crime to nonviolence, they sublimated their aggressive instincts into efforts to rid the ghettos of their criminal infestations. A reporter named Jack Alexander related this curious sidelight of the Peace Mission's crusade for civic spotlessness:

A patrolman of the West 123rd Street station house told me that the angels wait upon a neighbor who peddles dope or gin or operates a house of prostitution, and warn him to leave the vicinity. If he refuses, a couple of the more muscular angels shove him into a dark doorway some night and administer a seraphic swacking. Later, according to the cop, one of the angels will drop in at the police station and say: "Peace, Lieutenant! There is a gentleman sitting on the curb down the street and he is holding his head. I think it would be nice if someone called an ambulance. Thank you, Father. It is indeed wonderful."[22]

Father Divine encouraged this vigilante activity. He admonished Mayor La Guardia that if there were not sufficient police to arrest the thieves plaguing Harlem, he would do so on his own.[23] To his followers he often put the matter more euphemistically: "I will make you fishers of men, of both those that are endeavoring to be religious, and those that are unrighteous and wicked."[24]

What of nonviolence? Father Divine seemed undisturbed by the apparent incongruity of having his Peace Mission followers hunting criminals, though he instructed them to do so without weapons, relying on their faith and the justice of their cause to protect them:

[You should be] making yourselves a committee of one, as volunteer soldiers and troopers to capture every crook and every undesirable person in this community. . . . That is a citizen's duty. Whensoever you see one committing a crime, you can capture and handle him, with my spirit and my power, and nought can hurt nor harm you, even if they have guns. . . . That is, if you are filled with my power and use it constructively. . . .[25]

This departure from pure pacifism suffered virtually no censure from any religious or other "respectable" institution in the black community. The police, for their part, openly approved of the Peace Mission's extralegal defense of law and order. "I wish all of Harlem belonged," a New York detective enthused.[26] "Father Divine is never any trouble until he parades, and that merely makes work for the traffic bureau." Another officer expressed the prevalent police sentiment still more simply: "I am for this little guy, Divine."[27]

Education

Among black leaders during the thirties, no aspect of personal reformation received more attention than education. Many ghetto dwellers had
attended segregated schools in the South that had left them largely illiterate,
while northern-born blacks were only slightly more fortunate to attend
the squalid and underequipped schools in Harlem, Newark, and Bronzeville. To compensate, Urban League executives and others in the black
community helped organize special educational programs and urged adults
to enroll in city night schools in order to overcome the lacks in their earlier
instruction.[28]

Father Divine reflected this concern for educating ghetto residents and
he applied his unique organizing talents to the task. When Divine preached
for a return to public schools, his disciples responded in numbers bewildering to the night school administrators in New York. Of the 8,000 students enrolled in these schools in 1935, 98 percent were Negroes and about
20 percent, or 1,600 pupils, were followers of Father Divine.[29]

While the severe overcrowding led many night school students to drop
out, apparently none of them were from the Peace Mission centers. One
student, asked if she expected to be in school the following day, replied,
"Of course. Father Divine expects us to be here and what he expects must
be."[30]

Father Divine's followers evinced a strong appreciation for this chance
to resume formal study, with many recalling their early years of educational deprivation in the early South. Among the celebrated cases of individual achievement by students from the Peace Mission was the zealous
work of Brother Joseph, resuming his education at age ninety. Joseph
left the third grade some eighty years before but now sought to compensate for that lack. He explained, "There is always room to improve."[31]

Morris Siegel, director of evening and continuation schools in New York
City, described the disciples generally as eager to learn "and very attractive gentle people." Another administrator noted that David Levy, in
charge of the P.S. 89 night school, had gained great popularity with the
followers, in part by addressing them with the word "Peace." The official
added, "They rank him next to Father Divine himself."[32]

Levy in turn marveled at the enthusiasm that greeted his efforts. He
reported that the new students told him upon enrolling, "Father Divine
sent us here, so that we will have peace on earth by becoming better educated, so that we can understand our brothers in all parts of the world."
Levy noted that they had come in such numbers as to quickly exhaust the
available seats. Yet he was gratified by the trend Father Divine had started:
"It is up to me to thank him for overcrowding the school, and in the fall

we hope to have in it, three or four times as many classes as we have now, all due to the beloved Father."[33]

Divine and his aides also took steps to facilitate study by those who did not wish to attend public school evening classes. In July, 1935, the Peace Mission's "Educational Department" announced "good news for those that wish to keep on going to school in their own homes. Father Divine has enabled us to purchase used books for 5, 10 and 15 cents each. Arithmetic, reader and speller."[34] Divine also founded several private schools in the Peace Mission centers north of New York City. The schools drew their faculty mainly from disciples who were once school teachers, and the curriculum corresponded to that given in the public schools. Religious instruction was not included, partly because students could draw that from their environment and also because "the ideals of the Father Divine movement are not susceptible to catechism." According to the school administrators, the Peace Mission's tenets were best absorbed through the daily routine of communal life.[35]

Grading in the Peace Mission schools did not stop with the mundane score of 100 percent but reached to the more celestial region of 200 percent. Father Divine made it clear that his students should always aim for that 200 percent grade, no matter how difficult the subject.[36] Whatever the mathematical irregularities of such a grading system, it served one of the Peace Mission's chief goals: to stretch each follower's ambitions by raising his estimation of his own potential.

Little in the area of education escaped Father Divine's scrutiny. His concerns ranged to the exceptional and handicapped children as well as to the bulk of "normal" students. He protested to the commissioner of New York City's Board of Education against the threatened closing of the Townsend Harris High School for gifted children. That and any similar moves would be "indiscreet," he admonished. "There are other projects that could stand closing down, rather than this one on which hundreds have depended and through which they have gained strength and moral stability through the advantages of a common education."[37]

Father Divine's endless battle with racism deepened his concern with another group that suffered discrimination in the schools — the physically handicapped. Divine deplored the common practice of retarding and even denying graduation because of some physical disability. "This unjust condition exists in practically every community in the United States, but especially is it found in the school system of New York." It was not a matter of budgetary issues, he insisted to the cost-conscious commissioner, but a moral principle regarding the violation of students' rights for reasons unrelated to their ability to learn.[38]

Father Divine's thorough concern with the educational process was based in part on his belief that learning was essential to social mobility. This led him, for example, to call for more liberal admissions policies toward minority applicants for college study: "Colleges that close their doors to any downtrodden people are definitely breeders of immorality among men. They create unrest, and devitalize the energy and spirit of those who would advance themselves to become useful and profitable citizens of state and country."[39]

Divine's faith in education also related to the chance for personal growth that schools provided. Education fostered the qualities of independent judgment, a love of truth, and moral understanding that he was attempting to inculcate in his followers. He stated that even the search for religious wisdom might properly include the most unfettered analytic effort—a dangerous doctrine for any cult leader to dispense to his disciples. "If you have a mind that is termed an *intellectual mind*," he said, "that mind should be taught the wisdom and the mystery of God from a scientific and an intellectual point of view."[40] He merely asked that his followers remember that even the greatest scientific triumphs depended on a higher intelligence, for "God is the one who taught wisdom to Einstein."[41] Father Divine further tempered his calls for study by warning his learned disciples and guests never to disdain those followers with less knowledge:

> While listening to one of the testimonies down there, and many of these my followers at times, those of us who are humanly cultured to some degree . . . [may find it] a little embarrassing to hear the rest of us, or others of us, speak. When we talk, we may say, "You is," for "You are," . . . nevertheless God does not take the language of the saints, but the meaning of their groans.[42]

Father Divine's ambivalence about the value of intellectual sophistication may have stemmed from his own feelings of insecurity as a self-educated man who had never fully overcome the lacks in his early instruction. He could not endorse formal study unreservedly without placing his own limited education and untamed syntax in question. Divine therefore insisted that spiritual wisdom was ultimately all that mattered; in his case it released him from the constraints of mortal grammar:

> They may hang me on a grammatical cross. Aren't you glad? And you may say within yourself again, "If he is all intelligent," while I am on the grammatical cross of your consideration, "why is it he does not take himself down off of the grammatical cross? Why is it he splits so many verbs and makes so many grammatical errors?" I do as I please mentally, spiritually and physically. I am exempt. The law of diction cannot bind me. If the law of diction could bind me, I would be limited to the versions of men.[43]

This was not the stuff of which intellectual and scholastic role models are fashioned, but it represented only one aspect of Father Divine's character, based on defensiveness rather than conviction. In fact, Divine longed to be recognized as a rational leader and it was this quality that he stressed to his disciples. He once declared to a banquet gathering, "I could be classed at this time, not antique, but a modernistic, scientific scientist."[44] Because he genuinely valued learning, his self-consciousness generally led him to insist on his intellectual prowess rather than deny that it mattered. He stated to two visiting ministers, for example, that they should look beyond the apparent emotionalism of his talks to their deeper intellectual meaning: "When you hear me talk sometimes you may think it sounds like a whole lot of fanaticism, but I got a call from Texas the other week — they wanted me to come out there. Of course, the people seem to be deeply impressed with my work and they are convinced of the scientificness of my religious philosophy, you see."[45]

Father Divine was more whole-hearted about the moral, as opposed to intellectual, value of education. He believed that no truly learned person would be so prejudiced as to mistreat another because of his race or religious belief. No civilized society would permit discrimination to mar its laws and practices. Intellectual refinement had potential worth, but without a moral sense to guide one's behavior, ideas were ultimately hollow. Divine noted, as an example of such empty study, those who recited and revered the Constitution, yet did not support fully its principles of equal justice. He also commented that there were many who claimed to know and follow the doctrines of Christianity, yet displayed little love of humanity. This was not true knowledge, Divine observed, for "what need is it to get something theoretically and not get the reality of it?"[46]

Father Divine considered education a way to eliminate feelings of racial superiority or inferiority among his followers and all other people. He was therefore especially critical of educators in the public schools, who should have been setting examples to their students but who frequently were "ignorant enough to endorse vulgarity," or racial labels. "But from that version of our history and of our educational system, I came to emancipate you," he declared to a Peace Mission assembly in Harlem.[47]

Father Divine expounded his ideas on the moral value of education in a New York journal called *Better Schools* in 1939. He responded to an invitation by editor Brendan Byrne to write on his policies "If I Were a College Professor," by focusing on the need to cultivate tolerance among all people:

> Real education consists of more than merely teaching men the subjects taught in a school curriculum. . . . I should eliminate all reference to races, creeds and colors from my classes, and all considera-

tion of the same: thus nipping in the bud, wars and race riots, vices and crimes, segregation and discrimination, incipient in our educational system of today, which if allowed to develop would later be manifested in business and industry, in church and in politics, and in all society. I would eliminate the very segregated terms referring to races, creeds and colors found in our books of learning, and I would teach men that "of one blood God formed all nations."[48]

In sum, Father Divine considered education an important means of fostering racial equality rather than simply as a route to intellectual development. Public schools and universities were effective, in Divine's view, to the extent that they imparted skills needed by the underprivileged and made all people realize the essential unity of mankind. With these priorities in mind, Father Divine became one of the black community's foremost champions of educational opportunity and achievement.

Perspectives of Race

Underlying all Father Divine's efforts to remold character was his desire to have white and black people mingle in harmony and equality. To accomplish this, Father Divine had to eliminate not only prejudice among whites but also the racial self-hate that afflicted many ghetto dwellers. Jim Crow barriers and economic misery had long taught them that they were inferior. Before they could become fully independent and industrious, they needed to shed the caste consciousness that undermined their morale. This concern formed a key theme in Father Divine's preaching as he tried to inspire followers to a new pride in their common humanity.

There was but one race, Father Divine insisted, and that was the human race. He warned that to deny this basic truth was both immoral and self-destructive. "He that enslaves a person or a nation enslaves himself!" Divine preached in words that recalled Booker T. Washington's pragmatic appeals to the white South. "You cannot hold a man down in the ditch unless you stay down there with him."[49] In 1941, amid the American revulsion to Nazi doctrine, Father Divine put the same theme in more explicitly ideological terms, stating, "A free people cannot be free unless they are mentally and spiritually free from race superiority and race inferiority."[50] Unfortunately the nations of the world were mired in prejudice, so that "the wheels of progress do not go forward. They are burdened by the weight of human injustice, greed and intolerance."[51]

Father Divine objected to all racial designations as unwarranted and innately invidious. The term "Negro" in particular offended Divine's sensibilities as the word most commonly used to stereotype and restrict a group on account of color. Whatever neutral descriptive properties the term may once have held, it had long since forfeited them through a history of pejorative uses. "That which has been termed a race is NOT a race," Father Divine declared. ". . . It is a curse, and a cursed, vulgar name that was given you to low-rate you, in short, to DISGRACE you."[52] He especially objected to newspaper usage of the word "Negro" as generally gratuitous and unflattering, and he urged his followers to boycott papers that routinely used the term.

Divine was by no means alone in fighting to abolish the use of racial terms. While the majority of black leaders were seeking more prestigious racial or ethnic descriptions, a respectable minority thought the whole endeavor pure folly. Whether the black man called himself colored, black, Negro, Afro-American, or Moorish-American, he was merely devising a way to legitimize the segregated status that white society had imposed. George Schuyler, perhaps the foremost black journalist of the thirties, asserted in his characteristically mordant style:

> What we should have been striving for all along was not the capitalization of the "N" but the doing away entirely of the word [Negro].
> . . . What difference does it make whether a jim crow railroad waiting room is inscribed "Negro" or "negro" or "darkey"? All mean the same thing, i.e., a descendant of people once enslaved and now only half free, and whose complete emancipation is opposed by most white people and a large number of Negroes. It makes exactly as much difference as referring to an inmate of Leavenworth penitentiary as a "Convict" instead of a "convict." . . . I imagine one reason why white people have so readily acquiesced in capitalizing the "N" in Negro is because they realize that it is placing a further stamp of approval upon an inferior status. It gives the appearance of concession without any tangible reality.[53]

Schuyler's larger aim, to ensure that all people were judged by one standard of merit, united virtually all other civil rights activists. The Reverend Adam Clayton Powell, Sr., succinctly expressed this approach to racial justice: "I am not strong on 'Negro rights.' . . . I have only asked for the one right for my race, namely, the right of equal opportunity with all other American people."[54] Father Divine fully reflected these sentiments, urging "not only as it may be termed, an equal opportunity, but it should be the same opportunity. . . . We just want the one right!"[55]

To emphasize the point, Father Divine refused overtures to endorse activities and awards for "Negro" or "colored" progress. To a school in Bluefield, West Virginia, he wrote to acknowledge a speaking invitation at its fourth annual celebration of Negro achievement, but reminded the school's principal "that I stand for racial indiscrimination, and therefore would not be interested in anything that upholds segregation."[56] Similarly, when selected for an award in memory of black journalist Floyd J. Calvin, as "one of the ten distinguished Negroes in America" for 1939, he expressed appreciation for the kind intent but objected that his achievements would not have been possible had he limited himself simply to a certain category of people.[57]

By the standards of a later generation of blacks, accustomed to the proud and at times belligerent assurance that black is beautiful, the denial of race may appear more an expression of self-hate than real defiance. Yet during the thirties, when "Negro" more often than not prefaced the name of a segregated facility or identified social undesirables, a radical quality attached to demands for abolishing its use. Moreover, if Father Divine opposed racial pride, he also assailed any sign of racial shame. This was not to be taken for granted in an age when ghetto residents commonly employed hair straighteners and skin whiteners so as to resemble more closely the Nordic look of the dominant social stratum. Black businesses thrived on such cosmetic ventures, and Afro-American journals, whose editorials unfailingly called for black pride, routinely featured ads like the following from the *New York Amsterdam News:*

To be ATTRACTIVE you must CLEAR and LIGHTEN your complexion.

Above all, men admire a smooth, soft, light skin, because it is the basis of real beauty and feminine charm. Dr. Fred Palmer's Skin Whitener Ointment will give you this complexion by softening and lightening the skin, no matter how dark. . . . [Try] Skin Whitener Soap, Face Powder and Hair Dresser for further beautifying the complexion and hair. . . .[58]

Other journals also succumbed to the economic temptation to run such ads. Thus, for example, a range of black papers carried the good news about Nadinola Bleaching Cream, a wonder item that whitened the skin so that "your friends find you more charming, more attractive than ever."[59] Such odes to white aesthetic standards further eroded the self-esteem of many blacks who already felt strong pressures to admire the country's "superior" social caste and despise their own.

Father Divine, by contrast, effectively proscribed such cosmetics. He considered their use a sad attempt to flee one's true nature:

Of course, I do not tell people necessarily, "You cannot straighten your hair," but . . . practically all of my true followers abstain from the use of cosmetics and the custom of straightening their hair, or anything of that sort. . . . Of course, everybody should use soap and water to wash their face and hands and hair . . . but to use it excessively unnecessarily, to try to make themselves altogether different from what they really are—my true followers do not do those things![60]

Father Divine was no more willing to accept whites as moral tutors than as aesthetic models. Quite unlike those black clergymen who saw accommodation of white paternalism as the better part of valor, Divine quickly rebuked anyone who condescended toward black people. A landlord who praised him for "your upraising of the ethical code of your people" doubtless expected Father Divine to exude gratitude. Instead he received a typically stern rejoinder:

> [In] noting that you make mention of a particular people, for whom you declare I have raised the ethical code, I wish to advise and enlighten you. . . . My people are the peoples of the earth. And then I wish to ask, "Is the ethical code of righteousness, justice and truth the standard of all people and is it portrayed in the lives of those whom you would term are not my people?" We know it is not.[61]

The color-blind operation of the Peace Mission centers reinforced the impact of Father Divine's denunciations of all racial distinctions. Often for the first time in their lives, ghetto residents ate, prayed, worked, and socialized with whites on a basis of complete harmony and equality. All disciples, moreover, refrained from using racial terms as scrupulously as they avoided obscene and profane language. When necessary, a variety of euphemisms and circumlocutions were employed, including "complexion" for race or color, "light" for white, and "dark" for black or Negro.

The fact of Father Divine's leadership was perhaps the Peace Mission's most dramatic symbol highlighting the theme of racial equality. Here was a diminutive black parson whose slightest word constituted the supreme wisdom for white as well as black disciples. A follower experiencing this striking denial of society's established racial hierarchy could ask no more vivid confirmation of black worth. Nor, as he exulted in the power of this black messiah and sang hymns with his interracial brethren, could he doubt Divine's promise of a coming era of brotherhood for all mankind.

Father Divine's efforts to fashion independent, self-respecting people helped many in the ghettos to reach undreamed levels of achievement. Those who once viewed their complexion as a severe disadvantage, even a disgrace, now saw themselves as fully able, worthwhile individuals. Men and women who had never held steady employment or learned to read discovered that they could do these things, and much more: their potential had just been awakened.

For Father Divine these character reformations were encouraging in themselves and also a prelude to wider reform activity. He realized that once an underprivileged people had developed a positive and forceful self-image, collective action to obtain social justice could follow. Divine therefore used his Peace Mission movement as a base to promote an increasing number of social, economic, and political programs designed to ensure a new deal for the nation's oppressed minorities.

Disciples who came to Father Divine only to find relief from personal problems soon discovered that their devotion to him had to be expressed in service to others. As Divine met their individual needs, these regenerated followers enlisted by the thousands, with gratitude and boundless zeal, in his crusade for racial and economic equality. They acted in the firm belief that under Father Divine's leadership, they were to be pioneers of an American messianic age.

Notes to Chapter 4

1. Sermon of Jan. 13, 1935, in *SW,* Jan. 26, 1935, p. 2.

2. Father Divine to Harold Ickes, Feb. 1, 1936, in *SW,* Feb. 11, 1936, p. 17; also see Father Divine to Harry Hopkins, Feb. 25, 1936, in ibid., Feb. 29, 1936, p. 10, and Father Divine to Senator Royal Copeland, chairman of the Senate Commerce Committee, Feb. 4, 1936, in ibid., Feb. 15, 1936, p. 8. In each letter Divine requested repeal of the provision in federal employment relief legislation that prohibited citizens from receiving positions on any work project if they were not already on welfare. For Copeland's strongly sympathetic reply to Divine, see his letter of Feb. 8, 1936, in ibid., Feb. 15, 1936, p. 9.

3. Sermon of Sept. 23, 1937, in *ND,* Sept. 30, 1937, p. 25.

4. Sermon of July 29, 1936, in *SW,* Aug. 18, 1936, p. 27.

5. Father Divine to May Miller, May 13, 1935, in *SW,* June 1, 1935, p. 10.

6. Father Divine to William Aydelotte, May 24, 1935, in ibid.

7. Father Divine reportedly returned one donation valued at $460,000, from Moses Fickler of Montreal. See *Los Angeles News-Guardian,* Sept. 1, 1940, reprinted in *ND,* Sept. 26, 1940, p. 83.

8. See, for example, Henry Santrey to Father Divine, June 9, 1936, and Divine's reply of June 15, 1936, both in *SW,* June 16, 1936, p. 23. Santrey, of Cox Steel and Wire Company in Dallas, Tex., offered Divine a fee of $10,000 to go on a month's all-expense-paid lecture tour. Divine refused, stating that "to receive compensation from any angle expressible, is against my policy, as I am a free gift to the world, gratis to mankind." He assured that, if time permitted, he would be pleased to visit the cities in question without charge. See also Father Divine's comment on this exchange, in his sermon of June 17, 1936, in ibid., June 20, 1936, pp. 6-7.

9. See Father Divine to Alexander Corniffe, June 2, 1935, in *SW,* June 15, 1935, p. 8, and sermon of July 1, 1936, in ibid., July 7, 1936, p. 21.

10. *Daily News,* Aug. 6, 1939, p. 16.

11. Ethel Caldwell to George Haas and Sons of San Francisco, Apr. 6, 1936, cited by Hoshor, *God in a Rolls-Royce,* pp. 225-26.

12. *NYAN,* Oct. 10, 1936, p. 1.

13. Ibid.

14. *ND,* Oct. 15, 1942, p. 84.

15. Testimony by Fred Dickens at Peace Mission banquet, New York, Nov. 15, 1935, in *SW*, Nov. 23, 1935, p. 23.

16. Sermon of Oct. 28-29, 1950, in *ND*, Jan. 14, 1978, p. 19. The sermon synthesizes the major elements of Father Divine's views on liquor and tobacco as expressed over several decades; see also John Henrik Clarke, "Revolt of the Angels—A Short Story," in his edited work, *Harlem: A Community in Transition* (New York: Citadel Press, 1964), pp. 117-22, a satirical short story of how followers of Father Divine intimidated an unruly drunkard into sweet temperance.

17. *SW*, Mar. 16, 1935, p. 11.

18. Ibid., June 22, 1935, p. 19.

19. Report of commission appointed by Essex County Court of Common Pleas to investigate the Peace Mission movement, filed Dec. 11, 1933, in *AA*, Dec. 30, 1933, p. 12. The transcript printed in *AA* appears to contain printer's errors and other inaccuracies, and should be checked against the version in Hoshor, *God in a Rolls-Royce*, "Appendix." Text quotation is from Hoshor, p. 268.

20. Testimony of Chief Brady, Newark Peace Mission, Jan. 28, 1937, in *SW*, Mar. 6, 1937, p. 6. Ironically, this testimony came very shortly before Faithful Mary defected from the Peace Mission movement in a futile effort to set up her own cult group in New York and then Los Angeles.

21. Report of Newark commission.

22. Alexander, "All Father's Chillun," p. 69.

23. *SW*, Apr. 6, 1935, p. 1.

24. Sermon of Mar. 28, 1935, in ibid., p. 2.

25. Sermon of Feb. 16, 1937, in ibid., Mar. 2, 1937, p. 18.

26. Kelley, "Heaven Incorporated," p. 108.

27. Alexander, "All Father's Chillun," p. 69.

28. Efforts by Urban League branches to promote school attendance and to create or support educational programs for Negroes are noted in Nancy J. Weiss, *The National Urban League, 1910-1940* (New York: Oxford University Press, 1974), pp. 120, 169-72. Powell urged a return to night school courses, in "Soap Box," *NYAN*, Apr. 8, 1939, p. 10.

29. *Times*, Dec. 8, 1935, sec. 2, p. 9.

30. Ibid.

31. *SW*, May 11, 1935, p. 3.

32. Ibid., Mar. 30, 1935, p. 5.

33. Testimony by David Levy at Peace Mission banquet, New York, Apr. 3, 1935, in *SW*, Apr. 27, 1935, p. 1.

34. *SW*, July 6, 1935, p. 23.

35. *Times*, Mar. 20, 1937, p. 21.

36. Harris, *Father Divine*, p. 223.

37. Father Divine to Stephen F. Bayne, May 7, 1941, in *ND*, May 8, 1941, pp. 58-59.

38. Ibid.

39. Father Divine to Brendan Byrne, July 25, 1939, in *ND*, Feb. 11, 1978, p. 29.

40. Sermon of Nov. 14, 1935, in *SW*, Nov. 23, 1935, p. 26.

41. Sermon of Aug. 5-6, 1947, in *ND*, Aug. 4, 1973, p. 13.

42. Sermon of Nov. 14, 1935, in *SW*, Nov. 23, 1935, p. 25.

43. Sermon of Apr. 12, 1938, in *ND*, Apr. 21, 1938, p. 18.

44. Sermon of Sept. 25, 1935, in *SW*, Oct. 5, 1935, p. 26.

45. Interview given by Father Divine to the Reverends J. A. Manning and C. J.

Gadsden, High Falls, Oct. 29, 1938, in *ND,* Sept. 30, 1978, p. 6.

46. Sermon of Mar. 18-19, 1938, in *ND,* Mar. 31, 1938, p. 24.

47. Sermon of May 25, 1938, in *ND,* Aug. 4, 1973, p. 18.

48. Father Divine to Brendan Byrne, July 25, 1939, in *ND,* Feb. 11, 1978, p. 28.

49. Sermon of Feb. 23, 1941, in *ND,* Feb. 27, 1941, p. 8.

50. Father Divine to Kathryn Young, Oct. 4, 1941, in *ND,* Oct. 9, 1941, p. 88.

51. Father Divine to F. L. Jenkins, July 26, 1941, in *ND,* July 31, 1941, p. 83.

52. Sermon of Nov. 22, 1935, in *SW,* Dec. 7, 1935, p. 27.

53. George Schuyler, "Views and Reviews," *PC,* Nov. 7, 1936, sec. 1, p. 10.

54. Powell, *Against the Tide,* p. 180.

55. Interview given by Father Divine to the Reverend Bertha Harris, New York, Jan. 16, 1941, in *ND,* Nov. 5, 1977, p. 15.

56. Father Divine to Charles Thompson, of Jones Street School, Bluefield, W. Va., Mar. 5, 1941, in *ND,* Mar. 6, 1941, p. 103.

57. Father Divine to Mrs. Floyd Calvin of Calvin's Newspaper Service, New York, Jan. 26, 1940, in *ND,* Feb. 1, 1940, pp. 104-5.

58. *NYAN,* May 31, 1933, p. 5.

59. A sampling of black journals in a randomly selected week in 1933 reveals that this ad was featured in: *NYAN,* Feb. 15, p. 4; *AA,* Feb. 18, p. 18; *PC,* Feb. 18, p. 3; and *CD,* Feb. 18, p. 6.

60. Interview given by Father Divine to "Miss C," Newark, Jan. 28, 1951, in *ND,* Aug. 4, 1973, p. 22. See also similar comments by Divine in his sermon of Apr. 23, 1939, in ibid., Apr. 27, 1939, pp. 31-32; and his letter to a cosmetics salesman, Nathaniel E. Story, Mar. 23, 1940, in ibid., Feb. 9, 1980, pp. 12-13, in which he claimed that the money needed to buy cosmetics could better be put toward the purchase of necessities such as homes and land.

61. Father Divine to Jacob Kupperman, Sept. 6, 1937, in *ND,* Sept. 16, 1937, p. 11.

CHAPTER 5

The Challenge to Segregation

Racial integration was the cornerstone of the Peace Mission's social program. Father Divine hoped that the movement's example of interracial harmony and equality would inspire the wider society to emulate its achievement. Instead, surrounding communities often resisted bitterly and at times violently the establishment of Peace Mission branches, precisely because these centers challenged racist practices. The Peace Mission nevertheless pressed its message of brotherhood in white as well as black neighborhoods, as part of a small vanguard promoting civil rights on a direct and daily basis in American life.

The Peace Mission's approach to race relations was exceptional in an age when, even in the North, blacks were subject to separate and harshly unequal treatment. The vast majority lived in overcrowded ghettos, to which they were confined by poverty and restrictive housing covenants. Discrimination by employers, unions, and even government aid programs helped ensure their continued economic subordination. At the same time they endured exclusion by many restaurants, hotels, resorts, and stores. As late as 1941 the major clothing center in the nation's capital instructed salesmen to ban black patrons or, in the case of affluent blacks, to rush them in and out of fitting rooms so as to avoid the appearance of "a colored convention."[1]

The fear of racial integration was nationwide, and often most visibly acute in northern cities where caste barriers were relatively porous. During the early thirties, when the Civilian Conservation Corps established Negro camps, the most vociferous objections to hosting them came from communities outside the South, most stressing the alleged dangers of social mixing. Citizens in Thornhurst, Pennsylvania, for example, petitioned "righteously and vigorously" that no Negro camp be permitted to endanger their "unescorted women," despite the absence of a single instance of misconduct by Negroes in any CCC camp.[2]

The Peace Mission's spiritual orientation scarcely made its interracial membership more acceptable to the wider society. This was a time when over 99 percent of churches North and South guarded segregated corridors to Heaven. Nor was it clear during the Depression era that patterns of church membership—as opposed to abstract clerical pronouncements for tolerance—were becoming more progressive. In 1929 the Reverend William S. Blackshear of St. Matthew's Protestant Episcopal Church, Brooklyn, asked his Negro congregants to leave. Three years later the vestry of an Episcopalian church in New York ordered the church closed "for repairs," to prevent the minister from admitting Negroes to worship. These bold steps backward were matched by individuals in nearly all denominations, and occasionally by their highest leaders. The relatively tolerant Methodists, for example, united their northern and southern branches in 1939, but placed all Negro congregations in a separate jurisdiction regardless of geographic location.[3]

Almost any white clergyman in these years who dared call for full racial integration at best took a calculated risk with his career. The fate of Edward Thomas McGuire, a young white minister who expressed views similar to those of Father Divine, is a case in point. McGuire belonged to the Church of God in Christ, a sect that espoused racial equality. Days after he arrived in Tennessee, police arrested him without charge and held him incommunicado for two weeks. The city inspector of Memphis justified this treatment on the grounds that McGuire "had been hanging around town all hours of the night, frequenting Negro houses and establishments and generally acting in a suspicious manner." After the FBI cleared the minister of any wrongdoing, the inspector ordered him released—and expelled from the state. McGuire himself had no doubt as to why the authorities first suppressed and then deported him: "The real reason for my being treated so, I believe, is because of my religious faith which promotes racial equality. After I came to Memphis . . . I conducted services in several Negro churches. At some of them I preached to congregations which included both Negroes and whites of our faith."[4]

The boldness of the Peace Mission's stand on integration is further underscored by the absence of almost any other predominantly black church or cult that deliberately encouraged an interracial membership. Some, notably Marcus Garvey's Universal Negro Improvement Association and the black Jewish and Muslim groups, invested their separatist condition with ideological purpose. The majority of black religious leaders preferred racial separatism in the church mainly as expedient to their own authority and the independence of their congregations. R. C. Barbour, editor of the New Orleans *National Baptist Voice* and hailed by Adam Clayton Powell, Sr., as "the best editorial writer on religion and the race question the Negroes have in America,"[5] exemplified the self-segregationist position. In an open letter in 1937 Barbour admonished Divine for his alleged folly in daring to form an integrated religious movement: "You are taking Jesus too seriously in race matters. . . . Our advice to you is: that you, if you plan to preach in America, do what we Baptists are doing, develop a jim-crow church. No-one will harm you then; and then, too, you can get by with anything."[6]

Despite white opposition and black cautioning, Father Divine disdained the path of withdrawal from outside pressures. He refused to confine his leadership even to interracial centers within the black ghettos, but instead moved aggressively to establish Peace Mission branches in hitherto exclusively white neighborhoods. In brief, Divine intended not to flee American life for an insulated utopia but to foster nationwide integration as a means of overcoming the roots of prejudice.

To many whites, the Peace Mission's interracial membership and principles appeared as *prima facie* evidence of antisocial behavior. They responded with bitterness and savagery. In Ivywild, a suburb of Colorado Springs, vigilantes marched in front of a newly opened Peace Mission church, warning that they would have no "black and tan" groups in their town. The demonstrators surrounded the building and someone poured gasoline in the street and tossed a lighted match in it. Another hurled a rock through the window of the church. A tough-minded sheriff named Sam Deal dispersed the crowd with the aid of several deputies, but hostility remained intense and residents threatened more drastic action unless the Peace Mission members left the town.[7]

Colorado's Governor Edwin Johnson initially inclined toward the cause of Ivywild's vigilantes, whether from ignorance of the situation or political pressure. He declined to protect the Peace Mission members, while an aide ordered them to leave their church, thus encouraging the mob. Father Divine wrote several times to the governor, urgently requesting his administration "to safe-guard against mob-violence . . . [and] see that the Constitutional rights of your citizens are preserved. . . ." The governor's sole reply was to note that he was referring the matter to an aide.[8]

Police in other states sometimes initiated the persecution of Peace Mission members as part of a campaign to stifle all dissent and deviation from Jim Crow tradition. In Miami, Florida, police officers seized followers distributing copies of the *New Day,* kept them in detention, shouted obscenities at them, and threatened violence at the slightest lack of cooperation. One officer reportedly said, as he took fingerprints of the prisoners, "You ought to be hung, you will never get out of here." After vandalizing the followers' car, destroying copies of their journal, and collecting fines of $25 to $30, the officers ordered the disciples to leave town.[9]

Racial mixing in Divine's churches drew fire from veteran extremists, including some members of the Ku Klux Klan. These Klan followers, based in Los Angeles and seeking a foothold in New York City, distributed leaflets and letters vilifying the Peace Mission in areas where Divine's movement flourished. This hate literature stressed that it was an abomination for white women to worship a black cult leader. The Klan warned that "overtolerance" had permitted matters to get out of hand. In its view, white Americans had been too kind to the Negro for too long.[10]

With his shrewd sense of symbolism Father Divine had much the better of his propaganda fight with the Ku Klux Klan. In 1934 Divine personally negotiated the purchase of Hasbrouck Manor in upstate New York. Among the oldest homes in the United States, it had once been a base from which Klan members rode on cross-burning missions. Under Divine's new direction, the home became the headquarters for a series of integrated rural communities he established to the northwest of New York City, known to his followers as the "Promised Land."[11]

The Peace Mission frequently selected properties at least partly for their value in dramatizing the cause of interracial harmony. The salient example was Divine's purchase, in 1938, of Spencer's Point, an estate across the river from Franklin Roosevelt's Hyde Park mansion. By this stroke of public relations genius, the Father and his interracial following became known as the President's neighbors while also acquiring a luxurious, 500-acre property. Black journals hailed this as one of the year's notable events, while other papers also accorded the purchase front-page coverage as a stunning coup for the advocates of integration.[12]

The seeming sleight of hand by which Divine suddenly possessed Spencer's Point resulted from prolonged negotiation with owner Howland Spencer, an eccentric millionaire and bitter enemy of Franklin Roosevelt. Spencer objected to Roosevelt's "socialist" programs and a manner he likened to "an entire Trinity complex." Most of all, Spencer fumed at Roosevelt's appropriation of his land's historical title, "Krum Elbow." Spencer complained that he had unchallengeable credentials to that venerable title, but in 1933 "the Geodetic Survey—some Washington agency—came along the river" and conferred the coveted appellation on Roosevelt's estate. The surveyors assigned to Spencer's property the more parochial designation of "Spencer's Point."[13] His long-simmering bitterness found an opportunity for expression when the Peace Mission indicated interest in his property. The thought of converting that land into a political liability for Roosevelt, by giving him an interracial group of neighbors, helped induce Spencer to sell the estate.

Spencer reportedly surrendered the deed to his land for an absurdly low figure of $25,000, or some $50 an acre. Perhaps he was influenced by his professed admiration for the "wonderful work" Father Divine was doing.[14] There was also the fact that he had been unable in recent years to keep up the mortgage interest or taxes on the property.[15] His major aim, though, seems to have been his desire to cut at Roosevelt in some way. Spencer denied this motive, though he slyly added to reporters, "Whether we meant it or not, this really will annoy Franklin a great deal, won't it?"[16]

Roosevelt took the high road by ignoring Howland Spencer in public. There were indications, however, that he was less than pleased by Spencer's actions. One suspects that the president encouraged his wife's oblique mockery of Spencer in her syndicated column: "I always feel sorry for anyone who has to sell a country estate. It must, however, be pleasant to feel that in the future this place [Spencer's Point] will be 'heaven' to some people, even if it cannot be to its former owner."[17]

Father Divine found Spencer's attitude toward Roosevelt a problem, however useful it had been in pushing the deal to completion. Divine was concerned to elicit only positive responses from Roosevelt regarding the purchase. He was even more eager to elevate his purchase above the status of an "embarrassment," as Spencer and some observers described it. Divine announced to the press that he had no interest in any quarrel between Roosevelt and Spencer, only in "standing for the Constitution" until his followers gained their full rights as "real American citizens."[18]

Reporters were quick to note, however, that Divine implicitly sided with Spencer regarding the property's title, for he always referred to it as "Krum Elbow" rather than "Spencer's Point." Whether this had formed part of their business agreement is unknown. It was, in any event, a modest gesture for the chance to purchase, at nominal rates, 500 choice acres across from a presidential estate.

As Peace Mission members streamed in to upgrade the estate, Roosevelt faced a delicate political dilemma. He was already under fire from southern congressmen, who believed him too sympathetic to the cause of Negro rights. Moreover, a prominent southern senator, Allen Ellender from Louisiana, had denounced Father Divine earlier in the year as typifying the dangerous northern movement for racial equality. How then could Roosevelt respond—if at all—to the fact that his new neighbors included this very Negro leader, plus his considerable interracial following? The president's reaction was characteristically astute and low-key. He approved the purchase in general terms while making light of the whole situation. There was no special address on the subject to defend racial integration, nor did Roosevelt go out of his way to suggest respect for Divine's social or political views. After several speakers at the Roosevelt home club's annual reception had humorously referred to the new "Heaven," the president took the occasion to say, "I'm confident that the people in that 'heaven' in Ulster County will be good neighbors to us here in Dutchess County."[19] Divine was equally succinct and wry in dealing with reporters. Asked for a comment on his new acquisition, he quipped, "I couldn't have a finer neighbor, could I?"[20]

Father Divine later wrote to solicit the views of both the president and first lady regarding his movement's prospective purchase of another nearby property, the Vanderbilt estate.[21] Both replied — Mrs. Roosevelt personally and the president through his press secretary — that the fine trees on the estate made it best suited to becoming a public arboretum. Shortly thereafter, in fact, the federal government purchased the property for that purpose. Yet the president and his wife also expressed to Father Divine their belief that any citizen should be able to acquire whatever property he desired, and Divine immediately made the correspondence public.[22] He subsequently explained his motives in a private interview:

> [Many have said], "If President Roosevelt can be his neighbor, why not I?" Well now, if I get next to thousands of people that way, don't you see, I intend to bring a close relationship between so-called races, and I knew if the President would speak one way or the other, it would mean a whole lot — so I released it [Roosevelt's statement] to the press. . . . Now, I believe that has curbed a whole lot of antagonism.[23]

Divine added an understandably expansive afterthought: "And I am always thinking of something like that, you know."[24]

Father Divine moved swiftly but seldom directly to expand the Peace Mission's holdings in white neighborhoods throughout the thirties and early forties. In order to circumvent restrictive housing covenants, he had white followers act as secret emissaries to negotiate purchases for the movement. They often incorporated in deeds of sale the names of black as well as white followers of Father Divine, but made no mention of Divine or that the property would henceforth have an interracial ownership. After the transactions Divine often arrived to oversee the "house-warming" ceremonies with a racially mixed entourage, to the surprise and often dismay of the surrounding residents.

This predilection for secrecy extended even to the purchase of a building located on the edge of Harlem. In 1938 a man named Frank Warner paid $24,000 for a fifty-room mansion on Madison Avenue. The owner, Dr. Elihu Katz, had no notion that Warner was a follower of Divine and that his home had been chosen as a private residence for the Peace Mission leader, his twelve secretaries, and a few chosen disciples. Only some weeks after the contract had been signed did Father Divine appear at the home to introduce himself and request permission to look the place over. "I was astounded," Dr. Katz recalled. He gave Divine a full tour, while Divine peppered him with questions and remarks like, "It's wonderful." The overwhelmed physician acknowledged, "I never saw anything like it."[25]

If Divine's secretive mode of operations at times appeared overly elaborate, more often it reflected a sober appraisal of white attitudes toward "intruding" blacks. Divine's conquest of New Rochelle, a bastion of segregation north of New York City, illustrates the enormous difficulties of integrating a neighborhood in the face of bitter resistance by its residents.

While New Rochelle during the thirties contained "one of the largest Negro populations of any city of its size in the North," those residents were nearly all located several miles southwest of the exclusive area known as Sutton Manor. It is in this area that Divine, operating through his white intermediaries, dared in 1939 to acquire a spacious three-story home.

The Peace Mission's purchase of this home confirmed Divine's rare ability to find excellent real estate values for low prices and to acquire properties even in the most stubbornly racist and class-conscious neighborhoods. The Sutton Manor estate, including privileges at the nearby beach and yachting club, was assessed for 1939 at more than $37,000, but the difficulties of maintaining such a large home during the Depression had reduced its market price to a mere $7,500. The attorney representing the estate's executor, the Chase Manhattan Bank, "had no idea" that the prospective buyer was a follower of Father Divine.[26] As Negro as well as white followers began to arrive, bearing brooms, mops, and other aids for making the mansion spotless as well as luxurious, residents expressed horror at their first realization of Divine's presence.

Leading citizens of Sutton Manor quickly searched for ways to oust the Peace Mission members, apparently treating their existence in the town as ample provocation. State Supreme Court Justice Lee Parsons Davis referred vaguely to the possibility of zoning curbs, but was still acclimating to the distressing situation. "Give me a cigarette so I can stand the shock," he importuned an interviewer.[27]

Corporation counsel Aaron Simmons was more thorough than Davis. On behalf of numerous complaining residents, Simmons pored over legal volumes in hope of locating some law on which to base a campaign for eviction. This was perhaps a necessary means of operation given the absence of a ready-made pretext for indignation. "Something," Simmons grimly noted, "will have to be done to get them out."[28] It was simply a matter of finding a grievance.

Several legal routes impressed Simmons as possibilities for further exploration. If the Peace Mission's estate were declared a house of worship, then it would be illegal to sleep there. On the other hand, if the estate were used as a boarding house, this would violate existing zoning regulations. Either way, Simmons believed, the new owners might soon be pressed into reselling their property.[29]

Father Divine had no intention of leaving. His executive secretary, John Lamb, countered Simmons's charges: "The house will be occupied as a private residence. Of course, there will be guests. And undoubtedly the Father will be a guest there as often as he likes. I don't think they will find any way of evicting us."[30]

Sutton Manor's best citizens heightened the pressure by a concerted campaign to ostracize Divine's followers. Charles H. Griffiths, Republican chairman of Westchester County and a resident around the corner from Divine's new property, vowed to watch for a legal opening to force eviction. In the interim, as director and former president of the Sutton Manor Association, he declared that Peace Mission members would not be permitted to use the bathing beach or the boathouse at the manor's frontage on Long Island Sound: "We will amend the rules of the association, if necessary, to exclude them from membership."[31]

The Peace Mission members, inspired by Father Divine's support, serenely ignored the threats and slights. The ill-founded legal campaigns against them lost momentum once Divine made clear that neither he nor the owners would be intimidated. This, coupled with the continued well-being of Sutton Manor despite all manner of dire predictions, led the residents gradually to cease their efforts to expel the interracial newcomers.

The Peace Mission often acquired properties in order to challenge specific racial injustices, such as the exclusion of blacks from beaches and pools. This exclusion was a chronic source of racial friction during the early twentieth century. Black and white Americans each saw the practice as symbolic of broader efforts to deny "social equality" to the Negro. The violence at a Chicago beach, precipitating that city's race riot in 1919, was one of numerous similar incidents that periodically occurred in major urban centers.

Even to establish a separate beach for Negroes often required protracted struggle. It is a measure of the problem that the most significant achievement of the Interracial Commission in Norfolk, Virginia, was the establishment of a local Negro beach. All of Norfolk's beaches had long been reserved for whites only, and no private investor was willing to sell even a small beachfront for Negro use. At last, the municipality itself acquired the necessary frontal for such a beach, though it had to contend for some years thereafter with public recrimination and even litigation. It was the kind of segregationist benevolence that James Baldwin once likened to that of a well-meaning guide in hell, but in 1935 Norfolk officials proudly directed Negro residents to the city's first "colored" beach.[32]

The problem knew few regional distinctions. New Jersey, with many resort areas, was a major offender in the treatment of Negro vacationers. In Long Branch, for example, Negro bathers coming from all sections of the state to enjoy the July 4th holiday in 1939, were forbidden to use the best beaches because they were "for white people."[33] This was the general situation Father Divine sought to remedy when, in 1942, he supervised the purchase of the main hotel in Brigantine, New Jersey, together with rights to its excellent beaches and boardwalk near Atlantic City.

The acquisition of this choice property bore the hallmarks of Divine's distinctive methods. He selected a site of considerable value but his followers paid a relatively modest price for it — in this case, $75,000 for a 154-room, 154-bath, ten-story structure on a luxury island facing Atlantic City's famed boardwalk. The hotel was easily the dominant edifice in Brigantine and could be seen from a distance of five miles. White intermediaries made the purchase, ostensibly on their own initiative but with continued private recourse to Divine's counsel. Brigantine officials connected with the sale first learned of the Peace Mission's interest in the purchase after the contract had been signed and Divine had arrived to inspect the premises. The influx of black as well as white followers outraged the residents of the isle. With virtually one voice they demanded that the Peace Mission members resell their hotel to the city. The ensuing conflict between the new owners and the townsmen of Brigantine revealed Divine at his most ingenious and American racism at its most tenacious.

A mass meeting of the island's residents inaugurated hostilities. Brigantine Commissioner John Lloyd spoke against Father Divine's move, while some islanders threatened to rip up the boardwalk in front of the hotel. Divine, wearily accustomed to such receptions, said simply that his followers would build a connection of some kind to their private pier. Shortly thereafter Commissioner Lloyd formally stated the townspeople's objections to the presence of Divine and his interracial following as "seriously detrimental to property values in Brigantine."[34]

While racism, coupled with economic insecurity, motivated most objections to the sale, some businessmen had additional reason to promote discord. They protested that for more than a year they had been negotiating with the Army to buy the hotel for use as an Army hospital.[35] The combined pressures of mass prejudice and business influence led a municipal delegation to visit Divine at his new abode and discuss possibilities for its repurchase by the city.

Mayor Vincent Haneman of Brigantine, head of the delegation to Father Divine, was a well-intentioned man whose first principle appears to have been expediency in the face of conflict. He had used his political skills earlier in quieting the chronic racial tension that existed between Brigantine and a black neighborhood some eight miles away. Haneman feared a new explosion of racial violence if the townspeople of Brigantine were not quickly appeased. Not everyone was so progressive in these matters as he and Divine, Haneman explained to the minister. It was therefore necessary to face the reality of the situation and withdraw his followers at a fair price for the good of all concerned. The mayor added, in an attempt to cement his imagined rapport with Divine, "What we are talk-ing about is the practical results — not theoretical but practical results, whether it [remaining in Brigantine] will not defeat the ends that you are trying to obtain and I am trying to obtain." "Well, positively not!" Divine shot back, little disposed to humor Haneman's personal and political sense of caution. "Now is the time that you have co-operation and not just local co-operation but you have national co-operation," he encouraged the mayor. This was a time to put basic issues of human dignity to the test, not to cower to a group of prejudiced people. Divine suggested that Hane-man, if truly interested in preserving racial harmony, should himself mediate between the owners and the opponents of the sale, "and bring them in harmony by causing them to see and know of your personal con-tact . . . and let them know we are not idiots or someone just out of the wild woods, as lots of people may think — we have the most refined people. . . ."[36]

Commissioner John Lloyd also attended the conference and sternly lec-tured Father Divine on the importance of property values. Lloyd seemed unaware that Divine and his aides might not be so receptive to such con-siderations as the mob he had earlier helped incite with similar remarks. Lloyd apologized for the inconvenience to Divine's rights but expected that the minister would grasp the larger good of having his interracial fol-lowing withdrawn from Brigantine:

> We understand you are quite law-abiding people. . . . We recog-nize your legal right to be there, but for practical reasons we think that it would be more helpful to your movement if you chose not to come there. . . . [T]he entry of your followers into our town, into our little town, has the effect of taking from us property values. It has the effect of taking money from us just as much as if somebody dipped their hands into our pockets and took it out.[37]

The conference unsurprisingly produced no agreement between the two parties, but a few days later the hotel owners sent word to an anxious Mayor Haneman. Although they desired to remain, in the interest of mutual cooperation they would resell — for half a million dollars, in cash and not including the furniture. The owners expressed the hope that Hane-man would realize that this was "just and fair under the circumstances,"[38] a somewhat Draconian perspective of the offer. Instead, the municipal government adamantly refused and made plans to try other means of recovering their prize hotel.

Unfazed by the commotion surrounding the hotel, Father Divine presided over its grand opening in August, 1942. He spoke of this event as inaugurating a new era of privilege for the masses:

> [T]hose who are American citizens and decent and respectable; if they are willing to live evangelically while they are on the premises, matters not what or where you are from; even if you are from Harlem where I have been residing as well as in Tarrytown, you are welcome to come to this beach and enjoy the facilities such as we have open for the public, so long as you come decently and act respectably. . . . Some may not have had that privilege before. I am pleased to present that much to you, with the prospect and with the determination to give you more privilege in thousands of other places.[39]

The city's siege of the hotel, however, was still tightening. After Divine brusquely rejected threats to resell or face possible racial violence, he was confronted with a new form of attempted coercion: the prospect of a punitive tax revaluation of the hotel. In early September the mayor of Atlantic City presented to the County Tax Board a petition on behalf of Brigantine's residents, asking to raise retroactively the hotel's valuation for 1942 from $23,650 to $500,000. The residents based their appeal on an "error" by the Board of Assessors in the estimates for 1941 and 1942. At the proposed valuation the tax on the hotel would amount to some $67,000, or more than eighteen times the tax for the previous year.[40]

This maneuver did not take account of Father Divine's surpassing resourcefulness. In November he announced that the hotel owners, with his approval, were leasing the property for a dollar a year to the Coast Guard, through the duration of the war and upon assurances that the facilities would not be segregated. On the one hand, this was a move of sublime patriotic philanthropy. Coast Guard units in the area were desperately short of housing and had offered Father Divine $10,000 as an initial bid for the use of the hotel. Divine explained that the hotel was not his to sell, but he would ask the trustees to bring up the matter with the eighty-seven owners. This he did, pointing out that while they were clearly free to do as they thought best, if they cared to donate the use of the hotel to the Coast Guard, it would be a patriotic action that would have his full endorsement. Within days the owners met to lease the hotel for a nominal charge, and even insisted on paying the back taxes of some $3,000, despite the Coast Guard's offer to do so.[41]

As so often in Divine's career, selfless philanthropy was also brilliant strategy. His totally unforeseen maneuver draped the American flag around the standard of integration, generated national coverage of the controversy with Brigantine, and created pressure to abandon the proposed tax increases. The *Amsterdam News,* delighted to see the modern Br'er Rabbit again eluding his would-be oppressors, exulted over the latest turn of events:

> There is always someone trying to outsmart Father Divine and in turn getting all confused, mixed up, befuddled and in short, outsmarted himself. It's truly wonderful. The astute little cult leader had "gone and done it again. . . ." [The granting of the hotel] is a "purely voluntary, patriotic move. . . ." But incidentally, in addition to being patriotic, offering the hotel to the government would doubtless result in the withdrawal of the tax suit — at least until after the war when taxes presumably will be much lower. Peace, it's truly wonderful![42]

As anticipated, within two weeks of his "patriotic gesture," the Atlantic County Tax Board peremptorily dismissed the Brigantine appeal to "correct" the hotel's assessment for 1942.[43] Yet if Brigantine officials had reckoned without Divine's cunning, he in turn underestimated the unremitting intensity of Brigantine's prejudice. After a period of confusion Brigantine's representatives enacted a 400 percent increase on the assessment for 1943, from $26,500 to $107,540. The projected tax for the hotel was about $15,000.[44]

At last, seeing irrationality ascendant, Father Divine counseled his followers to resell their property, though he had one more surprise for the island of Brigantine. The new owner, a wealthy business executive, was a black woman associated with the Peace Mission. The price, fast becoming a staple for the hotel, was one dollar, and the purchaser, Sara Washington of the Apex News and Hair Company, agreed to assume unpaid taxes against the property amounting to about $21,000.[45]

The struggle in Brigantine resembled a contest between an irresistable principle and an immovable prejudice, and the verdict was divided. Some observers, noting the timidity of Brigantine's politicians in the face of racial prejudice, the huge financial loss to the Peace Mission, and the followers' withdrawal from Brigantine, saw the episode as a setback for Father Divine and the cause of toleration generally.

One doubts that Divine himself regarded the battle of Brigantine as a clear-cut victory, for he informed the Peace Mission members of the hotel's transfer only after the Coast Guard units left the building, with the close of the war. Until then, it appears, only selected aides had been apprised of the sale.[46]

Still, Father Divine was among the first to provide an integrated beachfront in the area of Atlantic City, and if his achievement was short-lived, it nevertheless helped spur the broader movement for racial integration. The

NAACP, for example, monitored the Brigantine incident and rejoiced to see Divine defy long-standing discrimination on that island. James Egert Allen of the NAACP's New York branch praised Divine in April, 1942, for his "masterful" argument to the Brigantine committees and his "courageous attitude" in confronting those "un-American" citizens who barred the path to full justice for all.[47] In reply, Father Divine emphasized the larger social aims that motivated all his actions:

> [M]y co-workers and followers are endeavoring to express our citizenry and enact the Bill of Rights in every activity and even in every community. . . . and we are endeavoring to open up the way for others to enjoy life, liberty and the reality of happiness. Hence, we mean to protect the civil liberties of the law-abiding American citizens in every community and give them a chance to enjoy some of the pleasures and liberties that the privileged few were only able to enjoy.[48]

On balance, Father Divine's campaign to integrate even the most exclusive northern white neighborhoods enjoyed considerable positive results. It is true that the severe and pervasive racism in the country limited the Peace Mission's efforts to enter new communities and remold national attitudes. Yet despite frustrations in Brigantine and elsewhere, followers who had known only constricted slum conditions were enabled to acquire homes in excellent residential areas formerly barred to them. The movement's purchases also demonstrated to white Americans that blacks would vigorously test their constitutional rights to live wherever they could afford. Perhaps most important, the Peace Mission inspired blacks within and outside the movement to realize that, through their determined efforts, they could make the seemingly impassable ghettos into points of departure for a better life.

Notes to Chapter 5

1. Roy Wilkins, "The Watchtower," *NYAN*, Aug. 16, 1941, p. 14.

2. John A. Salmond, "The Civilian Conservation Corps and the Negro," *Journal of American History* 52 (June, 1965):79-80.

3. Robert Moats Miller, "The Attitudes of American Protestantism toward the Negro, 1919-1936," *Journal of Negro History* 41 (July, 1956):219-20.

4. *PC*, Mar. 15, 1941, p. 2. The headline for this article fairly summarized a widespread social attitude as well as this incident: "Preached Racial Equality; Run Out of Town; Ordained Minister Told Not to Return."

5. Powell, *Against the Tide*, p. 241.

6. *Age*, May 29, 1937, p. 1.

7. Ibid., Apr. 13, 1935, pp. 1, 2.

8. Edwin Johnson to Father Divine, Apr. 11, 1935 (in reply to Divine's letter of Apr. 8, not reprinted), and Divine to Johnson, Apr. 14, 1935, both in *SW*,

Apr. 20, 1935, p. 10; Divine to Johnson, May 31, 1935, in ibid., June 8, 1935, p. 3. The quotation is from Divine's letter of May 31. Divine's disciples remained despite the harassment, Governor Johnson's attitude changed, and the situation gradually improved: see ibid., Jan. 21, 1936, p. 23.

9. Al Harwith (a Peace Mission member) to Peace Mission headquarters, Harlem, Mar. 4, 1939, in *ND*, Mar. 9, 1939, p. 88.

10. *NYAN*, Mar. 28, 1936, pp. 1, 4.

11. Hoshor, *God in a Rolls-Royce*, pp. 253-55.

12. See, for example, *Times*, July 29, 1938, p. 1, *PC*, Aug. 6, 1938, p. 1, and *NYAN*, Dec. 31, 1938, p. 1, all giving front-page coverage of the Peace Mission's purchase of Krum Elbow. The *Amsterdam News* cited this purchase as one of the twelve outstanding events in Afro-American history for 1938.

13. *ND*, Sept. 28, 1939, p. 16; *Times*, July 31, 1938, p. 5.

14. Ibid., July 30, 1938, p. 15.

15. Ibid., Aug. 6, 1938, p. 3.

16. "Black Elbow," *Time* 32 (Aug. 8, 1938):8.

17. Ibid.

18. *Times*, July 31, 1938, p. 5.

19. Ibid., Aug. 28, 1938, p. 1.

20. Ibid., Aug. 10, 1938, p. 3.

21. Father Divine to Franklin Roosevelt, telegram, Aug. 8, 1939, in *ND*, Aug. 17, 1939, p. 98; Father Divine to Eleanor Roosevelt, Aug. 7, 1939, in ibid., Aug. 17, 1939, p. 96.

22. Stephen Early to Father Divine, Aug. 14, 1939, in *ND*, Aug. 17, 1939, pp. 99-100; Eleanor Roosevelt to Father Divine, Aug. 12, 1939, in ibid., Aug. 17, 1939, p. 97.

23. Interview given by Father Divine to A. Mark Harris and Joshua Cockburn, in *ND*, Sept. 7, 1939, pp. 17-27. The quotation is on p. 23.

24. Ibid.

25. *Times*, Aug. 4, 1938, p. 3; *NYAN*, Aug. 13, 1938, p. 3.

26. *Times*, June 16, 1939, p. 48.

27. Ibid.

28. Ibid.

29. Ibid.

30. Ibid.

31. Ibid., June 17, 1939, p. 17.

32. Ralph Bunche, "The Programs, Ideologies, Tactics and Achievements of Negro Betterment and Interracial Organizations: A Research Memorandum," prepared for the Carnegie-Myrdal study of the Negro in America, pp. 469-70, in the Schomburg Collection of the New York Public Library; James Baldwin, *No Name in the Street* (New York: Oral, 1972), p. 72.

33. *NYAN*, July 15, 1939, p. 18.

34. Ibid., Mar. 21, 1942, p. 2.

35. Ibid.

36. Transcript of conference between Brigantine delegation and Father Divine, Mar. 20, 1942, in *ND*, Apr. 2, 1942, pp. 15-34. The quotations are on p. 23.

37. Ibid., p. 28.

38. Ibid., Apr. 2, 1942, p. 87.

39. Sermon of Aug. 8, 1942, in *ND*, Aug. 13, 1942, p. 77.

40. *Times*, Sept. 11, 1942, p. 16.

41. On Father Divine's offer to the Coast Guard, see *Times,* Nov. 23, 1942, p. 14, and *AA,* Nov. 28, 1942, p. 1. On Divine's persuasion of the owners to lease the hotel at a nominal charge to the Coast Guard, see *ND,* Nov. 26, 1942, pp. 21-22. Related statements by Coast Guard officers are in *ND,* Dec. 24, 1942, p. 33, and *Times,* Jan. 18, 1943, p. 17. On the Peace Mission's rejection of the Coast Guard's offer to pay taxes on the property, see *Times,* Jan. 22, 1943, p. 25.

42. *NYAN,* Nov. 28, 1942, p. 1.

43. *AA,* Dec. 12, 1942, p. 3.

44. *Times,* Jan. 13, 1943, p. 12.

45. Ibid., Sept. 11, 1944, p. 10.

46. Father Divine's speech at annual church meeting in 1945, in *ND,* Oct. 29, 1977, p. 3.

47. James Egert Allen to Father Divine, Apr. 9, 1942, in *ND,* Apr. 16, 1942, p. 62.

48. Father Divine to James Egert Allen, Apr. 14, 1942, in ibid., p. 63.

CHAPTER 6

A New Economic Order

While Father Divine considered integration essential to racial harmony, he believed that equality of opportunity must extend to the economic sphere. It is ironic that he is remembered largely for feeding and housing the indigent during the Depression, because he disdained the idea of relief as degrading to the recipient and a burden to society. Although Divine viewed his charitable work as a necessary humanitarian activity, he considered this only an interim measure. Prosperity through economic cooperation rather than mere subsistence remained the long-range goal of the Peace Mission's economic programs.

Cooperation

The cooperative ideal that Father Divine espoused was already widely popular among black leaders. Cooperation offered, first, a way to reduce consumer costs and promote the efficiency of Negro businesses. It also appealed to many in the black community as a means of fostering racial solidarity through mutual economic aid.[1] Father Divine's distinctive contribution lay in giving practical, large-scale expression to this ideal. His organizational wizardry led many, black and white, to agree with a prominent Negro educator who observed, "I am . . . waiving Father Divine's 'divinity,' but as a business genius, we must lift our hats to him."[2]

The Peace Mission was easily among the most impressive examples of cooperative enterprise in the nation. By the mid-1930s the Peace Mission had become the largest realty holder in Harlem, with three apartment houses, nine private houses, fifteen to twenty flats, and several meeting halls with dormitories on the upper floors. In addition, followers in Harlem operated some twenty-five restaurants, six groceries, ten barber shops,

122

ten cleaning stores, two dozen huckster wagons with clams and oysters or fresh vegetables, and a coal business with three trucks ranging from Harlem to the mines in Pennsylvania.[3] Divine's aide, Faithful Mary, alone directed over a dozen such enterprises in 1935, among them a large emporium for meat, fish, fowl, and vegetables, an ice cream and bakery establishment, and a tailor shop. A variety of Peace Mission businesses also operated in other areas from New England to California.[4]

Father Divine encouraged followers to enter business as a constructive act and a sign of their independence. The response was remarkable, as hundreds with minimal experience enthusiastically became merchants. Followers enjoyed wide latitude in selecting and operating businesses, yet seemed less interested in financial gain than in actively serving their movement. Most apparently returned their net profits to the common funds of the Peace Mission, relying on Father Divine's bounty to provide for their needs. Similarly, some followers voluntarily worked for others who had established businesses, yet received no wages except to cover transportation and other job-related expenses.

Among numerous paragons of the movement's entrepreneurial ethic was Priscilla Paul, one of the earliest followers from the years in Sayville. She responded to Father Divine's crusade for business initiative by opening a dress-making shop, with an "initial capitalization" of 75 cents and total resources of several patches of cloth. Profits from this outlay were reinvested in the business, and other followers volunteered to help as the turnover in merchandise increased. In time, Priscilla Paul's talented, original designs and low prices led to a flourishing concern, reportedly selling over $2,000 in clothing during the first five months of operation.[5]

Individual vendors displaying "Peace" buttons also proliferated during the thirties in the vicinity of the main kingdoms. They frequently stretched the most slender capital resources into healthy business ventures, as a visitor to the Harlem missions observed of one pushcart merchant dispensing frozen desserts: "He has a block of ice, some sort of metal shaver, and with this he scrapes the shavings into a cup, pours on the various colored syrups which he has in bottles, and there is your ice! These are sold for the trifling sum of three cents. Quite ingenious, the way some of the believers have succeeded in making themselves practical and independent."[6] Although these vendors clearly operated on a very modest scale, collectively they enjoyed substantial patronage, particularly in Harlem and Newark.

How did the Peace Mission businesses flourish amid the wreckage of so many other ghetto-based trades? The nature of the religious movement itself aided greatly, for it promoted the accumulation of capital. Communal living arrangements afforded important economies of scale in pur-

chasing food and housing the faithful snugly—often several to a room—
in "Peace Mission Evangelical hotels." Communal expenditures were pared
further by the injunctions against tobacco, liquor, cosmetics, and other
common but costly pleasures. Strictures against insurance plans truncated
still another possible siphon of funds from the common pool. It was therefore a relatively easy task for Peace Mission enterprises, in conjunction
with wages from outside work, to meet the basic needs of the members
and still provide a large supply of liquid capital. This in turn facilitated
investment in new properties and enterprises, always in cash payments to
avoid debt and the burden of interest on loans.

   These enterprises thrived, too, because Divine carefully avoided a mis-
take often fatal to black-owned businesses—dependence on racial solidarity
for patronage. Indeed, the sad record of such businesses during this period
suggests that many blacks preferred to deal with white merchants whose
chain stores undersold small black-operated shops and whose banks were
considered sounder than their minority-owned counterparts, a largely
self-fulfilling conviction.[7]

   Father Divine encouraged his disciples to seek patronage for their businesses by offering economic advantages rather than racial ideals. While
he left details of the Peace Mission's commercial ventures to the members, he urged them to keep prices at a minimum. Divine stressed, first,
the evangelical ethic of service, reminiscent of the Puritan view of business as a divine calling: "Do not go in business for the purpose of seeing
how much you will gain, but go in it to see how much you can give." This,
he assured his followers, "will give you a desirable result."[8]

   A clue as to what this "desirable result" signified is provided in a later
message, in which Divine spoke in hardheaded economic terms suitable
for a generation that had learned about spirituality from the pen of Bruce
Barton:

   When you can get a soda-pop for three cents, you come in at times
   and buy from four to five because they are only three cents. If you
   were obliged to pay ten cents for them, maybe you would not buy
   any. . . . Take Mr. Ford as a sample and as an example, building
   the cheapest car that could be built at one time. He did not build
   a car costing fifteen, twenty or thirty or thirty-five thousand dollars,
   yet he became to be the richest man in the world.[9]

Father Divine saw no contradiction between a spiritual calling and an economic reward. In his view religion was a practical ordering of one's life
to promote the common good—which would include one's own prosperity
as a result. His sermons envisioned a common march of prophet and profit
to a very earthly millennium.[10]

   Under Divine's guidance, Peace Mission members sold quality goods at fire-sale prices, taking advantage of the movement's low cost of living and relying on sheer volume of trade to sustain revenues. Peace Mission coal vendors charged for their wares $7.50 a ton in 1935, a full dollar below the prevailing market price. Peace Mission restaurants gained national renown for selling complete and nourishing meals for fifteen cents, a price substantially lower than found almost anywhere else in Harlem. Lodgings, too, were inexpensive at $1 to $2 a week; if quarters were often crowded, a comparison with most other dwellings in the same neighborhoods left virtually no cause for complaint.[11]

Although some competitors fumed at the Peace Mission's "unfair" pricing policies, shoppers took a rather different perspective of the public welfare. Divine's followers did a thriving trade with customers whose sole connection with the movement was an appreciation for low-priced goods. Given the high cost of living in the ghettos, these stores provided a vital service during the Depression by helping marginally independent workers make ends meet.

The "Promised Land"

The Peace Mission promoted rural cooperatives with equal energy, for reasons that involved cultural as well as economic factors. Even within the movement the process of adjustment to urban life was often painful and in some cases unavailing. This was particularly true of people who had only recently migrated from the rural South and yearned for at least some features of their old routine. For such people, whose background and needs were familiar to Father Divine, the Peace Mission offered the chance to resume a rural existence on properties it purchased in New York's Ulster County. These new farm settlements became known collectively to Divine's faithful as the "Promised Land."

Various land-oriented schemes of this nature had long received attention in the black community, but few had proven practicable. Back-to-Africa movements, most notably that inspired by Marcus Garvey, had arisen among black Americans since antebellum days, but all failed to persuade more than a tiny minority of blacks to emigrate. There were also efforts to found all-black towns in the South and Far West after Reconstruction, and an ill-fated plan to forge a black-governed state out of the Oklahoma territory. The idea of a black commonwealth within America persisted into the thirties, with separatist movements like the 49th-state crusade demanding that the federal government cede land for that purpose in Mississippi or some other heavily black region. Such movements received scant support from the black community, and no hearing at all in Washington. Mediating the conservative calls for flight and the politically surreal hopes for a black American nation were plans like that of Anthony "Prophet Costonie" Green, a black cult leader who in 1939 advocated forming a cooperative colony on an island off the Florida coast. He requested government aid for his projected island paradise, to be christened "New Dealia" because it would be a "haven for the forgotten man." Government officials reportedly studied plans for the project with Costonie. Like most such schemes, however, it did not materialize.[12]

Father Divine's colonizing project sought to avoid the twin visionary pitfalls of a "return"-to-Africa venture, which held scant appeal to black Americans except as a spur to racial pride, and the extreme political naiveté of the nation-within-a-nation enthusiasts. Instead he directed the investment of cooperative revenues in rich farmland located to the northwest of his Harlem kingdoms, focusing not on political goals but on economic progress. He assured his followers, "If perchance you have the means . . . to build a home, [then] the ground, the land, the lots, will be given to you free of cost, and you will have your deeds for them without a string tied to them. All the property I have purchased is free and clear."[13]

The purchase of a thirty-four-acre estate in 1935 inaugurated the Peace Mission's rural experiment in Ulster County. The scope of the enterprise quickly dwarfed the initial investment in terms of property, population, and production. Thousands became joint owners in these cooperative communities, each receiving small tracts of land, between five and ten acres. Those who worked in factories and offices could choose between communal homes and modest private residences. The communities soon began to produce fruits, vegetables, poultry, milk, and eventually—with more than a passing thought to the symbolism—honey.

An observer in 1939 recorded the "Promised Land's" transformation from a modest beginning as a single rural commune to a flourishing conglomerate:

> Since then [1935] the development of the Promised Land has become a large-scale real-estate operation. Today it consists of twenty-two parcels of property aggregating 2,000 acres, with no mortgages and all taxes paid up. Under Divine's supervision a total of $212,000 was expended in purchase money, and improvements costing between $50,000 and $100,000 have been, and are being, made. Some of the properties are choice estates, while others are farms, rooming houses, stores, garages and resort hotels.[14]

Followers frequently initiated the purchase of properties but routinely checked with Father Divine to inform him of their plans and ask his advice on the best real estate values. Divine seems to have spent much time consulting with legal aides and others in ascertaining the choicest sites and wisest bargains. He also had the comfortable advantage of having real estate agents besiege him with offers in all parts of New York. They knew he paid in cash for all deals, no matter the price, and always in advance. Armed with this financial leverage and an uncanny business sense, Divine often negotiated deals personally. He was reputed to drive sharp bargains and to scrutinize every detail of a prospective property before agreeing to a transaction. When satisfied, he sealed a contract with a single cash payment from a brown bag or satchel bursting with paper currency. This money represented part of the pooled savings of his followers. The deeds were invariably in the names of his disciples, never his own, though of course this was small sacrifice to a man whose followers believed that the earth was their lord's and the properties thereof. The deeds are significant, however, as evidence that a great many followers gained direct ownership and benefit from the expanding rural kingdoms.

The Ulster communes thrived from their inception. A reporter for the *Herald-Tribune* toured the Promised Land with Father Divine in 1936 and noted its progress: "Father Divine has bought no rundown farms. Rather, they are going concerns, equipped with electricity and baths, and completely furnished from radios to old pewter. Already at least a hundred of the brothers and sisters . . . have been taken up from the city in a fleet of five new station wagons, and as many limousines and trucks, to expand the settlements." The reporter also noted some sacrifices required of the followers to speed that progress: "Father Divine is a great one for economizing on space and, by putting up partitions and squeezing in beds, he can double the accommodations of the average house."[15]

The greatest economy was the near elimination of sloth among the inhabitants. Father Divine achieved this through continual exhortation and numerous visits by plane to his movement's various properties. To disciples awed by the Father's presence and grateful for this chance to work their own land, his surprise appearances were both inspirational and a chastening reminder that their efforts were subject to careful oversight.

Father Divine exhorted his followers, "Chickens and pigs should be multiplied the same as you have ever heard of locusts for the wicked." He also showed an acute sense of pragmatic planning in telling them, "If you love me so much as you say you do, let your love and devotion become to be practical, profitable, and good-for-something. . . . The love of God in the children of men is expressed or manifested in service to Him."[16] In short, Father Divine had no intention of presiding over the blissful disintegration of his community by having followers continually praise him while the land went untended and the properties neglected.

If the Father demanded a certain Spartan rigor from the rural settlers, he also displayed considerable self-discipline in refusing their offers of money for investment until the best possible bargains were at hand. His forbearance reflected the enlightened self-interest of an investment broker whose own fortunes were linked to those of his clients. Yet there was, in addition, a sense of personal pride in watching out for his followers, as he often expressed it, as a bird hovering over the nest.

Some affluent followers, too, displayed considerable idealism in pioneering these ventures, as Father Divine elaborated in revealing detail:

> [T]he first one who did it [purchased a settlement] was one who had worked for years and years and had saved up her earnings and purchased the New Paltz place. She did not pay very much for it compared to the actual value, but God was in it. . . . She was willing to give her service in that way, by purchasing, living [on] and developing this property and improving it. . . . [As followers] began to see how this was done, and they were well secured, then others began to come in cooperatively, and so the work still goes on.[17]

The work indeed went on, more rapidly than many residents in Ulster County could easily understand or accept. Farmers and businessmen were soon acting like the besieged defenders of a dwindling preserve, as Divine's agents acquired choice properties one after another. Scarcely a month elapsed without some new Peace Mission purchase, followed by some aggrieved Ulster official's dire warning. Harry G. Lamothe, president of the Kingston Chamber of Commerce, expressed the prevalent mood of resistance tinged with gloom: "We are strongly opposed to Father Divine's plan to make Ulster County into a 'model paradise.' Undoubtedly the question will come up for discussion at our May meeting." Lamothe prophesied that the migration of thousands of Harlem slum residents would ruin the hotel and boarding business throughout the county. Father Divine's right-hand lawyer, Arthur Madison, brushed aside this and similar belligerent comments by Ulster officials as irrelevant to the Peace Mission's plans. The movement, he assured reporters, would continue to obtain all available property in unsettled parts of the county, to start canneries, model dairy farms, and, in time, clothing and auto factories.[18]

By the time Divine's followers made their most spectacular crossing into the Promised Land, entering Krum Elbow in July, 1938, they had already established some 700 separate centers in New York state. These included farms, restaurants, barber shops, laundries, and other businesses. Krum Elbow was easily the most renowned addition to the heavenly cooperative system, in view of its proximity to the president's Hyde Park home. It was, however, one of many areas touched by this mass movement from ghetto to estate. Under Divine's supervision, the Promised Land came to include properties in New Rochelle, Newburgh, Milton, Kingston, Greenkill Park, Saugerties, West Saugerties, High Falls, Stone Ridge, and other places outside New York City.

The efficiency of the Peace Mission businesses enabled them to compete successfully even in these predominantly white communities, where initial sympathy for the movement was generally scant. Here, as in the ghettos, followers charged minimal rates for all commodities. Operators of gasoline stations, for example, were forbidden to make more than a penny profit on a gallon of gasoline. As a result, the many Peace Mission gas station owners lining the highways in Ulster County did a brisk business selling quality brands well below their competitors' prices.[19]

Throughout Ulster the Peace Mission generated economic growth that benefited entire communities. The *Amsterdam News* records the case of High Falls, twelve miles from Poughkeepsie, a village in sharp economic decline until the Peace Mission followers settled there in the mid-thirties:

> They moved in and bought up some of the best property in Ulster County. Today a flourishing shoe repair shop, a barber shop, a dressmaking concern where fine women's clothes are made; and a second hand clothing store where sterilized used clothing is sold, are operating full blast. Divine's restaurant does more business than any eating place in the village. His tailoring shop is considered as the largest custom-made tailoring establishment in the entire county. A grocery store does the major business in the village.[20]

Although High Falls residents at first feared that the Peace Mission's interracial following would destroy property values, they soon discovered a very different trend. As in other villages, "homes and buildings were renovated throughout and the example set by the Divinites launched a community-wide campaign for similar improvement. Property values, real-estate men reported, have increased and police said no disorders of any kind have come up in the Divine communities."[21]

In all, the Midas touch that the Divinites brought to their new settlements, as merchants, servants, renovators, and simply law-abiding citizens, assuaged decades of racism in those villages.[22] "Those fellows who follow Father Divine don't do anyone harm," one Poughkeepsie farmer expressed the mellowing attitude. "They're down there in High Falls doing something worthwhile."[23]

The heart of this worthwhile activity, to Father Divine, remained agricultural labor. For Divine, who still nursed memories of a sharecropper's wretched life, there was a special joy at seeing these fertile lands grow abundant and prosperous. Once, after inspecting a colossal, sixty-two-pound pumpkin, he gleefully reported to his Harlem followers, "The vegetable kingdom is willingly surrendering."[24] An oration at Rockland Palace in 1940 mixed that same enthusiasm with a reminder of the larger purpose behind the Promised Land experiment:

> Go out to Olive Bridge; I would like all of you to see all of that stock out there. Chickens and ducks and guineas and pigs and horses and cows and everything! It is just marvelous to see what God has

actually done, for the meek and the most insignificant, they are coming into possession of their rightful inheritance and shall no longer be in lacks, wants and limitations and in the slums and dirt and filth.[25]

The special pride Father Divine took in his colonizing project led some blacks to compare his work to that of Marcus Garvey; yet the Promised Land actually shared more in common with New Deal resettlement programs than with black nationalist efforts to retreat from American society. The existence of people on the margins of economic subsistence was a national problem that the Depression had greatly magnified. A salient aspect was the dislocation of tenant farmers and sharecroppers, who either continued to work submarginal lands for diminishing rewards or endured a harsh adjustment to city life. The federal government sought to relocate such people in model rural communities, which in their broad outlines were similar in purpose and method to the Peace Mission's rural colonies.

The Division of Homesteads was among the federal agencies designed to help people start a new, idyllic existence in specially created agricultural communities. Like the Promised Land, these communities ideally aimed to reintegrate struggling individuals into the American economic system by providing them with their own land and developing a diversified set of economic activities in addition to farming. The Division of Homesteads also shared another crucial goal with the Promised Land venture: it recognized the special need to encompass Negroes in its programs because of their generally weak economic position and their prominent representation among dislocated farmers.[26]

The lofty interracial ideals that resettlement administrators proclaimed were unfortunately quite helpless against the ravages of pressure groups and widespread racism. When, for example, the assistant supervisor of the homestead division assured blacks that "segregation and discrimination are not contemplated," he was referring only to planned settlements in areas that were already integrated. Settlements constructed in segregated locales were to observe Jim Crow customs in order to avoid the wrath of "problem areas."[27] Similar fears of offending whites reduced the number of projects implemented in integrated neighborhoods. Nor were blacks, even in segregated units, aided in proportion to their need, which might have weakened the program politically. As part of the administration's priority on economic recovery, the resettlement programs concentrated on individuals of some small means who represented a comparatively desirable investment for future prosperity. The very poorest strata, in which Negroes were disproportionately located, received scant assistance,[28] in accord with this approach to reform by triage.

The Promised Land experiment extended the benefits of resettlement programs to many whom politics and prejudice had placed on the edges of federal concern. Its integrated and predominantly black colonies reflected commitments that government officials often voiced but seldom fully achieved. Moreover, instead of focusing on those most likely to become successful independent farmers or merchants, as the federal programs did, Father Divine designed the Promised Land project especially for the socially outcast and the economically "hopeless." Free of political constraints himself — or, put another way, drawing his own constituency largely from an element too weak to influence Washington politics — the minister sought to aid those who, even during the New Deal, remained forgotten.

The Peace Mission and the Ghetto

While the Peace Mission built its own economic strength purely on business acumen, it did not neglect the calls to racial solidarity by black-owned enterprises. Father Divine justified his support of these businesses, however, not on racial grounds but on the severe economic disadvantages with which all ghetto residents contended.

The state of Negro business in the thirties was dismal even for a period of general economic depression. Fewer than 1,500 of the more than 200,000 American manufacturing establishments were controlled by blacks. Of those 1,500, about one-half made their revenues by selling hair straighteners and skin whiteners. The extent of black leadership in retail trade was similarly minute. Even among stores that catered to ghetto residents, blacks handled only some 2 percent of the retail business.[29]

Black entrepreneurs generally started with considerable handicaps. They suffered from meager capital resources and insufficient access to credit. Because most operated in ghettos, their clientele had sharply limited purchasing power. The Depression magnified these difficulties, to which black leaders reacted with heightened appeals to patronize "race businesses." The Peace Mission joined numerous church and secular groups in endorsing these appeals and pledging its members to shop at Negro-owned stores and buy goods produced by Negro workers.

A bread company with the somewhat incongruous name "Brown Bomber" was the leading focus of efforts to aid ghetto-based enterprise during the Depression. The name represented a cheerfully transparent attempt to attach the company's fortunes to the ring triumphs of Joe Louis; indeed, the firm became a fashionable symbol of black commercial aspirations more from its oft-cited name than its seldom noted bread. The ambitious publicity director, Walter Blair, secured endorsements by Negro leaders and special conferences on behalf of Brown Bomber Bread Company, out of all proportion to the firm's economic weight. Blair courted Father Divine, among other community figures, with characteristic energy. He spent more than a few nights entertained by the songs of Peace Mission followers, while singing his own praises of a bread at least "equal to any others." From a place of honor at Father Divine's own table, the publicity director assured the assembled Peace Mission followers that his company's aims were similar to Divine's — to promote economic achievement and the liberation of the race as a whole. Divine himself led the applause for Blair's words.[30]

The Peace Mission's principle of support for ghetto-based business operated freely even in the normally forbidden realm of cosmetics. Strictures against the use of such products receded by Divine fiat, as a variety of cleansing agents by the black-owned Apex News and Hair Company received his special sanction.

The dynamic and persuasive president of Apex Company, Sara Spencer Washington, seems to have contributed strongly to Father Divine's mellowing attitude toward cosmetic merchandise. Washington was among the most important business executives in the black community, with a reputation as a pioneer in promotional techniques. She was among the first Negro business leaders to establish a department of public relations. This department worked with Negro organizations in cities throughout the nation in order to explain the importance of supporting Negro business and buying products manufactured and distributed by Negroes. Washington cultivated the support of the Peace Mission with particular zeal, indeed, with a personal effort that seems to have far transcended business sense alone.

Washington denied being a disciple of Father Divine, claiming she lacked the self-discipline to be a true follower. Yet she attended numerous banquets, spoke of Divine with all the requisite awe of a devoted follower, and even became the honorary head of a Peace Mission church during the early forties. Divine, for his part, encouraged his followers to patronize Apex products. Certain of the more flamboyant cosmetics — hair straighteners and skin whiteners leading the list — remained taboo. But for the most part, followers adjusted to the notion that to purchase Apex cosmetics now marked them as dedicated rather than decadent.[31]

Father Divine realized, with most black leaders, that aiding black business had to form part of a wider effort to free the ghettos from economic hardship. By themselves, rallies for a ghetto-controlled firm or the success of a few selected corporations could not compensate for the continued outside ownership of most ghetto industries. Nor could it erase the complex pattern of discrimination that devastated black urban life. This required more militant community protest, and Father Divine strongly approved these "direct action" campaigns.

Few weeks went by without a new and usually tenuous coalition seeking Divine's aid. One of the more militant was the Consolidated Tenants League, which aimed to secure lower rents by threatening a rent strike throughout Harlem. The league sent representatives to Divine in September, 1936, urging him to have his followers march in solidarity with them. Divine explained that the problem was not so simple as confronting evil realtors, for they in turn contended with unjust tax assessments. Therefore the underlying need was to persuade city officials to abolish these discriminatory rates in the ghettos. Nevertheless, Divine agreed to bring his followers to the league's demonstration.[32] Peace Mission members formed the most numerous contingent in the league's march along Seventh Avenue in mid-October, and as rain scattered most other participants, the demonstration became almost wholly a Peace Mission activity.[33]

The interaction with the Consolidated Tenants League was characteristic of Divine's frequent but often strained dealings with most such coalitions. The league's delegates had little sympathy with the Peace Mission's religious tenets or Divine's self-appointed role as savior of the oppressed. Yet they needed the thousands of followers he could bring at a moment's notice to bolster a faltering cause. For Divine's part, the realization that groups sought him for his following, not for his leadership or tactical suggestions, must have rankled deeply. Yet these lobbyists did recognize his influence, while their work for racial justice confirmed his own sense of mission. Divine thus remained something of an outsider in Harlem's struggle for justice, even as he participated actively and in some ways quite effectively in the cause.

Direct action campaigns in the thirties centered on obtaining more jobs for blacks, for the Depression had greatly worsened an already existing unemployment crisis in the ghettos. Racism, the concentration of black workers in "marginal" positions like domestic service, and lack of seniority in industry all intensified for ghetto dwellers the problem of a contracting labor market that afflicted the entire country. Employment conditions in Harlem were reflected in the fierce determination with which residents eyed the most menial jobs. William Muraskin depicts the situation there during the first years of the Depression:

> Employment as a lowly grocery clerk became a desirable position, and even newsworthy. The New York *Age* of May 26, 1934, featured the news that there was "another Negro clerk in 125th Street," a Negro woman who had obtained employment as a salesgirl in a music store. On June 23 it carried a similar item in which the fortunate girl—the

daughter of a bandleader, no less — was congratulated for her good fortune. Such were the aspirations of the Negro social elite: the lower-class never dreamed so ambitiously.[34]

The frustrations of unemployment, confinement to menial work, and excessive costs of living combined, under the weight of the Depression, to spark a succession of boycott campaigns against stores that refused to employ blacks. Conservative leaders such as Kelly Miller and columnist Theophilus Lewis of the *Amsterdam News* spurned the boycott efforts for fear of white retaliation, by labor even more than business groups. The boycotts nevertheless received the endorsement of many organizations, including the Peace Mission.

The position Father Divine assumed in these campaigns is marked by a curious ambiguity. In principle he strongly favored all nonviolent direct action, including boycotting, to overcome discrimination. Yet there is scant evidence for Divine's active involvement in the picketing of targeted stores or in directing his followers to avoid purchases in such stores.

Divine did play at least a secondary role in the landmark Harlem boycott of 1934, in which a diverse coalition of black groups successfully pressured the owner of Blumstein's Department Store to hire black saleswomen. The initial organizer of this boycott was a fiery street orator and former cultist from Chicago named Sufi Abdul Hamid. In his bid for lower-class support of his boycott plan, he sought aid from Father Divine. While some believed that Sufi's notoriety for racist and anti-Semitic invective would preclude any basis for rapport with Divine, Sufi's judgment proved sound. Divine brought his followers to at least one of Sufi's rallies, on this occasion greatly outnumbering Sufi's own following.[35]

The unexpected harmony between the Peace Mission and Sufi's Negro Industrial Clerical Alliance centered on their common priority of obtaining fair treatment for blacks in retail stores. Father Divine may also have felt more comfortable dealing with another black crusader of lower-class origin who respectfully sought his aid, rather than with the genteel middle-class leaders, particularly ministers, who routinely spurned him and his followers.

Yet the entente between Father Divine and Sufi Hamid proved of short duration. This was partly because Divine evinced little concern to pressure Blumstein's store by picketing or by speaking more than generalities about his ideals at mass rallies. Then, too, Sufi deemed the final agreement between Blumstein's and the boycotting coalition to be grossly inadequate, providing no assurances that the poorer, darker-skinned blacks in the ghettos would be employed. Embittered by the conclusion of this campaign, Sufi ended his fragile concord with other leaders, including Father Divine. Divine, for his part, was almost certainly displeased by

Sufi's racist rhetoric and rabble-rousing that seemed increasingly divorced from issues vital to the Harlem community. The collapse of this alliance, however, did not dissuade the Father from stepping up his use of economic leverage to promote black rights.

As early as 1933, Father Divine began writing to selected companies operating in Harlem, demanding that they hire and promote more Afro-Americans, and implying that refusals would mean loss of patronage by his followers.[36] After the success of the boycott against Blumstein's, Divine even formed a staff of Peace Mission investigators to compile data on company employment patterns. He included this information in letters to corporate executives, in which he sharply questioned their hiring practices and insisted on improvement. Divine released the text of these letters and all company replies to the black press as well as to Peace Mission journals, thus seeking to pressure these firms into concessions.

Because Father Divine controlled a mass following that could in itself become a troublesome boycotting bloc, his polite communiqués always carried the veiled threat of sanctions should companies refuse his demands. His correspondence with New York's two major milk distributors, Borden and Sheffield, affords an example of his approach:

> Through nearly a week's research work, I do not find that you are employing chauffeurs, mechanics, and other skilled laborers [without discrimination]. . . . If your concern will [seek] to cooperate in abolishing discriminatory practices you will immediately [employ] more drivers of trucks of a different complexion and race than those that are mostly employed by you, especially in the streets of Harlem. By so doing, your concern will be looked upon from a different angle than what it is or has been, and we will be pleased to cooperate with it in every way possible to encourage the continuous friendship and respect by the public for your concern.[37]

The milk companies hastened to assure Divine that no discrimination obtained in their employment policies, but Divine insisted on specific commitments. His efforts drew wide attention among black leaders as he demonstrated how to place a racially biased firm under a sustained, embarrassing spotlight. Floyd Calvin of the *Pittsburgh Courier* observed, "It now looks like something more than the usual perfunctory gestures in Harlem's economic battles will come of the threatened boycott by Father Divine. . . ." Calvin saw Divine as working to bring a new age of concerted ghetto resistance against white economic exploitation.[38]

Yet it is unclear to what extent the Peace Mission actually went beyond words and boycotted the milk companies or other targeted firms. Although Divine certainly could have induced his followers to cease their patronage of any product, no direct evidence exists that he ever did so on the grounds of racism in hiring. It is possible that Divine, recognizing his weak ties with most other Harlem leaders, considered any unilateral boycott announcement a vain gesture that would be most harmful to the Peace Mission itself. In any case, he does not seem to have followed up his steps toward boycotting offending firms.

If Divine proved uncertain in the tactics of boycott campaigns, he nonetheless displayed a prescient grasp of their potential for overcoming discrimination by business leaders. In this regard it is significant to note the Peace Mission's written warning to a discriminatory bus company, some two decades before the Montgomery bus boycott of 1955-56, to protest Jim Crow seating arrangements:

> [Many followers] have not been accorded the same courtesy on board the busses, and when it came to dining they were positively forbidden, in places from Arizona to Pennsylvania, to eat with their fellow-passengers. Some have even been roughly handled by the restaurant keepers along the way. . . .
>
> These persons [Father Divine's followers] refuse to patronize anything that indulges in segregation. If their brethren cannot have the same accommodation they have, they will refrain from enjoying such accommodations themselves. If those who provide the accommodations do not employ all people alike without regard to complexion or nationality, they will not patronize them; and in this New Dispensation, such enterprises cannot be successful unless they do.[39]

On balance, Divine encouraged but did not decisively enter the ghetto's major boycott campaigns of the thirties. His efforts to implement plans for such boycotts generally remained halting and poorly coordinated with the activities of other groups. Still, his initiatives in documenting cases of racism and touting the weapon of selective patronage were widely publicized and highly praised in black journals, and they added to Harlem's mounting interest in the tactics of direct action.

Father Divine and Organized Labor

Father Divine's interest in mass action faltered most noticeably before the crucial issue of unionization. The organization of black workers, part of a larger trend among American laborers during the New Deal, was among the most dramatic signs of change in the ghettos. For half a century most of the major unions had excluded blacks through provisions in their constitutions or by other, marginally more subtle means. During the thirties, though, the importance of Negroes to labor groups increased sharply. Government encouragement of union growth and the membership drives by the AFL and the fledgling CIO accelerated the admittance of Negroes into labor organizations. Negro organizers such as A. Philip Randolph of the Brotherhood of Sleeping Car Porters, and Frank Crosswaith, who in 1935 founded the Negro Labor Committee to recruit in industries under contract with AFL unions, encouraged blacks to seize this new opportunity to ally with white workers. In this way, they hoped, class interests would at last overcome race prejudice and, subsequently, all economic exploitation. Yet in the midst of these trends Father Divine remained ambivalent toward unions and implicitly discouraged his followers from joining or aiding them.

The chief precipitant of conflict between Father Divine and organized labor was the resentment by union leaders at seeing Peace Mission members occupy jobs vacated by striking workers. Divine's stress on work, coupled with the lower cost of living for followers living communally, led his followers to readily accept employment for wage rates that union leaders deemed intolerable. Divine's followers did not deliberately seek out jobs opened to them by striking workers; they tended, instead, to ignore completely the conflicts between employers and unions, focusing their attention on the availability of employment. Frank Crosswaith termed Father Divine a "strikebreaker" for permitting his followers to accept sweatshop jobs in the garment industry. Divine thus "unwittingly allowed himself to be used by the people who have always exploited Negroes and all workers."[40] Frequently, union workers expressed their resentments against Peace Mission "scabs" more directly, beating them severely as a lesson not to interfere with union policies. The conflicts had varying short-term results, but their larger significance was to aggravate Divine's suspicions toward labor groups.

The hiring of Peace Mission members by the Street Coal Company in 1936 during a union strike sparked the bloodiest assaults against Divine's followers. Striking workers, able to obtain the addresses to which the new employees were delivering coal, rushed to those locations, hid in the coal cellars, and waylaid the drivers. Union workers also burst into the office from which delivery men were sent out, and beat victims at random.

The assaults tested the pacifist principles of the Peace Mission followers. One victim, testifying at a banquet about the viciousness of the union assailants, thanked Father Divine for giving him the strength to remain nonviolent. In former times, the man confessed, he would have "brutalized" his attacker. According to his and other testimony, some disciples held their would-be assailants in restraint, but none engaged in counterviolence.[41]

Father Divine himself was livid about "the brutality of those cursed organizations" that "interfere with law-abiding citizens." He even toyed briefly with the thought of physical retaliation, as he looked at the injured disciples in his entourage: "Although you have been converted to God, if I would release you and free you . . . although being apparently wickedness, it would be for righteousness in violence. . . . You would not have anything to fear. . . ."[42] Divine never did "release" any followers from their strictly nonviolent ways, but the fact that he wavered publicly over the possibility is a measure of his outrage at union tactics.

Divine blamed the assaults partly on the coal company, which had concealed the fact that a strike was in progress. Yet his fury focused overwhelmingly on the union's disregard for the law. He requested New York's Police Commissioner Lewis J. Valentine to protect his followers and took the opportunity to denounce both union violence and intimidation: "We feel the Constitutional rights of our great country have been molested and embarrassed and intruded upon by many of the union organizers, by taking advantage of the people thru fear of violence and by violence . . . to force non-union representatives out of positions. . . . I feel such should not be tolerated in this great country of our civilization."[43]

Divine and William Morrissey, president of the Coal Trimmers' Association, meanwhile corresponded in hope of ending this episode embarrassing to both parties. Morrissey outlined the benevolent activities of his union and solicited Divine's cooperation as a matter of economic self-interest. Yet his communications always contained the hint of further violence unless Peace Mission members agreed not to work for the coal company.[44] The subsequent resolution of the coal strike reduced the confrontation between the union and the Peace Mission, but mutual suspicion remained high.

A world of ideological differences notwithstanding, labor spokesmen continued to make overtures to Father Divine, in hope of winning to their cause the thousands of unskilled workers who supported him. In these efforts they enjoyed some successes, which were nevertheless sharply limited by their underlying — and ill-disguised — opposition to Divine's leadership.

Shortly after the coal workers' attacks on Peace Mission employees, labor leaders had occasion to deplore violence when picketers against the National Shoe Stores in New York were assaulted by police. A picketing delegate injured in the attack, Myrna Taylor, asked Father Divine to join a rally planned by the United Front of Labor Unions to protest police brutality. Her flattery of Divine as the one person who could put a stop to such brutality, together with her bandaged appearance, helped convince the minister to put aside past grievances and attend the meeting.[45] Yet the rally, far from mending old differences between Divine and major union figures in Harlem, instead revealed more glaringly than ever the depth of their mutual antagonism.

The rally's spirit of unity quickly disintegrated in the atmosphere of mistrust and resentment, exacerbated by some calculated union slights against Divine. First, union delegates had Divine placed at the end of the list of speakers. He acquiesced gracefully but found further snubs in store. While some union leaders welcomed him and expressed appreciation for his support, Frank Crosswaith adamantly refused even to sit on the same platform with him. A reporter for the Peace Mission painfully recorded that Crosswaith "waited in a back room until he was called upon to speak. When he came on the platform he completely ignored Father's presence and did not so much as refer to him. . . ."[46] Divine accepted these indignities, but the leaders of the assembled labor groups added another by extending the speaking list at the last moment and scheduling the newcomers ahead of him. A collection was also announced, which was the final insult to Divine. He claimed not to have been informed of this feature, to which his objections were well known. At that, Divine picked up his hat and prepared to leave the platform. The unnerved program director, union official Nathan Solomon, asked if Divine had anything to say. "Those who are leaving with me, kindly walk quickly and quietly out of the hall," he replied. Within three minutes the once-packed hall was virtually deserted and the meeting quickly adjourned on that account.[47]

Sniping between Divine and union leaders continued throughout the thirties. At times the issue was "scabbing," at others, union protests against Peace Mission centers that undersold union-produced goods and services. In Seattle, for example, Father Divine's Peace restaurants were among those picketed by union workers as unfair to organized labor.[48] Divine meanwhile continued to portray unions as subverting American democratic processes. He focused on specific practices such as the closed shop, but his references to unions were so uniformly disapproving and impassioned as to suggest that his opposition went beyond objective principles and democratic impulses. Indignation against union excesses had become nearly as much of an obsession as his hatred for Jim Crow.[49]

Divine's wary stance toward unions was strikingly at variance with his enthusiasm for many other forms of interracial cooperation, but it fairly typified black attitudes, stemming from a history of racist practices by organized labor. During the first decades of the twentieth century union exclusion of black workers was routine. So, too, was union violence against black strikebreakers who often were unable to gain employment in an industry under any other circumstances. These black workers usually accepted jobs in ignorance of raging labor conflicts and were caught in the middle of two cynical parties — one trying to exclude them from an industry, the other employing them at substandard wages to undermine union pressures.

Although the New Deal spurred the rise of industrial unions, which tended to recruit blacks on a basis of relative equality, the signs of racism within many older unions were still clearly visible. W. E. B. Du Bois, long an eminent champion of racial equality, observed in December, 1933, "The most sinister power that the N.R.A. has re-inforced is the American Federation of Labor."[50] Du Bois rightly considered the AFL highly reluctant to organize black workers, who were mostly unskilled, though their exclusionary policies did not keep them from issuing a barrage of cant on their avowed interracial good will. Herbert Northrup, a historian of blacks and labor unions in the 1930s, concludes that only in the latter part of the decade did unionism become more a help than a hindrance to Negro workers, and even then exceptions among unions abounded.[51]

It is therefore probable that Divine, whose central passion was racial justice and who for decades had witnessed union discrimination, exclusion, and violence against blacks, was inveterately suspicious of organized labor. Every new suggestion of prejudice and violence not only left its own deep mark but reinforced countless memories of past mistreatment.

Yet there may also have been more immediate considerations involved in Father Divine's opposition to union practices. Possibly Divine perceived unions, with their powerful economic and social influence on members, as a threat to his own otherwise uncontested control over his followers' allegiance. From this perspective, unions that accepted blacks on a basis of full equality may have heightened rather than assuaged Divine's suspicions of labor's encroaching power. In any case, it is notable that Divine, though highly sensitive to racism, focused his ire toward unions on their allegedly unfair control over workers rather than on discriminatory conduct.

Within the confines of his movement, Father Divine encouraged labor militance toward outside employers, which further suggests that his opposition to unions tended to be more personal than ideological. The struggle for the rights of laundry workers, many of whom followed Father Divine, illustrates the range of his leadership on labor issues. The laundry workers were among the worst-paid laborers in the country, in large part because they had no strong political or economic organization to protect their interests. With the invalidation of New York's minimum wage law in 1936, and subsequent drastic wage cuts against laundry workers, a full-scale campaign ensued to unionize these vulnerable employees. Rose Schneiderman of the Women's Trade Union League, Frank Crosswaith, chairman of the Negro Labor Committee, and William Mahoney, New York state organizer of the American Federation of Labor, cooperated with organizers for the incipient Laundry Workers' Union.[52] To some, Father Divine appeared to exercise a negative impact on this organizing drive. Union officials on recruiting missions frequently were told by laundry workers that they would not join a union because Father Divine said they did not need one.[53] Yet black columnist George Streator, probing more deeply than Divine's critics, pointed out that many people gave the Father credit "for awakening Northern laundry workers to their value in the industry. Staid trade-unionists followed Divine in this field, by no means preceded him."[54] Thus the followers' claim that they "did not need a union" had its basis in the fact that they were already organized in defense of their rights — with Divine as their labor leader.

The situation of domestic workers offers another instance in which Father Divine fostered organized labor militance to overcome exploitative conditions. The "Bronx Slave Market" was the most notorious example of the widespread mistreatment of domestic workers. Always a low-paid group, these workers suffered intensely from the Depression, where many former employers now regarded their services as dispensable. The result was to create a huge surplus of domestic laborers who lined up early each morning in front of homes that once regularly employed them. There these women would compete for the attention of housewives, often accepting work for 50 cents or even 35 cents a day. This seldom included lunch, transportation expenses, or any appreciable time off. Municipal investigations revealed the shocking conditions under which these women obtained work for minimal compensation, but the practices continued throughout the Depression. These conditions appalled and angered Father Divine. Many of his followers were domestic workers, and he instructed them never to accept employment for less than $10 a week — far above the prevailing wage. He exhorted them to defy the people who "want you to enslave yourselves," adding that "people are trying to get you to work for a dollar a day — it is an outrage. It is ridiculous." Aided by the shelter of the Peace Mission, which guaranteed their room and board, these workers followed Divine's advice and held out for better-paying jobs.[55] Divine thus appeared to sanction labor unity and assertiveness, so long as this remained subject to his direction.

Father Divine's reservations about unions also appear more moderate when viewed against the general attitudes of religious institutions of the period, particularly in the black community. When A. Philip Randolph was still struggling to build up the Brotherhood of Sleeping Car Porters during the twenties and early thirties, many churches were among the most reactionary opponents of his recruitment efforts in the ghetto.[56] Some clergymen viewed labor organization as beyond the legitimate sphere of church activity, while others feared unions as a threat to social stability and interest in religion generally. Often there were also more tangible inducements to champion the cause of business against that of union "agitators." Many ministers looked to white businessmen to contribute to their churches and could ill afford to alienate their monetary expressions of good will. Other preachers had subtler connections to corporate executives, as exemplified by the near unanimity of Detroit's black clergy in exalting Henry Ford's antiunion policies. Ford's use of character references from black pastors in selecting workers from a huge surplus of Negro applicants greatly enhanced the clergy's power and made it naturally loath to antagonize the source of this heightened authority.[57] Such corporate pressures, though seldom so intense as in Detroit, widely discouraged black ministers from revealing unionist sentiments.

In this context of antagonism between unions and most churches in the ghettos, the positive side of Divine's stormy relationship with organized labor, though modest, appears more notable. Divine refused corporate contributions (as he rejected all "outside" donations), denounced the exploitation of workers, and maintained at least sporadic contact with union leaders in order to promote common economic goals. He was, on balance, less antiunion than simply independent in pressing his vision of a society that respected the dignity of the workingman.

Whatever limits may be found to Divine's economic vision, the evidence suggests, in sum, that he undertook far more than simply providing relief for the poor. His programs extended employment, training, and business opportunities to ghetto residents, within the framework of a hugely successful and rapidly expanding cooperative organization. Divine even stirred, however tentatively, the class consciousness of his followers, a development hindered but not wholly negated by his ambivalence toward unions. In all, the Peace Mission helped its members not only to survive in the ghettos but to challenge the basic economic conditions of their confinement.

Notes to Chapter 6

1. J. G. St. Clair Drake, "Why Not 'Co-operate'?" *Opportunity* 14 (Aug., 1936): 231-34, 251, typifies numerous calls by black spokesmen for greater cooperative economic activity. See also E. Franklin Frazier, "Racial Self-Expression," in *Ebony and Topaz,* ed. Charles S. Johnson (New York: National Urban League, 1927), p. 121. Cornelius King gives two accounts of black cooperatives, in "Cooperation — Nothing New," *Opportunity* 18 (Nov., 1940):328-31, and " 'All-Negro Cooperative?' 'Mostly So,' " *Opportunity* 20 (June, 1942):172-74. Cooperative ideals entered into black fiction as well, for example, Anne Du Bignon, "The Farm on the Eastern Shore," *Crisis* 40 (Mar., 1933):61-62, 70, and (Apr., 1933):85-87.

2. *AA,* Sept. 20, 1939, p. 12, letter by Gordon B. Hancock, who otherwise disdained Divine.

3. McKelway and Liebling, "Who Is This King of Glory?" pt. 3, pp. 22, 23, 25, 26.

4. *SW,* Feb. 9, 1935, p. 15.

5. Parker, *Incredible Messiah,* pp. 165-66.

6. *SW,* Oct. 27, 1934, p. 13.

7. On the disappointing record of black-owned enterprises, see, for example, Ira De A. Reid, "Social Problems of Negro Businesses," *Crisis* 43 (June, 1936): 166-67, 186-87. On the subject of black-run banks, see Jesse B. Blayton, "Are Negro Banks Safe?" *Opportunity* 15 (May, 1937):139-41. A vivid illustration of black hesitancy to forgo the advantages of dealing with white merchants is provided by Louis E. Lomax in *The Negro Revolt* (New York: New American Library of World Literature, 1963), p. 52.

8. Sermon of Feb. 7, 1937, in *ND,* Sept. 28, 1974, p. 5.

9. Sermon of May 25, 1938, in *ND,* Aug. 4, 1973, p. 19.

10. Father Divine assured his followers that "the time will come, as cooperation continues and my spirit is recognized and realized within you, when mankind will be able to purchase a box of candy, a pound of candy, and the manufacturer will not want but a penny on the box — a penny profit, just for the overhead expense; and it will be sufficient through my spirit and my work and my activities, to carry the work on perfectly and expertly and cause you to be super-successful. It may not be at that stage just yet, but as you abide in me. . . ." Sermon of Feb. 7, 1937, in *ND,* Sept. 28, 1974, p. 5.

11. Father Divine went so far as to brand the government's imposition of minimum price laws "an unjust ruling" and suggested some barely legal means to circumvent them. See his sermon of Sept. 5, 1936, in *ND,* Jan. 22, 1977, p. 7.

12. *AA,* May 20, 1939, pp. 1, 2.

13. Hoshor, *God in a Rolls-Royce,* p. 254.

14. Alexander, "All Father's Chillun," p. 64.

15. *New York Herald Tribune,* Apr. 6, 1936, p. 13.

16. Hoshor, *God in a Rolls-Royce,* p. 254.

17. Sermon of Sept. 23, 1937, in *ND,* Sept. 30, 1937, p. 26.

18. *Times,* Apr. 27, 1937, p. 25.

19. *AA,* Aug. 5, 1939, p. 17.

20. *NYAN,* Aug. 6, 1938, p. 10.

21. Ibid.

22. *AA,* Aug. 5, 1939, p. 17, details how personal contact with Peace Mission members changed the attitudes of Ulster's white residents from "bitter opposition into tolerance and hospitality."

23. *NYAN,* Aug. 6, 1938, p. 10.

24. Sermon of Oct. 18, 1936, in *SW,* Nov. 3, 1936, p. 28.

25. Sermon of Oct. 20, 1940, in *ND,* Feb. 3, 1979, p. 10.

26. John P. Murchison, "The Subsistence Homesteads Experiment and the Negro," *Opportunity* 12 (Aug., 1934):244-45.

27. Ibid., p. 245.

28. See Donald Holley, "The Negro in the New Deal Resettlement Program," *Agricultural History* 45 (July, 1971):179-93, and reply by Robert E. Nipp, in the same issue, "The Negro in the New Deal Resettlement Program: A Comment," pp. 195-200.

29. Vincent, *Black Power and the Garvey Movement,* p. 53.

30. *NYAN,* Jan. 24, 1942, p. 10; Sept. 6, 1941, p. 15.

31. Ibid., Sept. 6, 1941, p. 15, outlines Washington's record as a business executive. On her views of Father Divine's ministry, see ibid., June 21, 1941, p. 2. An account of a visit by Washington to a Peace Mission banquet is given in *AA,* Aug.

1, 1942, p. 17. Father Divine endorsed varied Apex products in a "sermon" on Mar. 9, 1941, in *ND,* Mar. 13, 1941, p. 16.

32. Interview given by Father Divine to delegates from the Consolidated Tenants League, in *SW,* Sept. 22, 1936, p. 14.

33. Sermon of Oct. 10, 1936, in *SW,* Oct. 17, 1936, p. 19; *SW,* Oct. 20, 1936, p. 17.

34. William Muraskin, "The Harlem Boycott of 1934: Black Nationalism and the Rise of Labor-Union Consciousness," *Labor History* 13 (Summer, 1972):362.

35. *AA,* Nov. 3, 1934, p. 2.

36. See Father Divine to president of the 20th Century Bus Company in New York, Sept. 1, 1933, and Father Divine to R. Peck of the Rialko Bus Corporation in New York, Sept. 6, 1933, both in *ND,* Nov. 4, 1937, p. 10.

37. Father Divine to C. E. Cuddeback, sales manager of Sheffield's Farm Products Company, May 28, 1935, in *SW,* June 15, 1935, p. 9. A similar letter to the Borden Corporation appears in the same issue, pp. 8-9.

38. Fauset, *Black Gods,* p. 94; *PC,* June 29, 1935, sec. 1, p. 2.

39. Father Divine's Peace Mission (a staff letter) to All American Bus Lines in Chicago, Dec. 27, 1937, in *ND,* Jan. 13, 1938, p. 30.

40. *NYAN,* Oct. 23, 1937, p. 23.

41. *SW,* Feb. 8, 1936, p. 23.

42. Sermon of Feb. 1-2, 1936, in ibid., pp. 20-21.

43. Father Divine to Lewis J. Valentine, Feb. 3, 1936, in ibid., p. 11.

44. William Morrissey to Father Divine, Jan. 31, 1936, in ibid., p. 24. See also Father Divine's reply on the same date, in ibid.

45. *SW,* Feb. 4, 1936, p. 17.

46. Ibid.

47. *NYAN,* Feb. 8, 1936, p. 5.

48. *ND,* Feb. 16, 1939, pp. 91-92.

49. Father Divine continued over the years to heighten his attacks on union practices, till by the early fifties he was suggesting that major strikes were subversive and communist-inspired. See, for example, his sermon of Feb. 6, 1951, in *ND,* Dec. 2, 1978, p. 7.

50. W. E. B. Du Bois, "Postscript," *Crisis* 40 (Dec., 1933):292.

51. Herbert R. Northrup, "Organized Labor and Negro Workers," *Journal of Political Economy* 51 (June, 1943):221.

52. *NYAN,* June 6, 1936, p. 1.

53. Henry Lee Moon, "Thank You, Father So Sweet," *New Republic* 88 (Sept. 16, 1936):149.

54. George Streator, "Father Divine," *Commonweal* 31 (Dec. 15, 1939):178.

55. Parker, *Incredible Messiah,* p. 230. See also *NYAN,* Jan. 7, 1939, p. 20, in which a former Peace Mission member claimed that Divine had effectively formed "one of the strongest domestic workers unions in America, even though it wasn't known as such."

56. Jervis Anderson, *A. Philip Randolph: A Biographical Portrait* (New York: Harcourt Brace Jovanovich, 1973), pp. 183-84, 368, documents the indifference and hostility to unions by black ministers.

57. On Ford's influence with the black churches, see Horace A. White, "Who Owns the Negro Churches?" *Christian Century* 55 (Feb. 9, 1938):176-77; August Meier and Elliott Rudwick, *Black Detroit and the Rise of the UAW* (New York: Oxford University Press, 1979), pp. 59-60; and Herbert R. Northrup, *Organized Labor and the Negro* (New York: Harper and Bros., 1944), pp. 193-94.

CHAPTER 7

The Politics of Racial Justice

The desire to foster fundamental changes in race relations increasingly drew Father Divine into politics. Unlike some black cult leaders such as Elijah Muhammad of the Muslims, who rejected all white institutions, Divine deeply believed in American political ideals and processes. Moreover, unlike many Negro clergymen, whose interest in racial uplift tended to fade at the point of political protest, he insisted that the struggle for justice was the highest religious calling.[1]

Coalitions against Racism

As the leader of a potentially important voting bloc in the ghettos, Father Divine faced a dilemma common to aspiring black politicians: whether to give priority to advancing racial equality or to alignment with one of the major parties. To the extent that he resolved this tension, Divine chose the former course. Largely as a result of this strategy, he was able to infuse the burgeoning civil rights activities in the ghettos with added vigor, without ever achieving his personal ambitions to influence elections and control political officials.

The Peace Mission exerted its greatest political influence in Harlem, where it promoted a wider trend among blacks toward organization in defense of racial interests. Lobbying groups drew Divine's primary attention, for he could supply numerical and verbal support to causes he favored and which already enjoyed widespread organizational commitment.

To help combat racism in municipal politics, Divine supported local coalitions representing a broad spectrum of community institutions and political ideologies. One such group was the All People's party (APP), which Father Divine helped found in June, 1936. The Peace Mission was one of eighty-nine Harlem-based organizations, including five religious

145

bodies, to pledge support for the new party, representing over 100,000 people.[2]

Peace Mission journals gave substantial and favorable coverage to the APP, whose central objective was to improve the lives of Harlem residents. The party's twelve-point platform included demands for an end to gerrymandering of Harlem, fuller employment at trade union wages for ghetto dwellers, increased unemployment relief, and 40 percent rent reductions. The APP also endorsed a small slate of radical candidates in 1936, including the white Communist Vito Marcantonio and the black Communist and labor organizer Angelo Herndon. Although the party failed to place its candidates in office, it did provide a widely respected forum in Harlem for some of the more radical voices among the civil rights leadership.[3]

The Harlem Political Union (HPU), a confederation of sixty-five civil organizations formed in 1935, also received the enthusiastic support of the Peace Mission. Like the All People's party, this coalition aimed for ideological and social inclusiveness, so that delegates from the Communist party, various fraternal orders, and several churches all mingled, however uneasily, in its meeting halls. The diverse membership found common ground chiefly in lobbying for reapportionment of Harlem to give blacks more equitable representation.[4]

Divine's relations with the Harlem Political Union illustrated the pattern of mutual need but equally strong mistrust that described most of his efforts to work with local coalitions. At virtually all meetings of the union his followers predominated. They could be relied upon to pack an assembly hall or demonstrate anywhere for the union's objectives. Yet many leaders in the union, particularly clergymen, viewed Divine more as an intruder than a savior. They were in the curious position of avoiding Divine at almost all other times, only to find him in their midst during these meetings. In order to placate these disgruntled delegates, organizers for the union usually scheduled Divine's speeches as the last item of business at their conventions. This enabled the Father's detractors to attend the meetings without having to sit through his often rambling and egocentric discourses.[5]

Despite the slights he endured, Father Divine consistently aided the Harlem Political Union's activities. He also complemented its lobbying efforts by his own feverish correspondence with virtually every important political leader in New York. He bestowed on Mayor Fiorello La Guardia the most voluminous parcels of advice, generally to accord greater recognition to blacks in appointing government officials.[6]

Notwithstanding later expansive claims by the Peace Mission, there is no evidence that La Guardia received Divine's requests with especial interest, let alone urgency. Yet the cumulative pressure by a variety of black groups and civil rights organizations, to which the Peace Mission vigorously added its voice, moved La Guardia to set many precedents in appointing qualified blacks to city offices. One such appointment, of a prominent Catholic layman and civil rights activist named Myles Paige, must have been especially gratifying to Father Divine. Paige, who became the city's first black magistrate, was a frequent visitor to the Peace Mission and an open admirer of Divine's work.[7]

Some of the most active political coalitions in the ghettos during the 1930s centered on campaigns to rescue individual victims of southern "justice." The Peace Mission participated in these efforts, including two that gained sustained national attention as tests of strength between civil rights advocates and a racist judicial system.

The more famous of these campaigns involved the "Scottsboro boys," nine Negro youths convicted in Alabama on dubious evidence of having raped two white girls. Although some observers professed to discern progress in that the youths were not immediately slaughtered by mob violence, the blatant racism of the proceedings illustrated what W. E. B. Du Bois once called a "judicial lynching." Although the efforts to aid the Scottsboro boys mitigated their lot only to a limited degree, they did much to impress upon the nation the evils of a caste system that had subjected nine bewildered and likely innocent youths to years of prison, public degradation, and imminent jeopardy to their lives.[8]

Father Divine conveyed his concern over the plight of the Scottsboro youths in sermons, interviews, and letters. His strong statements and ability to galvanize mass action induced a fiery social activist but bitter clerical opponent, Thomas H. Harten of New York's Holy Trinity Baptist Church, to join forces with Divine. They appeared together at a rally to raise money for the Scottsboro prisoners and dramatize their plight. Both ministers explained to their audience that personal and theological differences were irrelevant to them, so long as they could contribute to the cause of racial justice.[9]

Another black prisoner who became a rallying symbol for the civil rights movement, Angelo Herndon, also attracted Father Divine's support. Herndon was arrested in Georgia for attempting to organize black workers and was convicted of incitement to insurrection based on an antebellum statute designed to prevent slave revolts. The court's sentence of eighteen years of hard labor sparked an outpouring of sympathy for Herndon and outrage against Georgia's judicial system among civil libertarians nationwide. Divine made headlines in Harlem for his vigorous support of a petition campaign for Herndon's release. He also had his followers demonstrate on Herndon's behalf.[10]

The delicacy of Herndon's legal situation led the organizers working for his freedom to restrain all personal criticism of Georgia's Governor Eugene Talmadge. Instead, a supplicatory and respectful tone pervaded virtually all public lobbying efforts directed to his office. Divine, too, showed that he could adapt to the niceties of interstate diplomacy. He addressed an appeal to the governor that substituted praise for indignation and modesty for his usual flamboyant rhetoric.[11] What went through Divine's mind as he described the land of his early encounters with racism and chain gangs as a "great state," one can only surmise. It was but one of many instances in which he put aside personal resentment to further a larger cause.

It appears that the collective efforts by Father Divine and many other leaders on Herndon's behalf did have some positive impact, though not by securing southern clemency. Rather, the persistent calls for Herndon's freedom kept this issue before the national conscience until, in 1937, the Supreme Court reversed the conviction, two years after initially dismissing Herndon's appeal.[12]

Within limits imposed by nonviolent principles, Father Divine pursued lobbying activities and coalitions more controversial than many civil rights leaders deemed wise. He incurred especially vehement criticism by associating actively and warmly with the Communist party, beginning in 1934 and for several years thereafter.

The party and the Peace Mission might at first appear "natural enemies," and in fact the differences in principles were vast. Few could fail to note the incongruities between Divine's pantheism and the Communists' dogmatic atheism, between his advocacy of nonviolence and their eager anticipation of the workers' revolution, and between his wariness of unions and their stress on labor organization. Yet the two sides also shared powerful bonds, which related to the wider ties between the Communists and the Negro community during the thirties.

The Communists perceived black Americans as a natural constituency of oppressed people. If, as some skeptical blacks charged, the Communists embraced the cause of black rights out of opportunism, they nevertheless aided that cause during the thirties more effectively than conservative groups like the NAACP were ever willing to admit. While few blacks became Communists, many praised the party's activism on behalf of racial equality, considering this more important than the questionable soundness of Communist dialectic. Adam Clayton Powell, Jr., spoke for a substantial segment of the black community in stating that a Communist was the same as a Holy Roller, Republican, or Elk, in that he was to be judged chiefly on one question: did he back full equality for blacks?[13]

Father Divine recognized that the Communists, more than the major political parties, were aggressively battling against discrimination. He there-fore risked opprobrium from white as well as black liberal sympathizers by participating in numerous Communist-backed rallies. For their part, the Communists eyed Divine's mass support like famished predators spot-ting a favored species crossing their path. Divine appeared to them as a key to their hopes for incorporating urban blacks into a strong proletarian coalition. Both sides were prepared to make substantial compromises in order to work together, the one to further civil rights and the other to promote class revolution. Ultimately their radically different goals drove them apart, but in the interim they marched together and staunchly de-fended each other's work against the many critics of the alliance.

Joint parades of Peace Mission and Communist party members began in late 1934, around such common values as opposition to fascism and war. The "American League against War and Fascism," a Communist-supported group, led nearly 10,000 in a march through Harlem that August, with some 3,000 Divinites participating. Yet it was evident that the two groups were harmonizing in only the most superficial sense. Their memberships remained distinct at all times, while the disparities in their behavior were striking, as one journalist recorded:

> Harlem's religious fervor, paradoxically, was the stabilizing force yesterday in a Communist demonstration which began in Columbus Circle and ended with violent speech-making and "Amens!" in a massed throng of 15,000 persons in Madison Square. . . .
> The monotonous chanting of "Fight-fight — against war — and fas-cism" in harmony with the marching feet of the Communists was inter-spersed with "Keep on praying for the rain — keep on praying for the rain," a singing prayer of "Father" Divine's flock.[14]

Although the Divinites marched in the common procession, they seemed to have little regard for Communist aims. One told a reporter, "I'm not worryin' about no war. I would like to see peace. That's all I want. I won't talk to these Communists. They don't believe in God, and that's all there is to it."[15]

The attitudes of Peace Mission members at these rallies was not lost on the Communist party leaders. Some could find no stock vituperation strong enough to express their horror at allying with such a "reactionary" influence on thousands of ghetto dwellers. Their denunciations sent the normally factious Communist party into a particularly bitter round of in-house polemic. A senior party member attempted to dispel any confusion as to the correct party line with this sharp rebuke administered through the *Daily Worker:*

> [S]ome of our comrades were startled and confused. . . . They failed to realize that for the first time so many thousands of Negroes

were participating in a central, downtown demonstration in New York City against war and Fascism. They did not consider the effect of this mighty anti-war anti-Fascist demonstration on the followers of Father Divine. They saw only "Father Divine is God" and they questioned the correctness of a united front policy that brought these people to the demonstration, obviously forgetting that great masses of workers, small farmers, sharecroppers, etc. who must be won by us, are still under the influence of religious beliefs.[16]

For nearly two years thereafter the diminutive leader of the Peace Mission continued to cast a long shadow across Communist party ranks. His ties with the party also provided Socialists with a golden issue on which to assail their rivals on the left as ideologically inconsistent. Such charges stung badly enough to draw the Communists' most prestigious polemical fighters into the fray. The American party head, Earl Browder, insisted to a gathering of the Central Committee in September, 1934, that it was totally consistent and essential for the Communist party to unite all elements of the working class, necessarily including the "backward masses" following Father Divine.[17] Several months later a leading black Communist, James Ford, praised Browder's approach as "absolutely correct." Ford added: "Indeed, Father Divine reacts to the pressures of the masses on Scottsboro more than these bureaucratic gentlemen," referring to assorted sniping Socialists.[18]

The controversy heated up with the election campaign in 1936. The Communists launched a major drive for the Negro vote, placing Ford as vice-presidential candidate and championing every militant Negro cause from total abolition of discriminatory laws to the creation of a separate black republic within the United States. As part of this effort the Communists also renewed the courtship of Father Divine. This left them vulnerable to continual criticisms by the Socialists, as in Gus Tyler's acid polemic, "God Attacks the Unions," mocking the regressive lengths to which Communist party members would go to broaden their coalition.[19]

Having committed their party to support Father Divine, Communist leaders now made him into a symbol of their differences with the Socialists. Ben Davis, Jr., enlivened the *Daily Worker* in February, 1936, with a searing reply to Tyler. He observed that Father Divine and his followers were marching for the freedom of Angelo Herndon while Norman Thomas, the current Socialist nominee for president, was hesitating over whether to enter the united front demanding Herndon's release. Davis concluded:

> We put the question to Tyler. Does it make no ripple on your simon pure class-consciousness to have thousands of religious minded white and colored workers, followers of Father Divine or of anyone else, in motion against lynching, discrimination, segregation, wage differentials, and jim-crow oppression?

If the progressive features of Divine's program are demagogy (etc.) then let us have more of such.[20]

Divine for his part praised the Communists for helping to secure individual rights and for taking commendable stands on practically every issue. He expressed his firm intent to cooperate "with any organization that will stand for the right and deal justly. I know the higher-ups are oppressing the people and I will end this by righteousness, not by violence. I find fault with the Communist methods, but not their aims."[21]

New York alderman Lambert Fairchild was among Divine's white admirers who were highly distraught at the minister's pro-Communist actions. How could Divine claim to champion peace, Fairchild wrote him, if he supported a group dedicated to the overthrow of the government? Divine, naively perhaps, insisted that his association with the Communists was limited to respectable areas of mutual agreement. Moreover, "The platform of the Communist Party as we understand it, is the brotherhood of man, the abolition of war and equal opportunity." Therefore, Divine suggested to all the Republicans, Democrats, and Socialists, "Give me something better than the Communists have and I will endorse it."[22]

The association between Father Divine and the Communist party dissolved during the later thirties, under the cumulative pressure of their fundamental differences. The party's failure to invite Divine to join its "united front" march in 1936 marked a cautious rethinking of the value of allying with the Peace Mission. Divine's refusal to give the party a definite endorsement in that year's national elections further accelerated the decline in amity. The underlying problems, though, were the Communist disappointment with Divine's unchanging skepticism about the value of unionization, and Divine's growing perception of the Communists as more totalitarian than democratic. By 1939 Divine scarcely defended the Communists except to say that the oppressed minorities were already so disillusioned by the major political parties that they naturally reached out for the promises tendered by the Communists. "They will grab after a straw, as you say," quite a devaluation of his once beaming approval of Communist rhetoric.[23] By 1940 even this faint praise disappeared, as Divine became wholly disenchanted with the unqualified Communist (and Socialist) support for labor unions and their class-based tactics. He also concluded that the party's proclamations for racial equality were insincere, that these radicals merely played on racial division for subversive ends rather than seeking to bring the nation closer together.[24] When Divine reached this stage in his thinking, the already weakened association between him and the Communists was altogether doomed.

The remarkable aspect about the Peace Mission's tortuous relationship with the Communists is not, however, its increasing bitterness and ultimate rupture; rather, it is that it endured for so long and despite so many obstacles of ideology and practicality. Their alliance over several years underscored the fact that Divine's North Star, in politics as in all else, was racial advancement, in which cause he would tend to overlook almost all other problems and contradictions.

The Righteous Government Convention

Father Divine's varied ideas for overcoming social injustice in America found their most systematic expression at a three-day convention of his disciples in January, 1936. Six thousand followers, including many from California and several from Europe, gathered in Harlem's Rockland Palace to endorse and amplify Father Divine's new political testament. The document that emerged from these proceedings, hailed as a "Righteous Government Platform" by Peace Mission members, aimed chiefly to create full equality of opportunity, unmarred by race prejudice or violence.

Numerous representatives of left-wing, pacifist, and civil rights organizations attended the ceremonies. Had Divine keyed his expectations to the scope of his invitations, he might have been disappointed by the absence of such notables as the President of the United States. Yet some lesser luminaries addressed the gathering, among them Myles A. Paige, then active in the Joint Conference against Discriminatory Practices; Ray C. Heber, for the Townsend movement; James W. Ford, the Communist party official; educator Willis Huggins, recently returned from Ethiopia after representing that country at Geneva; and long-time well-wisher Lambert Fairchild, alderman of New York City. Benjamin Howe, of the city's Fusion party, gave the keynote address on the first day. As befitted the Peace Mission's principles, he refrained from partisan appeals and instead delivered an impassioned speech on the need to end all war.[25]

Divine dominated the meeting. He proposed most planks, guided the procedure, and even led the wild applause that punctuated his revelations. The unanimous vocal thunder for a follower's resolution declaring the Father to be a God on earth fairly set the pattern of command at the convention.

For all the flamboyance and excess, the Peace Mission assembly seriously addressed difficult issues of justice and social planning. Few evils, from segregation to unemployment, escaped detailed analysis and equally detailed plans to remedy them.

Ten of the fourteen introductory planks in the Righteous Government Platform (RGP) related, directly or indirectly, to correcting racial inequities. The most important plank proposed sweeping civil rights legislation

> making it a crime to discriminate in any public place against any individual on account of race, creed, or color, abolishing all segregated

neighborhoods in cities and towns, making it a crime for landlords or hotels to refuse tenants on such grounds; abolishing all segregated schools and colleges, and all segregated areas in churches, theatres, public conveyances, and other public areas.[26]

Most of the remaining planks in the RGP's introductory section were inserted to promote and protect the Peace Mission's religious tenets, particularly that of nonviolence. One plank urged international abolition of all weapons, save for domestic law enforcement. Moreover, "true followers of Father Divine will refuse to fight their fellowman for any cause whatsoever." The principle of nonviolence also contributed to inclusion of the planks to end lynching and capital punishment.[27]

The RGP's section on general principles also gave vent to Divine's antiunion bias. Long extracts from past sermons elaborated on the danger posed by undemocratic union leaders, while one plank called for severe restriction of unions unless they could guarantee all goals for which they charged dues and ordered strikes. It was small surprise, therefore, that the wide-ranging section on economics that immediately followed scarcely noted the presence of unions in its design for a better society.[28]

The RGP's economic program proposed to guarantee full employment within a voluntary cooperative framework. In case the private sector proved unable to ensure these conditions, the government would have authority to intervene on a temporary basis. The heart of the twelve-point program demanded "governmental control of all idle plants and machinery, tools and equipment, where owners are unwilling to operate them at full capacity; such facilities to be made available to workers on a cooperative, non-profit basis under supervision of government experts, with temporary provision for materials. . . ."[29] The RGP thus sought to maintain reasonable prosperity for the common worker, whatever the fluctuations affecting corporate enterprise. Among other measures to reinforce this policy was a proposal to establish a minimum-wage scale. This was two years before a similar bill passed Congress, in weakened form, as the Fair Labor Standards act.[30]

One other proposal the RGP shared with numerous other reform groups that otherwise stopped short of socialism was the nationalization of banking.[31] The Depression helped make this idea respectable, for hundreds of banks had already closed from unsound management or lack of confidence by depositors. Bankers themselves were a class whose once-great prestige had gone the way of their financial operations; the way was clear for measures to invest control of the nation's monetary system in public hands. Roosevelt stopped short of this course, though he initiated major new regulations of private banking. Yet even some of his close advisers never ceased to hope that the president might yet follow a more thorough policy of government control, to prevent the kind of sharp business cycles that had contributed to the Depression.

More than most contemporary radical reformers, Divine showed at least as much interest in fostering productivity as in redistributing opportunity. Two proposals in the RGP's economic section implicitly assailed the restrictive programs of the early New Deal, urging an end to government-mandated crop controls, destruction of foodstuffs and other goods, and minimum price requirements. The RGP aimed to achieve national prosperity through increased purchasing power among the laboring classes, never by eliminating an "excess" of goods or striving to raise their cost. The presence of so many needy workers in his movement strongly affected Divine's view on this matter, for it made the policy of planned scarcity repellent no matter what the alleged benefits to producers. Just below the text of one proposal to end restrictive approaches to recovery, Divine is quoted as saying: "The spectacle of hungry people in a land of plenty is worse than uncivilized."[32]

The RGP's political section was surprisingly brief but contained the memorable suggestion that candidates for office be required to show their qualifications "not as politicians but [as] technical experts."[33] This may have startled some for whom the recent administration of Herbert Hoover — elected as the nation's ultimate technocrat — remained a vivid memory of disaster. Yet Divine believed that scientific behavior was an essential complement to any quality, be it religious moralism or political skill. Therefore, virtually alone among the Isaiahs and Jeremiahs who wandered the fringes of American political reform, he stressed that the prime requisite of a government official was a careful understanding of society's complex problems and the practical possibilities for resolving them. Only then, in combination with a righteous spirit, to be sure, would society attain both justice and prosperity.

The RGP's concluding section, on education, required free universal education, the exclusion of school texts that glorified war or promoted racial superiority, and the standardization of the greeting "Peace," to reinforce an abhorrence of war for generations to come.[34] The section thus recapitulated the essence of the entire document — equal opportunity, racial harmony, and nonviolence.

Like most plans to perfect society, the Righteous Government Platform displayed glaring flaws. Despite the comprehensive quality of its program, it offered no clear political or economic priorities. Rather, it deposited a shopping list of causes for Americans to champion, with no apparent distinctions in emphasis. Then, too, the document was muddled in important aspects of political philosophy. Was the coming utopia to be capitalist, socialist, or communist? What institutional guidelines would determine which alternative, or combination of alternatives, would emerge? Was the cooperative commonwealth envisioned by the Peace Mission dependent on evangelical conversion on a national or worldwide basis? In the interim, would presumably enlightened leaders seek to compel such cooperation, or resign themselves to an indefinite period — perhaps centuries — of only partly restrained capitalism?

A further difficulty with the RGP was its apparent self-contradiction regarding the rights of labor. The document presented itself as a Magna Carta for the common man, yet it assailed or slighted the fledgling organizations that, with new-found government support, were at last conferring dignity and bargaining power on industrial workers. Technically, the RGP condemned only the abuses of union power, not unions *per se,* but distinctions blurred amid a consistently hostile tone and unrealistic demands for union reform. The RGP, in effect, undermined the major weapon of the very group deemed most in need of its support.

Compounding the RGP's difficulties was the continued ego intrusion of Father Divine. The convention that produced this platform did not merely endorse its leader; it deified him. Whatever the merits of Peace Mission theology, from a political viewpoint this was a tactical blunder. Even a staunch advocate of cooperative association, racial justice, and nonviolence might well have hesitated before endorsing a movement that insisted on Divine's status as messiah, if not higher.

Despite these conspicuous problems, the Righteous Government Platform was significant for its insight into the needs of the poor and minorities, and the potential for constructive federal action. Like the best reform documents, it anticipated much of government policy and concern over subsequent decades. Many of its prescriptions, later championed independently by other groups, were incorporated into federal programs in civil rights, aid to education, and urban planning. In particular, the concept of federal responsibility for ensuring desegregation and full employment appeared in far bolder form in the RGP than in government circles for decades afterward.

The RGP also surpassed the efforts of most contemporary civil rights groups to focus on lower-class economic needs as well as middle-class social concerns. Notwithstanding its antiunion policies, the RGP still outdistanced groups like the NAACP in detailing an ideology for social change that included proposals not only for integration and legal equality but also for redistribution of economic opportunity.

Finally, in judging the RGP's economic prescriptions, one must consider the circumstances in which they were formulated. The catastrophes of the Depression had shattered the ethos of extreme individualism that had characterized the country during the twenties. Many feared that the wave of the future would be either communism or fascism. The temper of the period, then, was to devise a system that avoided the excessive self-indulgence of earlier years without succumbing to the totalitarian evils of Stalinism or Hitlerism. The Righteous Government Platform, seen as an economic document, was one innovative attempt among many to reach this elusive middle ground. It sought to give new expression to American values by broadening economic opportunity while maintaining political freedom. As such, the RGP's stress on voluntary cooperativism, with strong government incentives but in a largely capitalist framework, conformed in spirit if not in detail to the New Deal itself.

If the RGP was often ambiguous and inconsistent in its economic outlines, it was hardly alone in this regard. The Depression years brought forth much groping by certified economic experts as well as alleged demagogues. Roosevelt's New Deal, once one gazed beyond its general principles of reform capitalism, revealed a bewildering succession of piecemeal and often apparently incongruous experiments. Roosevelt himself frequently was at a loss to characterize, let alone defend, his programs in consistent ideological terms. Instead he gamely made a virtue of his inconsistencies, as in his joking admission that the TVA, that imaginative hybrid of capitalism and socialism, was "neither fish nor fowl," but "it will taste awfully good to the people of the Tennessee Valley." Contemporary critics, including the government-appointed investigator of the National Recovery Administration, Clarence Darrow, found the New Deal a compendium of economic contradictions. Even some of Roosevelt's advisers, from conservative ideologues like Raymond Moley to centralizing planners like Rexford Tugwell, searched in vain for a clarifying Rosetta Stone to the president's maze of programs, and gaped in dismay at his routine trampling of their economic models.

For all this, the New Deal was a vastly more practical approach to the problems of the Depression than the RGP, though for political rather than economic reasons. The swarm of interest groups covering Roosevelt, his advisers, and the Congress at virtually every stage in formulating new government programs severely limited the latitude of official decision making. Yet the RGP blithely ignored the ubiquitous political constraints the government faced. This was particularly true of its proposals for voluntary cooperative economics, which somewhat dogmatically sought to remodel all of American society after the Peace Mission's own vastly successful economic system. In effect, it projected reforms based on the evangelization and moral rebirth of some 130 million Americans along lines of the same communal idealism that marked the Peace Mission membership. The RGP's model society was indeed economically efficient — in theory and as exemplified on a small scale by Divine's following. Yet it was so aloof from the realities of American political conservatism as to confine itself largely to the distant realm of utopia.

The Campaign against Lynching

The major immediate accomplishment of the Righteous Government Convention was to strengthen the Peace Mission's various lobbying efforts for civil rights. First, it served notice that Father Divine and his followers would henceforth play an active role in national politics. At the same time, the RGP provided a broad philosophical foundation for the petition campaigns, marches, and other activities in which Peace Mission members engaged.

Divine's efforts to enact RGP proposals focused chiefly on aid to the growing campaign for a federal antilynching law. Such bills had been proposed in Congress since 1919, at the strong initiative of the NAACP, only to be quashed by southern filibusters. During the 1930s many civil rights advocates accorded priority to this issue, even more than to employment, housing, and other matters of immediate importance to black Americans, because it was a particularly dramatic aspect of racism at its most lawless. A federal antilynching bill commanded wide public support, and even in the South there was increasing opposition to mob violence. Civil rights leaders, particularly in the NAACP, believed that a triumph by antilynching forces would inject new vigor and morale into a range of other campaigns against racial injustice.[35]

Lynchings were becoming rare during the 1930s, a fact to which some southern legislators frequently pointed in ridiculing the need for a bill that would increase federal interference with state "law enforcement." This, of course, minimized the crucial fact that the potential to kill Negroes outside the law but with assurance of community sanction must have created an atmosphere of intimidation, whatever the annual statistical rate of mob violence.[36] Lynching was in some respects a functional equivalent of slave whippings in antebellum times, in that it not only punished individuals for reputed crimes but dramatized and reinforced the hierarchical pattern of race relations in an entire region. If the NAACP leadership in the thirties insisted on making antilynching legislation the major symbol of the civil rights cause, it was responding largely to the fact that the white South had long since made lynching a symbolic underpinning of white supremacy.

Father Divine was quick to grasp the symbolic import of the NAACP's battle against lynching, perceiving a higher contest between the forces of law and equity and those of passion and prejudice. He readily conceded to critics that a federal antilynching bill actually would do little to prevent lynchings. That, he said, would require conversion of "the minds and hearts and lives of the people," for that "will do more over night, than making legislation of such would do inside of years." Nevertheless, the bill should be passed, "so that we will go on record as a nation refusing to endorse lynching, or murder, without due process of law, which is not according to the Constitution. . . ."[37]

Divine worked vigorously to impress on his followers the importance of the antilynching campaign, infusing it with both spiritual and political dimensions. He preached, with a fervor possibly born of personal experience, that lynching represented the antithesis of the Peace Mission's central goal of "eradicating prejudice, segregation, and division from among the people."[38] At the banquet tables psalms of praise mingled with antilynching songs that envisioned an America freed from racial violence. A typical song fused religious and social themes into a picture of future tolerance throughout the South:

Away down in Texas and in the farthest parts of the South
We shall eat and drink together, racism shall be wiped out.
There will be no more race riots and lynchings,
There will be no more division or strife
When they recognize God's Body, they will value each other's life.
Father will make them love each other so much with or without an
    anti-lynching bill
They will know that they are brothers and will not desire to kill.
Away down in Texas and in the farthest parts of the South
They will enact the Bill of Rights in every community,
Racialism shall be wiped out![39]

These sentiments had their active political counterparts in varied lobbying efforts for antilynching legislation. Divine and aides drafted a model bill in 1936 and later, in slightly revised form, had it introduced in Congress by a representative from Westchester, New York. It was stronger than the Wagner bill then pending in the Senate, as well as the Gavagan bill, which the House had just passed. It specified that every member of a lynch mob be tried and, if convicted, sentenced accordingly for first-degree murder, no matter what the motives involved. Divine's bill, like the strongest congressional proposals, also insisted on a minimum $10,000 fine on any county in which a lynching occurred. The money was to compensate families of lynching victims.[40]

The Peace Mission's activism on behalf of antilynching legislation is unquestionable, but its influence is much more suspect. The fact that Father Divine endorsed a bill imparted to it added controversy—the last thing sponsors of antilynching legislation wanted. There resulted the curious situation of supporters going to great lengths to ignore Divine's persistent aid, while opponents amply compensated by declaring him a prime mover in the struggle for passage.

Senator Robert F. Wagner, Democrat from New York and a co-sponsor of the antilynching bill, determinedly avoided acknowledging Divine's contributions to the cause, though the senator publicly thanked minor local groups such as the North Harlem Community Council. Wagner also disregarded a barrage of epistolary advice from Father Divine on the antilynching bill, although these letters contained far more than exhortation. They displayed a deep understanding of the textual minutiae as well as the moral import of the bill and were probably prepared after considerable consultation with the Peace Mission's legal aides. Again on tactical grounds, the senator declined invitations from the Peace Mission to speak on the subject of lynching, explaining somewhat lamely that his legislative duties ruled out all public appearances outside the capital.[41]

In attempting to reduce Father Divine to a nonentity, Wagner reckoned with Allen Ellender, junior senator from Louisiana and one of the great masters of filibustering in conservative causes. Ellender was surely aware that the NAACP had been the dominant lobbying group on behalf of the antilynching bill, and that Father Divine's role was peripheral. Yet he devoted more than fifteen pages in the *Congressional Record* to a discussion of Divine's influence in Harlem and why this posed a mortal threat to the southern way of life. The senator ridiculed the worship of Divine — for its racial rather than its religious implications: "Imagine a people in America seriously believing that the son of a slave is God!" Ellender also attacked Divine's association with Communists, not as an evil in itself but because Divine gave as his reason, "The Communist Party stands for social equality."[42] As an avowed defender of southern civilization, Ellender professed horror at what leaders like Divine were steadily promoting:

> [I] would be willing to vote tomorrow for the repeal of the fifteenth amendment granting the Negro suffrage, because if all States of the Union give political equality to the colored people, leaders like "god," and others in those cities, who control a little clique of voters here, and another over there will seek more and more social equality, and what I am warning of [the downfall of American society] will come to pass. . . . I am speaking now for future generations and for the progress of America.[43]

Buttressed by this bigotry that admitted no rational retort, Ellender vowed to filibuster to death the proposed antilynching bill, and continued to paint a dire picture of Father Divine's opposition to all the South held segregated.[44]

The foes of a federal antilynching law stood firm on the Senate ramparts, vanquishing the bill by filibuster early in 1938. Yet its sponsors did not acknowledge final defeat. They reintroduced a similar bill in 1940 and pressed with greater urgency to effect its passage. Again, Divine's followers contributed energetically to this effort. In New York alone the disciples gathered a quarter of a million signatures on copies of a petition urging immediate passage of the bill.[45] Many accompanied Divine to Washington, D.C., to present the petition to Senator Wagner. Unknown to these faithful pilgrims, Congress had adjourned and Wagner was not in his office. The honor of receiving the Peace Mission contingent fell to an aide. Heavy rains and a shortage of parking space in the capital completed the fiasco. For Divine, the keenest disappointment may actually have been the absence of Senator Ellender, whose office he made it a point to visit.[46]

One can only wonder at the motives that led Father Divine to seek out the company of a man who so despised him. His public explanation was that he sought to canvass Ellender's sentiments on the antilynching bill, but this obviously is absurd, for the senator had already made his views unmistakably clear. Moral and personal indignation, a tactical ploy, publicity seeking, a gesture of courage, a desire to re-enact some challenge from his youth, perhaps an element of martyrdom — some or all of these may have pressed Divine to make this most unlikely courtesy call. Or, perhaps, Divine was in some perverse way flattered by the attention and aura of power Ellender had bestowed upon him. Certainly Divine relished the irony that while Senator Wagner had studiously ignored him, "the opposing Senator, the filibuster [sic]," tells "of my being the sole inspiration and the author of the anti-lynching bill."[47]

One reason that southern filibusters against civil rights measures generally succeeded is that they encountered only perfunctory opposition from most northern legislators. Father Divine attempted to change this situation by confronting congressmen who claimed liberal sympathies but appeared resigned to let the antilynching bill once more be buried alive in verbiage. In a nationally publicized correspondence with Arthur Vandenberg, Republican senator from Illinois, Divine challenged the senator's claim that filibustering was essential to preserve minority rights. Divine suggested that it was merely an abuse of a congressional majority's right to vote on a major social issue.[48] Far from constituting freedom of speech or any of the other virtues Vandenberg claimed for it, filibustering appeared merely an attempt to "obstruct justice."[49]

The obstructors in the Senate once more filibustered the antilynching bill to defeat, after the House had passed it by a resounding margin of 252 to 131. There were, however, long-range consolations. The campaign brought civil rights issues closer to the center of public attention, and induced some southern states to pass their own measures against lynching in order to defuse pressure for a federal bill. The campaign also served as a testing ground for the civil rights movement. The historian of blacks during the New Deal, Harvard Sitkoff, describes it as a "baptism of fire" from which "the movement learned the intricacies of modern public relations, fund-raising, and legislative lobbying."[50] Father Divine fostered this process by providing an outlet for black proletarians to express their resentments against lynching and racism in constructive political ways: as petitioners, marchers, and Washington lobbyists. If the techniques they and other civil rights workers employed were too often unpolished and unheeded, they were still gathering force for campaigns and triumphs to come.

Electoral Politics

Father Divine's usually active leadership seemed to falter in the realm of electoral politics. Since his emergence from a jail cell in Mineola with his reputation enhanced and his following larger than ever, Divine was courted assiduously by candidates for municipal and even national office. Yet his recurrent hesitation to endorse any political figure or party, whether from a manifest disdain for compromise or a possible reluctance to expose the limits of his influence, kept him on the sidelines of election campaigns throughout the Depression decade.

The pattern of eager partisan competition for Father Divine's support, followed by the Peace Mission leader's abstention from endorsing any nominee, was first seen in the New York City mayoralty campaign of 1933. Both of the leading aspirants for that office made the uptown hegira to the Peace Mission's headquarters at 155th Street in Harlem, to bid for Divine's political blessing. The Democratic incumbent, John O'Brien, at a loss for winning over Divine's followers with a straight political appeal, retreated to a fulsome endorsement of Divine's "great work."[51] Fiorello La Guardia, running on a liberal Fusion ticket, was still more expansive, pledging his unqualified aid to Divine's course of action:

> I say, Father Divine, no matter what you do, I will support you. I came in that spirit, and I came here tonight, not to ask but to give, for I believe, Father Divine, in what you say.
> This city must be cleaned up and I am willing to clean it up, and I ask for Father Divine's help and counsel, because he knows the spots that have to be cleaned. I want to pay my tribute to Father Divine, and say peace be with you. . . .[52]

Despite these competing fusillades of flattery, Divine displayed uncharacteristic caution. "At this juncture, I would not feel justified to commit myself," he informed a reporter by phone. Would he vote at all? A long silence ensued. The repeated question produced further hesitancy, then admission of uncertainty: "Well, if I do, it will be a final decision on the impulse of the moment." And would he then let his followers act according to individual conscience without his direction? "That's it exactly," Divine answered.[53]

The election appeared to draw few Divinites to the polls. Divine explained his refusal to commit himself as due to the absence of political figures who met his standards of idealism and moral courage. More cynical pundits suggested that Divine simply did not wish to risk choosing among candidates in a close race and possibly disillusioning his followers should his blessing and their votes prove insufficient.[54] Yet at heart he seemed to prefer the outsider's role as political prophet to that of ward boss for any party, no matter how certain of electoral victory.

Divine's failure to endorse any candidate or produce a sizable vote curbed his impact on municipal politics for years after. Fusion party representatives maintained contact with Divine, but La Guardia no longer considered him a major force in Harlem politics. Divine's letters to him appear to have remained largely, perhaps entirely, unanswered, as the mayor instead sought other contacts more widely respected in Harlem.

Despite Divine's indecision in 1933, he could not be wholly ignored, because his potential voting strength remained unclear and might still prove significant in future elections. Many municipal, state, and even national representatives, judges, commissioners, and other government officials continued to stream into Peace Mission centers to praise Divine's civic accomplishments, discuss current issues, and often solicit support for their political campaigns. Myles Paige was among the frequent visitors to Divine's gatherings. Another was Jonah Goldstein, an independent-minded judge of rare ability who served on the Court of Special Sessions. Ben Howe, a founder and chairman of the Fusion party, spoke many times at Divine's banquets and rallies. Veteran Republican partisan George Harris regularly featured Father Divine's speeches in his black-oriented journal, the *New York News*. Charles Mitchell, former minister to Liberia and another staunch Republican, also maintained regular contacts with the Peace Mission. In neighboring New Jersey politicians in heavily black districts paid especial attention to the movement, convinced that Father Divine held the balance of power in any close election.[55]

Political observers were perhaps most impressed by the steady intensification of Father Divine's political activity during the early thirties, which soon diminished memories of his aloofness from the New York mayoralty campaign in 1933. At that time he was just beginning to join and in some cases establish reform coalitions on the municipal level. By late 1934 he forged his brief alliance with Sufi Hamid and the next year he deepened his cooperation with the Communist party. Although he still produced few votes, he gave every indication of preparing to send his followers *en masse* to the polls for the presidential election in 1936. Thus, within three years of his relative eclipse in New York City politics, Divine emerged more widely influential than ever before.

The year 1936 promised in every way to be the Peace Mission's *annus mirabilis*. In January the movement issued its Righteous Government Platform, prescribing comprehensive reform of American society, amid national publicity and strong coverage in the black press. Subsequently the Peace Mission became the object of considerable courting by the major parties nationwide. This time, many observers agreed, if only Divine chose sides — and wisely — the Peace Mission seemed ready to become a formidable political force.

Democratic solicitors for Divine's vote attempted to show that the Roosevelt administration favored his reform program. Senator Wagner directed an aide to assure Divine that Vice-President John Nance Garner had arranged for the Righteous Government Platform to be read into the *Congressional Record*.[56] There is no evidence to show that this was done, though the gesture toward Divine indicates a healthy regard for his potential command of votes.

An aide in the Roosevelt campaign, W. A. Graham, traveled secretly from Washington, D.C., to Divine's Harlem headquarters in order to bid for his support less than a month before the election. Graham repeated so frequently that he came merely as a private citizen and not from Democratic headquarters that one suspects that his words, so well rehearsed, were provided by higher authorities. Graham engaged in a long, often repetitive discussion with Divine on political issues and tactics, urging from every practical angle that Divine work for change within the Democratic party. Graham never once came to grips with the fact that in Divine he was confronting a prophet rather than a machine politician, for he kept insisting to Divine that none of the minor parties could be a winner in 1936. Divine replied to such attempted pressure: "We are not as much interested in winners as we are in having the leaders get a view of what we consider the new philosophy of government." He asked Graham whether the Democratic party was prepared to endorse his Righteous Government Platform, by name or by individual proposals. Graham squirmed desperately away from such a commitment, to which Divine as relentlessly returned. The Democratic emissary seemed to become increasingly frustrated with Divine's position. He apparently considered it a remarkable imposition for Divine to hold up an endorsement of so worthy a candidate as Roosevelt over a matter of principles. Toward the end of the protracted meeting, the two mutually incredulous individuals exchanged these comments: "Well in other words, Father, as I understand you, you will not give your support to any party unless they support you." "Why should I?" The meeting concluded on the same note of futility.[57]

Republicans meanwhile wooed Divine's followers with full-page ads in the *Spoken Word* and the *New Day,* lauding the talents of presidential nominee Alfred Landon. Ladies from the Women's Republican Club also visited Divine's Harlem headquarters to commend his teachings and denounce the Democrats.[58]

Divine at times leaned tentatively toward the Democratic ticket, if only as the lesser of two evils. "The Republican Party has been in power for years and years," he told a supplicant for his endorsement, "[but] how much segregation have they eradicated from among us? They claim to be the ones who endorsed emancipation for the slaves, nevertheless, they have gone back . . . and are more prejudiced than the Democrats."[59]

As in 1933, though, Divine resisted the courtship of both major parties. Neither had publicly endorsed the RGP, nor even an antilynching bill, which he had deemed the minimal price of his support. By late October Divine was already preparing both his followers and political onlookers for a grand retreat: "Then I say the time has come, we must stay our hands until I give you the command. No doubt it will be 1940!"[60] This anticlimax to years of preparation foreshadowed a further let-down at the polls. Although Divine ostentatiously had instructed his followers "to strike," or boycott, the polls, on election day, his followers were inconspicuous by their absence, as Harlem's two assembly districts ran up record vote totals.

Initially, the fact that Divine controlled few votes made no headway against the powerfully rooted myth of a teeming political following. Even that bastion of careful, understated reporting, the *New York Times,* generously attributed the absentee strength of Harlem's Divinites at 50,000, "observing" that the polls in Harlem were "virtually deserted at his [Divine's] command."[61] This precipitated an avalanche of angry criticism by Negro leaders, who pointed out that Harlem's voting turnout was easily its greatest ever.[62] The *Times* then officially buried the corpse of Divine's political ambitions by printing a retraction and detailing the unprecedented vote in Harlem's 19th and 21st Assembly Districts. It concluded that Divine's voting strength after all was not much above a thousand individuals.[63]

Where did Father Divine fail in his bid for the elusive wreath of Caesar? Part of the answer lies in factors over which Divine had little control, particularly the harassment of followers attempting to register under their newly assumed spiritual names. The bureaucrats who supervised the electoral rolls were largely Tammany appointees, who realized that the Peace Mission opposed the kind of machine politics they represented. Whether under orders or on their own initiative, they claimed that Divine's followers had taken names that could not legally be accepted for purposes of registration or voting.

After bitter protest by the Peace Mission, a decision by the New York State Supreme Court in 1935 seemingly put the matter to rest, by ruling in favor of the movement. Judge Albert Cohn instructed that so long as an individual's voting qualifications could be verified, he had the right to use whatever name he wished.[64] This the Peace Mission hailed as a significant victory, but civil authorities repeatedly and flagrantly violated the ruling.

One group of women followers actually was arrested in Harlem while attempting to register in October, 1936. In response, some 300 Divinites conducted a sit-in at the registration center, just a few doors from Father Divine's main headquarters. Crowding the center to the point where no one else could register, they resolved not to be moved until authorities recognized their legal right to vote. The followers chanted, "Peace, Father," continually and remained until police dispersed them by charging the crowd on horseback. Twenty-four persons were taken to the police station and were later joined by five more followers who asked to be arrested as well.[65]

Once more the Peace Mission won a judicial reprieve. A local court dismissed charges against the arrested followers, and shortly afterward Justice William T. Collins of the State Supreme Court reinforced the legal guarantees already given to Divine's disciples. "The law concerns itself with persons — with human beings rather than with names," he pointed out in a rebuke to the Board of Elections for its extralegal conduct against the Peace Mission.[66]

The esteem in which politicians then held Divine's influence may be gauged by the appearance in Collins's court of observers from the law committees of the Democratic, Republican, and All People's parties. These "watchers" obtained permission of the court to have their party names entered on the record as "interested spectators." The Republican counsel in particular was apparently there to impede, if possible, the registration of spiritual names, aware that the Divinites were leaning, if at all, toward Democratic and All People's party candidates.[67]

Although the Peace Mission won a decisive theoretical victory in the courts, partisan bureaucrats continued — in 1936 and for years after — to hamper its registration efforts. These impediments were compounded by subsequent court rulings that often contradicted each other. Perhaps most disturbing was a decision by the same Judge Collins, who in October, 1937, cryptically reversed his earlier ruling and prohibited Peace Mission petitioners from registering under their acquired spiritual names.[68]

Aside from bureaucratic barriers, Father Divine simply was too openly opinionated to make an effective political leader. He was not only a

utopian social ideologue with communist tendencies but a fervent theo-
crat, a self-declared messiah, and an uncompromising champion of temperance. Not much of a constituency remained after that, but for good
measure Divine was also a crusader for celibacy.

Further, as the economic situation improved, if only marginally, from
1933 through 1936, Divine's image as a major leader of Harlem's destitute masses faded somewhat in comparison with his role as a cult leader.
As such, the base of his hard-core support must have narrowed because
the unifying force of hunger was obscured by the fragmenting tendency
of all cult leadership. Thus Divine, through no major change on his own
part, likely became a more parochial figure to the people of Harlem in
1936 than he had been four years earlier.

Finally, Divine picked the wrong circumstances in which to declare a
boycott of the polls. Voter registration drives in Harlem were at a peak,
Franklin Roosevelt enjoyed overwhelming favor in the ghettos, and many
who cooperated with Divine on specific social issues could not be counted
upon to adhere uniformly to his personal commands. It is doubtful that
any leader or organization could have slowed measurably the rush to re-
elect Roosevelt, who—whatever his faults—provided employment and
relief, housing and even pride to many urban blacks. One finds little evidence, for example, that the *New York Age,* which arrogantly dismissed
Divine's influence after the election, itself swayed any more votes with
its editorials that blacks should not support Roosevelt. The *Age* based
this vain plea on reasoning similar to Divine's—that FDR had "sold out"
to the South in refusing to support the antilynching bill then in Congress.[69]
Clearly, any Harlem opponent of Franklin Roosevelt in 1936 was hopelessly out of step with the masses.

The New York mayoralty campaign of 1937 gave a local omen of
Divine's fading political stature in the wake of his ill-timed boycott. La
Guardia was bidding to become the first anti-Tammany candidate to suc-
ceed himself. Although he had once fawned over Divine as an insurgent
in 1933, he now declined even to visit Divine, although Divine had all but
guaranteed an endorsement if only the mayor would appear at his Harlem headquarters. In pique, Divine threw his support to Judge Jeremiah
T. Mahoney, who had also disavowed Tammany.[70] La Guardia, however,
knew his Harlem. With his progressive record and superb campaign style,
he won the black vote easily and also a decisive re-election. In the process he further relegated Divine's say in Harlem politics to a peripheral
status.

There were signs during the late thirties that Father Divine's political
influence might yet approach the potential many had envisioned in 1936.
The fight for an antilynching law seemed to elicit from Divine new levels

of energy and commitment. Also during this time, the Peace Mission continued to receive a steady stream of local officials apparently still convinced that Divine's blessings and voting bloc might help bring them victory. There were even some fanciful rumors, emanating mainly from the site of Divine's rapidly expanding estates in Ulster County, that he was considering a race for the presidency on a "Peace" platform. The common assumption that he had the financial resources to mount such a campaign gave the rumors a surface credibility.[71]

The hoped-for resurgence never came. Divine would have risked far too humiliating an exposure of his limited base had he run as a protest candidate for president. Therefore, despite some tantalizing remarks about public requests that he declare his candidacy, Divine never came close to doing so.

The preacher also failed to obtain public recognition from either Roosevelt or his Republican challenger, Wendell Willkie, in 1940. Their partisans solicited Divine's endorsement but considered him simply too controversial a figure to risk reciprocating.

The chairman of the Republican National Committee, Joseph Martin, Jr., wrote Divine to inform him that Willkie's platform "embodies all the virtues and principles that you request" and that Willkie "asks that you, Father Divine, urge your followers to register and to vote for him and the Republican party." But Martin stopped short of acceding to Divine's subsequent demand that Willkie first publicly endorse his political principles.[72]

Another advocate for Willkie permitted a telling truth to slip out, as he courted Divine while evading his request for a more open association: "Everybody is afraid of you who doesn't know you. I have met you before, I know your friends—I am not afraid of you, but lots of people are. . . ."[73]

Roosevelt, like Willkie, was inaccessible to Divine, who appeared sympathetic to the president's candidacy but conditioned his endorsement, once again, on a public stand for antilynching legislation. Divine sought Roosevelt's open support on this issue because, "as one of the greatest statesmen of all history," the president's word would have a great effect on the masses. Roosevelt was disinclined, however, to risk alienating southern support for his foreign policy. He was even more reluctant to deal directly with Harlem's controversial cult leader, lest he magnify the "Ellender effect" of too-recent memory and further stir up the racist forces in Congress.[74]

Roosevelt's artful windings on civil rights issues continued to exasperate Divine throughout 1940. The creation of separate Negro training units for national defense, as a means of introducing blacks into formerly all-white military branches, was galling in the extreme. In effect, Roosevelt proposed to advance black rights through segregation. It was, in Divine's view, "as a cow that has given a good pail of milk and kicked it all over and trampled into it on the ground and made mud out of the milk."[75]

Divine also expressed keen disappointment that Roosevelt, "my friend and your friend, my neighbor and the neighbor of a good many of you refused to commit himself on the anti-lynching bill." Had Roosevelt only supported this and a plan to unite the Americas for hemispheric defense, "no doubt I would have personally, publicly endorsed him." Divine thought the situation especially regrettable, "for I admire the boldness and determination of a man such as he is and I admire his stand on many points."[76] Instead, Divine again refrained from supporting any presidential candidate, preferring to observe the contest from a more Olympian moral height.

The election of 1940, which Roosevelt won, though more narrowly than in 1932 and 1936, confirmed the limitations of Divine's power at the polls. Even Divine himself appeared more fully aware of his marginal role, although he indicated his awareness only subliminally amid gusts of bravado. "We do not believe there will be many of my immediate followers who will vote," he conceded to Joseph Martin in late October, "although there are thousands and millions of others who are not immediate followers of mine [who] will lean in the way and the direction I am inclined."[77] By this time, however, few outside that immediate following still believed in the myth of Divine's electoral power, as many otherwise shrewd politicians had through early November, 1936. When Harlem's residents flocked to the polls in 1940, the absence of Divine's disciples caused scarcely a ripple of interest among the public, politicians, or journalists. His national political ambitions had lost even the facade of realistic calculation.

Political Educator

If Divine's attempts at electoral brokering met frustration, he enjoyed significantly greater impact as a political educator, a role more suited to his evangelical temperament. Many of his followers had spent decades in the South, where political activity and knowledge were considered the exclusive domain of white men. Although some followers had come to the Peace Mission partly because of concern with civil rights, others might with equal likelihood have joined a religious movement of wholly spiritual bent. It required all Divine's effort to instill in those people a sense of political awareness and activism.

The predominantly cultlike character of Peace Mission protest marches confirms that only Father Divine's wishes could lead his followers into such unfamiliar political realms. It is impossible to ascertain what proportion grasped the problems and circumstances surrounding these marches. A substantial number, though, clearly viewed them as opportunities to praise Father Divine and the bliss they had found in his movement. They likely had a general notion that they were in some way working against racism and, more simply, evil. Yet they evinced no further tie to politics or protest than their willingness to follow Father Divine's directives in the belief that he was working for their welfare. These disciples had thus entered a transition between the spiritual escapism of their past and full political commitment, with Divine as their bridge to further development.

The Peace Mission's participation in rallies sponsored by political coalitions highlighted the still rudimentary social awareness of many followers. A demonstration which the American League against War and Fascism sponsored in 1935 offers a vivid example. The prominent black Protestant minister, William Lloyd Imes, chaired the Harlem-based event, which featured some 50,000 people from forty organizations. All gathered for the expressed purpose of protesting the world's indifference to the Italian invasion of Ethiopia. The Peace Mission members formed a sizable contingent in the march, yet seemed largely aloof from the spirit of the proceedings, as a reporter for the *New York Herald-Tribune* witnessed:

> While the rest of the paraders chanted "The Internationale" or shouted "Hands off Ethiopia" or "Down with War and Fascism" Father Divine's followers, led by a nine-piece orchestra, sang such songs as "Ain't Going to Study War no More," "We shall have a Righteous Government," "Take all your troubles to Father Divine" and numerous others. At other times they chanted lustily, "He's God, He's God—He's God, God, God."
> . . . With the calm of those who had found true guidance they remained blissfully aloof from the issues of the day, ignoring the bitter problems of Fascism and unemployment, war and race prejudice and all the other questions which troubled the minds of their fellow marchers. They strode along singing in unison:
> "We don't have to worry, We don't have to worry,
> We don't have to worry no more, For God has come in a bodily form,
> We don't have to worry no more, Hallelujah!"[78]

Doubtless other groups had their own ends as well. One suspects, for example, that the communist paraders sought to promote much more than the disengagement of forces in Ethiopia: they were marching for the bliss of a common front as specified by Moscow. The Elks lodges, too, had their own interests: the impressiveness of their respective delegations and orchestras. The rally, in short, featured one common aim and a host of differing ones. The insulation of the Divinites therefore should not obscure the fact of their participation in reform campaigns. It does suggest, however, that Divine was somehow fashioning a crusade for justice out of raw troops many of whom appeared content simply to worship their general.

Divine expressed acute awareness that some might think it "absurd" for a minister to place such importance on political activity. He answered that the whole point of his leadership was to free people from their oppressions, not merely to preside over the oppressed. And to do that he had first to awaken the latent militance in followers long resigned to second-class citizenship: "You know you want your emancipation, you know you want your constitutional rights, you know you want social equality, you know you want religious liberty, you know you want health and happiness, and you know positively well you also want a chance to earn a living, the same as everybody else. That is what I came for."[79]

Divine exhorted his followers "to help emancipate Harlem from political bondage, the same as we mean to emancipate all people. . . ." He assured them that he would not coerce disciples into political actions against their consciences, but urged that no one rest content simply because he or she was now living well. He asked his followers to become "co-workers with me" to aid every oppressed individual, "that he might have his freedom even as we have it."[80]

That Divine was able to marshal a previously supine element to mass action was itself a formidable achievement. Divine wanted more, however: greater political awareness and commitment among his disciples, independent of his own hortatory directives. Therefore Divine held up to his followers a standard of informed citizenship in a way some religions reserve for the goal of nirvana, salvation, or some other state of grace. The effect on many Peace Mission members was visibly great, for they developed an interest in serving and shaping their country as never before.

For the large number of Peace Mission adherents of West Indian and other foreign origin, Father Divine's injunction to become good citizens had immediate and literal significance. At his urging, they sought naturalized status in such numbers as to disconcert New York's municipal bureaucracy. Divine gently reassured Rudolph Reimer, Commissioner of Emigration at Ellis Island, that the overflow of recent applications for citizenship in 1935 was not for the purpose of qualifying for government aid, as Reimer suspected. "If you trace the applicants," Divine wrote him, ". . . you will see it was encouraged by my Peace Mission, not for the purpose of receiving Old Age pensions, neither for welfare protection nor compensation, but to the extreme contrary. These . . . have been influenced by me, to become to be American citizens."[81] This injunction similarly sparked the rush by disciples to enroll in night school courses, the sooner to qualify for the most valuable prize of citizenship, the ballot.[82]

Disciples were encouraged not only to help select their political leaders but to qualify for government service themselves. The Peace Mission's own "Civil Service Preparatory Class" — a branch of the "Vocational Guidance Department of Righteous Government" — met twice weekly to familiarize interested members with the format of civil service tests and "to stress at all times the worth of a Civil Service position."[83] The long discrimination against blacks for civil service posts gave these classes a deeper significance. Father Divine was again attempting not only to provide employment and instill patriotism but to break the color line in one more area of American life.

The Peace Mission by 1933 made political instruction an integral part of its activities. State and municipal officials, from whatever combination of civic duty and hopes of storing up future electoral treasures, regularly addressed Peace Mission gatherings. They spoke on current political issues and the mechanics of government in the United States. These talks effectively made many of the movement's festive banquets into political seminars that coexisted with sessions of frenzied religious praise.

Divine furthered this educational renaissance by organizing formal classes on basic political science within the Peace Mission centers. The class called "U.S.A.," for example, offered instruction in "Americanism," citizenship, and government, and required students to learn the Declaration of Independence and the Constitution verbatim. The reason for this scrupulous attention to basic American political documents was illuminated by a young member of the Peace Mission, who described her old school in Georgia this way: "The light-complected school had a course called 'civics.' We didn't, though. We had one called 'character building.' While the children of the lighter complexion learned about the Constitution and all, we learned what they called 'courtesy' and 'humility.' "[84] Divine, possibly remembering the effects of his own scant education in the South, was determined to spare his followers the same enforced ignorance and timidity. He wished to give people a sense, for the first time, that they could play an active, constructive role in shaping their destinies and the character of their society. In this he touched many lives, and it marked, perhaps, the real height of his political career.

Notes to Chapter 7

1. See, for example, Father Divine's sermon of Jan. 1, 1936, in *SW,* Jan. 11, 1936, p. 13, in which he stated, "I have *more* right in politics than I have in the church," in order to ensure righteous leadership in government.
2. *NYAN,* June 27, 1936, p. 3; *Times,* June 21, 1936, p. 5, June 22, 1936, p. 2.
3. Herndon, for example, won only 327 votes, yet his extensive campaign in the 21st Assembly District in Harlem "attracted much attention" with his "ringing appeals" for justice, according to *NYAN,* Nov. 28, 1936, p. 2. See also Marcan-

tonio's postelection call for a third-party coalition of farmers and laborers in a speech to the All People's party, in *Times,* Nov. 23, 1936, p. 42.

4. Parker, *Incredible Messiah,* p. 242.

5. *SW,* Mar. 16, 1935, p. 9, editor's note, details the treatment of Father Divine at these conventions.

6. See, for example, Father Divine to Fiorello La Guardia, May 10, 1935, in *SW,* June 1, 1935, pp. 10-11.

7. See *NYAN,* Sept. 5, 1936, p. 1, on Paige's career and his appointment as magistrate.

8. For a comprehensive examination of the Scottsboro controversy, see Dan T. Carter, *Scottsboro: A Tragedy of the American South* (New York: Oxford University Press, 1969).

9. *AA,* Sept. 11, 1937, p. 32.

10. *NYAN,* July 27, 1935, p. 17. See also Father Divine to Angelo Herndon, Oct. 1, 1935, assuring Herndon of his concern, in *SW,* Oct. 12, 1935, p. 23.

11. The appeal stated:

"I write as I wish to advise, I, Rev. M. J. Divine, my Peace Mission and other cooperating organizations, with thousands of humane workers, do hereby appeal the honor of your office to please kindly release Angelo Herndon by reversing the decision of the Supreme Court of your great state, from the sentence of eighteen to twenty years in prison for the violation of the State Insurrection Law, of which I sincerely believe Mr. Herndon was ignorant to the fact that he was actually violating the State Law.

"Thanking your Honor in advance for your kind consideration in this great humane act, that you and all might be even as I am,

"Respectfully and sincere, I am, Rev. M. J. Divine (Better known as Father Divine)."

See Father Divine to Eugene D. Talmadge, Oct. 24, 1935, in *SW,* Nov. 2, 1935, p. 22.

12. For a thorough account of Herndon's ordeal, see Charles H. Martin, *The Angelo Herndon Case and Southern Justice* (Baton Rouge: Louisiana State University Press, 1976).

13. Adam Clayton Powell, Jr., *Marching Blacks,* rev. ed. (New York: Dial Press, 1973), p. 68.

14. *Times,* Aug. 5, 1934, sec. 2, p. 3.

15. *Times,* Aug. 5, 1934, sec. 2, p. 3.

16. "Father Devine Is God," *Daily Worker,* Aug. 6, 1934, p. 6.

17. Earl Browder, "The Struggle for the United Front (report to meeting of the Central Committee of the Communist Party, September 5-6, 1934)," *Communist* 10 (Oct., 1934):959-60.

18. James W. Ford, "The United Front in Negro Work," *Communist* 14 (Feb., 1935):171.

19. *Socialist Call,* Feb. 8, 1936, p. 9.

20. *Daily Worker,* Feb. 11, 1936, p. 1.

21. Sermon of Mar. 2, 1935, in *SW,* Mar. 16, 1935, p. 2; Hoshor, *God in a Rolls-Royce,* p. 252.

22. Lambert Fairchild to Orol Wiltshire, Oct. 24, 1935, and Orol Wiltshire (endorsed by Father Divine) to Lambert Fairchild, Oct. 26, 1935, both in *SW,* Nov. 2, 1935, p. 23.

23. Interview given by Father Divine to Graham Booz and Oden Fox, New York, Mar. 1, 1939, in *ND,* Mar. 16, 1939, p. 8.

24. Father Divine to Mrs. W. P. Yarnell, Oct. 22, 1940, in *ND,* Oct. 24, 1940, pp. 81-82.

25. "Highlights of International Righteous Government Convention," *SW,* Jan. 14, 1936, p. 20.

26. Righteous Government Platform (hereinafter RGP), Introductory Plank 2. The RGP has been reprinted in numerous issues of *SW* and *ND,* beginning with *SW,* Jan. 14, 1936, pp. 7-16.

Of the nine remaining planks concerned with racial justice, the one whose link is least evident is Plank 10: "Immediate return to owners of all stolen goods or their equivalent, not only by individuals but by nations; this is to include all territories taken by force from other nations." This should be understood in light of Father Divine's occasional references to just compensation for the descendants of slave laborers, and to the indignant reaction of the black community to the recent Italian invasion of Ethiopia.

27. RGP, Introductory Plank 3 advocated destruction of armaments and unqualified pacifism. Plank 6 proscribed capital punishment and Plank 8 dealt with lynching.

28. The RGP section "Principles" included such statements as, "Why should the unions try to control the people and put them in slavery?" With obvious if implicit reference to the harsh treatment of strikebreakers, it also objected to "the unions coming in and snatching men and women up from their work, when they are working getting an honest living." It further recorded Father Divine as warning, "I will call a strike on the unions! They have oppressed the widow and the orphan, and the hireling in his wages, long enough."

29. RGP, Economic Section, Plank 2.

30. Ibid., Plank 1.

31. Ibid., Plank 10.

32. Ibid., Plank 5.

33. RGP, Political Section, Plank 1.

34. RGP, Educational Section, Planks 1 (on free education) and 2 (barring racist and martial texts).

35. On the NAACP's crucial role in this campaign, see Robert L. Zangrando, *The NAACP Crusade against Lynching, 1909-1950* (Philadelphia: Temple University Press, 1980).

36. The intimidation was greater for the many racist justifications of lynchings. Among the alleged offenses for which Negroes paid with their lives were: incitement to racial troubles; trying to act like a white man; seeking employment in a restaurant; denouncing a sailor's part in the Chicago race riot; being a member of the Non-Partisan League to promote racial tolerance; and expressing sympathy with a lynched Negro. See Arthur F. Raper, *The Tragedy of Lynching* (1933; reprinted New York: Dover, 1970), pp. 36-37.

37. Interview given by Father Divine to Graham Booz and Oden Fox, Mar. 1, 1939, in *ND,* Mar. 16, 1939, pp. 10-11.

38. The quotation is from the RGP section on "Principles."

39. Braden, *These Also Believe,* pp. 19-20.

40. See *SW,* Apr. 20, 1937, pp. 3, 6-7. The House bill was HR 4547.

41. See John Lamb to Congressman Joseph Gavagan, Nov. 23, 1937, complaining of Senator Wagner's disregard of the Peace Mission's contributions to the cause of antilynching, in *ND,* Nov. 25, 1937, p. 14; and John Lamb to Congressman Gavagan, Dec. 27, 1937, in *ND,* Jan. 13, 1938, p. 30. Regarding Divine's messages to Senator Wagner, see, for example, Father Divine's staff (endorsed by

Father Divine) to Senator Robert Wagner, Apr. 17, 1937, in *SW,* Apr. 20, 1937, pp. 6-7. On Wagner's evasiveness toward Peace Mission overtures, see Robert Wagner to Orol Freedom, Jan. 11, 1937, in *SW,* Jan. 19, 1937, p. 13.

42. *Congressional Record,* 75th Cong., 3d sess., 83, Jan. 19, 1938, p. 763, and Jan. 20, 1938, p. 833.

43. Ibid., Jan. 20, 1938, p. 833.

44. Ellender's full remarks on Father Divine are in ibid., Jan. 19, 1938, pp. 752, 753, 761-63, and Jan. 20, 1938, pp. 818-33.

45. "Is It Wonderful?" editorial in *AA,* July 20, 1940, p. 4.

46. Sermon of Oct. 30, 1940, in *ND,* Oct. 31, 1940, p. 45.

47. Sermon of Jan. 29, 1938, in *ND,* Feb. 17, 1938, p. 19. Divine exaggerates here, though Ellender did claim that the Peace Mission leader was a strong advocate of the bill, whose provisions strongly resembled Divine's own proposals for antilynching legislation.

48. *Times,* Feb. 27, 1940, p. 14.

49. Sermon of Mar. 3, 1940, in *ND,* Mar. 7, 1940, p. 6.

50. Harvard I. Sitkoff, *A New Deal for Blacks* (New York: Oxford University Press, 1978), p. 295.

51. *Times,* Nov. 6, 1933, p. 3.

52. *ND,* Nov. 4, 1937, p. 12; a similar though abridged version of La Guardia's speech to the Peace Mission assembly in Harlem is given in *Times,* Nov. 6, 1933, p. 3.

53. *Times,* Nov. 7, 1933, p. 18.

54. "Not That Kind of a God," editorial in *AA,* Nov. 18, 1933, p. 16, typifies such disparagement.

55. *AA,* July 20, 1935, p. 12, on Father Divine's impact on New Jersey's black ward leaders.

56. Hoshor, *God in a Rolls-Royce,* p. 251. The vice-president did apparently put before the Senate a resolution of the Righteous Government Convention remonstrating against war, the sale or manufacture of war materials in the United States, and the loan of money to any warring nation. This is noted in *Congressional Record,* 75th Cong., 3d sess., 83, Jan. 20, 1938, p. 832.

57. Interview given by Father Divine to W. A. Graham, New York, Oct. 21, 1936, in *SW,* Oct. 27, 1936, pp. 17-23, 26. The quotations are on pp. 18 and 26.

58. Parker, *Incredible Messiah,* p. 250.

59. Interview given by Father Divine to the Reverend Harrison Lamb, New York, July 5, 1936, in *SW,* July 25, 1936, p. 19.

60. Sermon of Oct. 26, 1936, in *SW,* Oct. 27, 1936, p. 6.

61. *Times,* Nov. 4, 1936, p. 12.

62. *NYAN,* Nov. 14, 1936, p. 2, reveals Divine's weakness.

63. *Times,* Nov. 8, 1936, sec. 2, p. 3.

64. Parker, *Incredible Messiah,* p. 160, reprints Judge Cohn's ruling in its entirety.

65. *NYAN,* Oct. 10, 1936, pp. 1, 24.

66. Ibid., Oct. 17, 1936, p. 3.

67. *SW,* Oct. 10, 1936, p. 3.

68. *ND,* Mar. 13, 1971, p. 8.

69. The *New York Age* deprecated Father Divine's political influence in its editorial "Divinites Sidestep Showdown," Nov. 14, 1936, p. 6. Its earlier, apparently unheeded editorial against Roosevelt, "A Forgotten Issue," Oct. 24, 1936, p. 6,

concluded: "The only safe way for the Negro is to vote Republican and to elect Governor [Alfred] Landon as President and Col. [Franklin] Knox as Vice-President."

70. *ND,* Nov. 4, 1937, p. 32.

71. *NYAN,* Aug. 6, 1938, pp. 1, 4. See also *ND,* July 25, 1940, p. 93, referring to a curious plea from the *Savannah Journal,* July 7, 1940, calling on Divine to run for president.

72. Joseph Martin to Father Divine, Sept. 27, 1940, in *ND,* Oct. 24, 1940, p. 78. See also Father Divine to Joseph Martin, Oct. 23, 1940, in *ND,* Oct. 24, 1940, pp. 79-80.

73. Interview given by Father Divine to Kenneth Patterson and Colonel Little (both from Wendell Willkie's campaign organization), New York, Nov. 3, 1940, in *ND,* Nov. 7, 1940, pp. 41-48. The quotation is from remarks by Patterson, on p. 45.

74. Neither Roosevelt nor his press secretary, Stephen Early, replied to Father Divine's correspondence after 1939. Eleanor Roosevelt made one brief, impersonal reply to an effusive letter by Father Divine (praising Franklin Roosevelt while calling for passage of federal antilynching legislation), Feb. 26, 1940, in *ND,* Mar. 7, 1940, p. 83.

75. Sermon of Oct. 17-18, 1940, in *ND,* Oct. 24, 1940, p. 19.

76. Sermon of Oct. 30, 1940, in *ND,* Oct. 31, 1940, p. 45.

77. Father Divine to Joseph Martin, Oct. 23, 1940, in *ND,* Oct. 24, 1940, p. 79.

78. *New York Herald-Tribune,* Aug. 4, 1935, p. 21.

79. Sermon of Nov. 29, 1934, in *SW,* Dec. 8, 1934, p. 4.

80. Sermon of Feb. 9, 1935, in *SW,* Feb. 23, 1935, p. 3.

81. Father Divine to Rudolph Reimer, Mar. 20, 1935, in *SW,* Apr. 6, 1935, p. 4.

82. *Times,* Dec. 8, 1935, sec. 2, p. 9.

83. *SW,* Dec. 7, 1935, pp. 17-18.

84. Harris, *Father Divine,* p. 224.

CHAPTER 8

Father Divine and the Black Community

Father Divine exerted a strong, though sharply mixed, impact on the black community during the Depression. As the cult head of a largely proletarian group, Divine discomfited and embarrassed the more refined elements of ghetto society. Ministers of conventional churches particularly feared his Peace Mission movement as a pernicious influence on their congregants. At the same time, however, the preacher impressed all but the most blindly critical with his social achievements, which imparted a luster to his ministry few orthodox pastors could match. As a result, Divine symbolized for many black leaders the possibilities for civil rights reform through the churches, even as the black community as a whole shunned him as a demagogue or worse.

Father Divine and the Black Bourgeoisie

In June, 1936, two opinion makers in the black community exchanged sharp arguments about the value of Father Divine's ministry and his personal character. Adam Clayton Powell, Jr., termed Divine "the colossal farce of the twentieth century" and added, "The type of person who follows him proves the issue." Powell viewed Divine's disciples as dwelling "on the fringes of life, hanging between sanity and insanity." They were "truly a lost generation."[1]

The following week a featured columnist in the *Amsterdam News,* Dr. Wilfrid Rankin, retorted that while he had "no sympathy for the ecstatic enthusiasm and other strange characteristics of the votaries of Father Divine," he had "profound admiration" for the man himself. Rankin saw him as a saintly man "who, disregarding the violent insults hurled at him by other Negro ministers, continues to pursue the even tenor of his way in his endeavor to provide food, shelter and other forms of succor for suffering and starving Negroes whose woes could otherwise never be a source of concern to those who delight to rail at him."[2]

The dispute confirmed Father Divine's rare ability to generate vigorous controversy, eye-catching headlines, and comments by prominent figures in black America. Perhaps even more significant as a gauge of his impact on the ghettos, it revealed the remarkably limited spectrum of debate over Divine's movement. Powell and Rankin, for all their lively disagreement, shared more deep-seated sentiments than either appeared to know. Both viewed the Peace Mission through middle-class perspectives of affluence, education, and decorum, and found Divine's followers sadly wanting in all respects. Apart from the moot point of whether a leader should be judged independently from the people he attracts, the fact is that few in the black community made that distinction in the case of Father Divine. The proletarian character of his movement colored almost every appraisal of it and, in general, stigmatized Divine's ministry in a way he could never fully overcome.

Middle- and lower-middle-class blacks tended to view the Peace Mission primarily in terms of caste considerations. According to E. Franklin Frazier, the typical black bourgeois "avoids the fantastic extravagances of Father Divine's cult, partly because lower-class Negroes are associated with it. He concedes, however, that Father Divine 'does some good' because his followers are 'honest and faithful domestic servants.' "[3]

Ralph Mathews, the Afro-American's version of H. L. Mencken in his jaundiced appraisals of the masses, typified the black bourgeoisie's view of Father Divine's ministry. Mathews derided the emotionalism and flamboyance of cult worship, and he considered Father Divine one of the chief perpetrators of all that was wrong with the state of Negro religion:

> Religion has become overcrowded with various sorts of upstarts who have evolved just one kind of hokum after another. The good Father Divine won his claim to divinity by a direct appeal to the stomachs of the down-and-outers and it is no hard job for a hungry man to believe in anything that relieves his cramps. . . . All of these gentlemen [Divine, Elder Michaux, Daddy Grace] are drawing the mobs and the shekels while the pews of the orthodox places of worship are empty. This merely proves that people are not so much concerned about being good as they are in seeing a good show.[4]

The matter of Divine's aid to the poor and oppressed, Mathews dismissed with the condescending but not wholly inaccurate appraisal, "Father Divine impresses me as God's ward-healer." Like the political bosses who did favors for constituents, "Father Divine is God's fixer."[5] Mathews projected a more uncompromising conservatism than most other critics of the Peace Mission. Yet his basic cultural and class elitism resonated with the mood of the ghetto's "respectable" elements.

Pastors of conventional churches were the group most implacably hostile toward Father Divine. They resented his inroads into their spheres of authority and saw his brand of religion as an affront to their own. These sentiments, which had surfaced while Divine was still a fledgling leader in Sayville, became much more widely voiced as the Peace Mission extended across Harlem and other ghettos. Divine seldom responded in kind to such attacks, after the sharp exchange with Bishop Lawson in 1932, but he seemed wounded by the efforts of other ministers to ostracize him. He summarized matters with uncharacteristic understatement when he told two visiting pastors in 1938, "I really enjoyed meeting you gentlemen, because for the last five or six years there are not so many of the clergy class who have met me harmoniously. . . ."[6]

The Reverend E. W. White, who in 1933 told a Baptist ministers' conference that Divine should be jailed for "99 years and a few more days," set the tone of most clerical speeches on Divine throughout the Depression decade. Ministers at that conference joined in condemning Divine and all religious figures who "conceal themselves behind the cloak of the ministry" to engage in racketeering.[7]

Of particular concern to many clergymen was the apparent travesty of traditional worship perpetrated by the followers of Father Divine and other cultists. One minister said that when he went by a Peace Mission center once, he heard "angels" making parodies of well-known hymns and parading with placards, all declaring that "Father Divine is God." The same minister, in a sermon implicitly striking at the theme of "Antichrist," related that a man returned from a Peace Mission home saying, "Reverend, I went up there myself and I heard Father Divine three days, and I tell you, there is something that gets a hold of you." Then the minister added ominously, "[But] that something is not God."[8] To such clergymen, Father Divine was a devil to be exorcised from their congregations.

As Harlem's list of cult priests, prophets, and deities lengthened in response to Depression conditions and Father Divine's success, the orthodox clergy intensified its criticisms of these leaders in sermons and interviews. Their denunciations reached a peak in 1938, during the short-lived challenge by "Daddy Grace" for control of Harlem's cult followers. The Reverend Ethelred Brown of the Harlem Unitarian Church expressed the sentiments of many ministers in placing both Grace and Divine "under the same category" as nothing more than "exploiters of the ignorance of poor people." He added, "They can't last, but while they do operate, they are a disgrace to all decent-minded communities. The sooner they go the better." Adam Clayton Powell was similarly scathing as he equated the rise of Daddy Grace with that of Father Divine before him. "Nothing to it," he scoffed. "Just another of the long line of imposters who have each only lasted for a brief season."[9]

Powell's attacks must have been especially disheartening to Father Divine. The young Baptist minister was a man of demonstrated leadership qualities and social concern; he could scarcely be brushed aside like Bishop Lawson and others of his limited caliber. The two men in fact espoused enough of the same reform objectives to have been potentially close allies, but Powell's blistering sarcasm toward Divine simply overwhelmed any basis for rapport. It is likely that he saw Divine not simply as a charlatan — though this sentiment was definitely present — but also as a competitor possessing many of his own dearest resources: charisma, organizational talent, and a mass base in Harlem.

For years Powell limited his notice of Harlem's most famous cult leader to carefully crafted invective. This, of course, made little impact on Divine's disciples, who knew that their leader was God on earth. Then, too, Powell's reputation for altercations with other leaders drained his polemics against Divine of their full force.[10] Nevertheless, this Baptist preacher was probably Harlem's foremost minister, partly because of the numerous and wealthy congregation he inherited from his father and partly as the result of his own dynamic nature. His unrelenting opposition to Father Divine greatly encouraged other clergymen and middle-class blacks generally to treat the cult leader as a pariah.

The vigor of status distinctions even among members of an oppressed people is clear from the way black middle-class neighbors reacted to the arrival of Father Divine's proletarian flock. "Striver's Row" in Harlem was perhaps the epitome of black bourgeois values. Famous as the most exclusive residential block in black Manhattan, this area between Seventh and Eighth Avenues on 139th Street self-consciously exhibited the best of Negro middle-class life within the limits of a segregated existence. In 1934 members of the Peace Mission acquired a property in that district. Possibly they expected that the residents of Striver's Row would welcome with open arms a group similarly dedicated to securing full civil rights and a law-abiding and industrious existence for Negroes. Instead the agonized and angry responses revealed a deep-rooted disdain for those of lower-class origins and cultural patterns.

Almost from the outset, when a sign in blazing red and blue letters proclaimed "Peace" to all the refined residents of Striver's Row, the Peace Mission members outraged the neighborhood with their unrestrained exuberance. Several thousand followers shouted and loudly chanted praises at an opening-night celebration further enlivened by the Father's personal appearance. Neighbors accustomed to a more golden level of aural comfort frantically called the police. Patrols came on two occasions but accomplished little because of the great numbers involved. Some neighbors found parking a difficulty because of the huge buses and the cars transporting Peace Mission members to and from their new residence.

These factors alone cannot fully explain the depth of opposition to the presence of Peace Mission members, for these annoyances were largely temporary. The banquets, which began as all-night affairs, soon routinely wound down promptly at ten o'clock, in response to frequent police interruptions. The initial bustle of Peace Mission vehicles also subsided once the new residents settled in. The atmosphere, in short, was conducive to compromise, if only because the Peace Mission recognized its interest in cooperation with the authorities. Moreover, the followers were inculcated with essentially middle-class principles of thrift and diligence that paralleled the values extolled by the veteran inhabitants of Striver's Row.

There were other discomforts, though, which were mainly psychological but perhaps for that reason much more grievous and intractable. Some expressed displeasure at inhaling odors of sparerib stew and frying pork chops. These were foods from the old, never-to-be-remembered days in the rural South. While many black migrants had naturally carried such cultural baggage with them to the ghettos, the families on Striver's Row deliberately renounced "soul" food and all the degrading conditions they associated with it. Now Divine and his proletarian Negro followers were reintroducing these discarded, hated ways back into their lives.

Discussions in Striver's Row focused for months upon the horror of the Peace Mission's presence in the neighborhood. Angry words over this "disgrace" and "outrage" complemented hopeful rumors that a petition for court measures to oust Divine and his following might soon rescue the area from these invading elements. The specific charges by residents of the Row suggest that the black bourgeoisie, when put to the test, considered itself more bourgeois than black. There are, for example, the revealing comments by the wife of William Pickens—the civil rights leader who later praised Father Divine's efforts for integration. Mrs. Pickens forcefully explained the objections of her fellow residents in tones reflecting fear for hard-earned property values and status:

> Shouting and singing draw crowds, and everybody knows that a crowd makes a place public and common and lowers the tone of a residential block. It is not that we feel that we are better or a group apart from any other group. We are simply trying to prove to the world that a group of Negroes can keep up a model residential block. Property is bound to depreciate with all this hue and cry, and some of us, like my family, have got every cent we have invested in these walls. Do you blame us for protesting?[11]

Despite this eloquent effort to identify opposition to the Peace Mission with the greater good of the Negro race, others in the black community were skeptical. It was, after all, something of an embarrassment to blacks, particularly the more affluent elements active in seeking civil rights, to indulge in their own segregating and discriminating rituals. A guest columnist in the *Amsterdam News* lamented the actions of "society hypocrites" and asked "what the result will be when a Negro takes his next segregation case to court."[12] Another scathing protest against the snobbery of Striver's Row also noted the economic folly of excluding a financially solvent group from the opportunity to patronize black professionals:

> How dare Father Divine and his uncouth horde to descend upon that thoroughfare of culture known as Striver's Row? Not long ago most of the aristocrats of the Striver's clan were doing menial labor for a living, but that makes no difference and Father Divine should realize that they are his betters. If the dear father desires social equality he should send the sick of his horde to white doctors and let colored doctors starve.[13]

The strife at Striver's Row suggests that zeal for minority rights often stops at the edge of class consciousness as abruptly as it pauses before race prejudice. For Father Divine, who cared for the most underprivileged souls in the ghetto, this meant enduring the role of perpetual outsider among its "better elements," despite making their rights a prime focus of his concern.

Father Divine and the Struggle for Civil Rights

Even from the periphery of established black society, Father Divine's ministry substantially aided the development of new religious patterns in the ghettos. His ability to attract congregants from the conventional churches helped awaken pastors to the need for practical social programs to benefit the masses. So, too, did the fact that lay leaders frequently lauded his ministry as a model of civil rights activism to which other clergymen should aspire. Thus, while Divine largely failed to gain the clergy's personal approval, he determined their manner of rivalry with him: only by extending their commitments to racial equality and care for the poor could these ministers maintain their stature in the black community.

Father Divine's burgeoning influence in the ghettos was a source of consternation and, at times, sober reflection for ministers of the regular churches. Some concluded, with Baptist Reverend Miles Mark Fisher, that movements such as the Peace Mission were in some respects more progressive than the conventional denominations and that "the churches have much to learn from the cults."[14] A Methodist pastor in Little Grove, Pennsylvania, told his presiding elder, "We have got to take some lessons from Father Divine. . . . He is feeding the people, and that is what He [Jesus] meant for us to do."[15] At a New York ministers' conference a Methodist bishop urged his colleagues to "use more the technique of Father Divine," warning, "You can't defeat Father Divine by mere criticism, we must get more of his spirit."[16]

The chorus of hosannas for Father Divine in clerical circles was admittedly confined to a very small choir. More often, ministers fearful of Divine's inroads into their congregations thundered against him from their pulpits in the manner of Bishop Lawson or the Reverend White. Yet most soon discovered that they could not curb his popular appeal by ministerial maledictions alone. As long as Divine remained in the vanguard of clerical activists for racial advancement, he could continue freely to gather disaffected churchgoers under his banner.

Divine's impermeability to clerical venom is revealed in the sobering experience of L. K. Williams, president of the National Baptist Convention. At the organization's national meeting in Philadelphia in 1939, Williams devoted part of his keynote address to a denunciation of the Peace Mission. He urged ministers to "indoctrinate" their followers against Father Divine's influence and warned, "You cannot build a religion on a bread and butter brigade." Williams received hearty applause but, to his acute embarrassment, could not prevent scores of attending Baptist pastors from flocking to the nearby Peace Mission center throughout the week in order to avail themselves of the inexpensive food and lodgings. For 15 cents these preachers, many of them living on very modest earnings, enjoyed meals at the Peace Mission as nourishing as the ones which the convention sold for 50 cents.[17] The episode led Harlem's leading journal to inquire whether the old, purely spiritual orientation of the black churches any longer sufficed in the changing ghetto communities.[18]

In the face of considerable mass support for the Peace Mission, even the highest ranks of the clergy failed to maintain a fully solid front against Father Divine. Two years after the Baptist embarrassment in Philadelphia, the denomination convened to choose a successor to L. K. Williams, the victim of a plane crash in late summer 1941. One of the two candidates for the office, J. C. Austin of Chicago, sought to enhance his dim chances by consulting Father Divine and asking his blessing.[19] Austin's action drew predictable rebukes from many Baptist leaders, and he eventually met a sound defeat by his rival, whose home state of Alabama provided over 40 percent of the convention delegates.[20] Yet the fact that a man so important in the black Baptist hierarchy courted Divine's aid suggests the mystique this cult leader projected even among circles generally hostile to his ministry.

Pastors could no more rely on lay support to help curtail Divine's influence than they could count on a united clerical front or the loyalty of their own congregants. The clergy of Bronzeville in Chicago discovered this truth in shattering fashion when they attempted to prevent Father

Divine from visiting their neighborhoods. Their intervention with Chicago's political leaders drew a crushing public reproach from Bronzeville's mayor, Robert Miller. He defended Father Divine's "religion of the human ideal and the good social order" and condemned the protests against him as the "detestable" work of a group of "religious parasites." Miller wondered, too, if these clergymen feared "that the coming of Father Divine is powerful enough to open the eyes of their congregations. . . . Father Divine has a program — what have those who would like to keep him out of Chicago?"[21]

A substantial number of lay leaders within the black community to some degree shared Miller's assessment. It may at first appear inconsistent that Divine's support should have come chiefly from the laity, since few indeed professed kinship with his religious tenets or approved — any more than most ministers — of the cultlike enthusiasm of his followers. Yet because these leaders had little vested interest in preserving existing church hierarchies, they favored socially progressive movements like the Peace Mission despite the "subversive" character often attached to them.

Among those impressed by Divine's accomplishment was W. E. B. Du Bois, pre-eminent among civil rights activists during the early twentieth century. After visiting Krum Elbow in 1942, Du Bois reserved judgment on whether the Peace Mission's methods held "any promise of permanency," but left no doubt as to the movement's positive character:

> Certainly the Father Divine movement differs from numbers of religious cults. It is not noisy and obtrusive. It does do a great deal (just how much no one knows) of charity in feeding people and giving them work. It is (and this is most curious of all) interracial; and interracial among people of the laboring and middle-class. . . . It can certainly be said that of the various religious movements of our day, there is least in this that one may criticize; and as a social movement there can be no question but that it has helped many people who need help. . . .[22]

Du Bois's generally laudatory reaction to the Peace Mission corresponds with his conception of a minister as a wide-ranging executive concerned equally with temporal and spiritual matters. His idealized portrayal of the black preacher in *The Souls of Black Folk,* written forty years before his visit to Krum Elbow, might well be taken for a summary of Father Divine's ministry:

> The preacher is the most unique personality developed by the Negro on American soil. A leader, a politician, an orator, a "boss," an intriguer, an idealist, — all these he is, and ever, too, the centre of a group of men, now twenty, now a thousand in number. The combination of a certain adroitness with deep-seated earnestness, of tact with

consummate ability, gave him his preëminence, and helps him maintain it.[23]

Du Bois may well have seen in Divine a revival of that versatile social leadership which had long imparted to the church its pervasive importance in black communal life.

The black lay leaders who praised Divine frequently shared little ideological affinity beyond their mutual interest in securing racial advancement. Some, like James Egert Allen, president of the NAACP's New York chapter, focused on Divine's work in the area of social rights. Allen wrote Divine in 1942 "to congratulate you on your achievements and trust that you will continue to point the way of true democracy to those most in need of it." He added his appreciation "for your continued efforts to enact an anti-lynching bill."[24]

Others emphasized the Peace Mission's economic progress as a major basis for their support of the movement. George Schuyler, the foremost black journalist who combined a wide interest in racial problems with a devastating satirical style, exemplified this group of well-wishers. He had long crusaded for measures to ease the plight of the poorer classes, from welfare to cooperativism. Though generally disdainful toward religious institutions for their backwardness on social issues, Schuyler made an exception of Father Divine's ministry:

> The obvious reason for his fame is that he really has a great message and program for the world. . . . People were hungry, so he fed them. No cards to fill out. No embarrassing questions to answer. No petty officials to keep you standing in line. You just sat down and ate. This made poor people — poor in body and in spirit — happy. They sang and shouted, while those who despised them ridiculed the activities. . . . Through economic co-operation with a Christian basis, Father Divine's followers own scores of [businesses]. . . . Who else has done more, or even nearly as much? And yet there are people who laugh![25]

Many blacks, whether or not they fully approved of Father Divine's work, defended him out of a sense of racial solidarity. They perceived him as a prominent target of prejudice because he dared to show independence of wealth and spirit in a white-dominated society. Even Adam Clayton Powell, who disliked wasting a kind word on Divine, once complained that white society was not treating him justly.[26] With more sustained enthusiasm, Roy Wilkins described Divine as a decent man whose success and assertiveness exceeded the fragile tolerance levels of the average American. He lamented that "the good little father" had forgotten that anyone who tried "to bring the two races together on a plane of equality [was] subject to suspicion and perhaps to persecution."[27]

If civil rights leaders like Wilkins grieved at the injustices Divine suffered, others displayed a vicarious pride in his ability to thwart racist officials and invert the usual social and economic hierarchies. William Pickens
of the NAACP, who had little personal regard for the Peace Mission's
religious principles, nevertheless gleefully reviewed Father Divine's artful
maneuvers against lawyers probing his source of funds. "There may be
shrewder men than Father Divine," Pickens exulted, "but they are not in
the New York office of the United States Revenue Service." As for Divine,
he was a serenely heroic rebel against the white power structure, "all the
time . . . smilingly good-natured and polite, never excited, never 'rattled',
— as imperturbable as the deity or the devil." Then Pickens abandoned
all pretense of objectivity as he relished Divine's mockery of white
supremacy:

> Generations to come will laugh about how this little bald-headed
> black man of the twentieth century "spiritually" and financially van-
> quished an arrogant revenue agent. Marcus Garvey was a phenome-
> non, but he was not half way to Divine; Garvey made God black,
> and the Devil white. That was revolutionary in an age of Nordic
> gospel.
> But Father Divine has not simply made God black; he has made
> a black man God, — and a humble American lynchable black man at
> that. Garvey had black devotees to worship his black God; Divine
> has white men to bow to his deified Black Man. "Peace" — to every-
> body except the internal revenue collector. For "It is indeed wonder-
> ful!"[28]

The press in the black community tended to reinforce the positive view
that civil rights activists expressed toward Father Divine. A greater
ambivalence obtained here, because the flamboyance of the cult leader
and the excesses of his followers invited sensational headlines and condescending feature columns. The press also had a stake in covering the
activities of the ghetto's conventional churches and maintaining good
standing with their pastors and parishioners. Yet, on balance, the major
journals, especially Harlem's own *Amsterdam News,* sympathetically portrayed Divine's efforts to establish a socially conscious religion.

The most eloquent editorial tribute to Father Divine came from the *Pittsburgh Courier,* the most respected weekly journal in the black community,
which usually took the high road regarding cult figures — by ignoring them.
This aloofness traced to the journal's relatively restrained format but also
to the absence in Pittsburgh of exotic leaders on the order of a Father
Divine, Daddy Grace, or Rosa Horn. Yet even the *Courier* took note of
Father Divine's contribution to the underprivileged. In 1937 — notwithstanding Divine's deepening legal woes — the *Courier* admiringly described

"Divine's Challenge to the Church." It noted that while Divine's movement "may not be 'respectable', . . . it is certainly tackling problems of the greatest importance to poor people, regardless of color, and making a pretty good job of it."[29]

Father Divine, of course, had his detractors among the laity, as did virtually every contemporary black leader from Du Bois to the junior Powell. Tactical misjudgments, such as his vacillations in electoral politics, and personal excesses, seen to greatest disadvantage in his messianic posturing, alienated many potential allies. So, too, did his embrace of a baffling variety of controversial causes from chastity to faith healing, all having at best a dubious relationship to black welfare. In this he recalled those antebellum reformers who seemed to multiply panaceas over the years, impeding a full devotion of energy to any one goal. Yet in Divine's case, what is remarkable about most of his far-ranging activities is the extent to which they were guided by the end of achieving racial equality. A broad spectrum of eminent black spokesmen, who otherwise felt little attachment to the Peace Mission, were prepared, like Du Bois, Wilkins, and others, to commend Divine's ministry on the basis of this central, common concern.

Divine himself recognized that his actions were a frequent focus of debate on the direction of clerical leadership in the ghettos, and he offered perhaps the most incisive apologia for his legacy as a minister preaching salvation in this world. While he refrained from attacking any clergyman by name, he observed the central fallacy of those religious leaders who anticipated heavenly reward in redemption for present bondage:

> I would not give five cents for a God who could not help me here on the earth, for such a God is not a God at hand. He is only an imagination. It is a false delusion — trying to make you think you had just as well go ahead and suffer and be enslaved and be lynched and everything else here, and after a while you are going to Heaven someplace. If God cannot prepare Heaven here for you, you are not going anywhere.[30]

Divine thus crystallized the premise underlying all his activities as leader of the Peace Mission: the belief that an oppressed people could not productively separate religion from the struggle for social justice.

In all, Father Divine reflected and helped foster the growing militance among urban blacks during the Depression. He set a formidable standard of social activism that other ministers, keenly aware of his fast-spreading popularity, increasingly sought to match, whether to emulate or compete with him. At the same time, by aiding and uniting the most disadvantaged elements of ghetto society, he reminded middle-class Negroes that racial justice rested as much on alleviating poverty and unemployment as on eliminating Jim Crow practices. His ministry thus formed a distinctive part of the process by which black religious leaders moved from an era of absorbing spirituality to one of vital commitment to the struggle for equality. It was a trend whose influence on race relations in America was to become ever more visible—and decisive—in succeeding decades.

Notes to Chapter 8

1. Adam Clayton Powell, Jr., "The Soapbox," *NYAN,* June 6, 1936, p. 12.
2. Wilfrid Rankin, "The Watchtower," *NYAN,* June 13, 1936, p. 12.
3. E. Franklin Frazier, *Black Bourgeoisie: The Rise of a New Middle Class* (New York: Free Press, 1957), p. 209.
4. Ralph Mathews, "Watching the Big Parade," *AA,* Dec. 1, 1934, p. 4. See also a similarly acerbic essay by Mathews on Father Divine, in ibid., Jan. 8, 1938, p. 4.
5. *AA,* Apr. 8, 1933, p. 6.
6. Interview given by Father Divine to the Reverends J. A. Manning and C. J. Gadsden, High Falls, Oct. 29, 1938, in *ND,* Sept. 30, 1978, p. 6.
7. *AA,* Dec. 2, 1933, p. 12.
8. *NYAN,* June 6, 1936, p. 1, quoting the Reverend W. L. Johnson of the Allen A.M.E. Church in Philadelphia.
9. *NYAN,* Mar. 12, 1938, p. 1.
10. See, for example, ibid., Nov. 15, 1941, p. 13, on the end of a bitter feud between Powell and the Reverend Thomas Harten. The senior Powell admitted to amazement that the two actually reconciled.
11. *NYAN,* July 21, 1934, p. 2.
12. Eugene D. Johnson, "Divine's Invasion," *NYAN,* Sept. 1, 1934, p. 8.
13. Stanley Deas, letter to *NYAN,* July 28, 1934, p. 8.
14. Fisher, "Organized Religion and the Cults," p. 10.
15. Matthew H. Nutter of A.M.E. Church, Little Grove, Pa., Feb. 4, 1941, in *ND,* Feb. 13, 1941, p. 49.
16. Bishop W. J. Walls, quoted in *PC,* Feb. 21, 1942, p. 15.
17. *NYAN,* Sept. 16, 1939, p. 1.
18. "Divine and the Baptists," editorial, *NYAN,* Oct. 7, 1939, p. 6.
19. *AA,* Sept. 6, 1941, p. 1.
20. "Dr. Austin and Father Divine," editorial, *AA,* Sept. 6, 1941, p. 4; *AA,* Sept. 20, 1941, p. 1. See also Father Divine to J. C. Austin, Sept. 9, 1941, in *ND,* Sept. 18, 1941, p. 89.
21. Robert H. Miller, "This Week with the Mayor of Bronzeville," *CD,* Sept. 2, 1939, in *ND,* Sept. 14, 1939, pp. 99-100. This article was not printed in the edition of the *Defender* put on microfilm; in view of the otherwise great exactitude shown by the *New Day* in quoting other sources, it is plausible that Miller's essay did appear in another edition of the Bronzeville journal. See also Robert H. Miller to Father Divine, Sept. 8, 1939, and Father Divine to Robert H. Miller, Sept. 11, 1939, both in *ND,* Sept. 14, 1939, p. 99.
22. W. E. B. Du Bois, "As the Crow Flies," *NYAN,* May 23, 1942, p. 6.
23. W. E. B. Du Bois, *The Souls of Black Folk* (Philadelphia: A. C. McClurg, 1903), pp. 190-91.

24. James Egert Allen to Father Divine, Apr. 9, 1942, in *ND,* Apr. 16, 1942, p. 62.

25. George Schuyler, "Views and Reviews," *PC,* Sept. 12, 1942, p. 13.

26. Adam Clayton Powell, Jr., "The Soapbox," *NYAN,* May 1, 1937, p. 12.

27. Roy Wilkins, "The Watchtower," *NYAN,* May 1, 1937, p. 12.

28. *AA,* Oct. 10, 1936, p. 9.

29. "Divine's Challenge to the Church," editorial, *PC,* Mar. 27, 1937, sec. 1, p. 10.

30. Sermon of Feb. 20, 1938, in *ND,* Mar. 3, 1938, p. 20.

Angela Drennen observed a striking and perhaps not incidental resemblance between this photograph of Father Divine and the pose President Roosevelt made famous in this period.

Arriving in Philadelphia, September, 1939. Although black ministers objected to his visit, crowds gathered wherever Divine appeared.

In the "Promised Land," Ulster County, New York.

In the late 1930s, Father Divine urged Americans to repel Nazism everywhere.

Signing a petition, sponsored by the Peace Mission in 1940, to support pending anti-lynching legislation.

With Mother Divine, taken during the early 1960s.

CHAPTER 9

American Reformer

Father Divine was unique among black cult figures of the Depression in that he had a national impact as a reform leader. He enjoyed a following of affluent, educated whites as well as poor urban blacks. His activities were covered in leading national journals and in the black press. He exchanged views on issues of race relations with prominent political figures. Most important, he had greater success in lifting followers from poverty and in breaking down the color line, in white suburbs and black ghettos, than any other religious leader of the day.

One major reason that Father Divine exerted such influence is that he, more than any other of the ghetto's innumerable cultists, built on a faith in American society and its capacity for peaceful change. By referring often to the nation's democratic values, as embodied by the Constitution and the Declaration of Independence, he struck a responsive chord among blacks and whites. By asserting that a growing American idealism could overcome even racism and poverty, he conveyed a present-centered hope perfectly suited to an era marked by both social crisis and buoyant reform leadership.

Father Divine denied being a "race leader" and claimed instead to be an emissary of democracy. Still, in voicing his belief in the validity of the American dream, he seemed to capture the prevalent mood among Afro-Americans as well. With whatever admixture of cynicism stemming from long oppression, black Americans clung to the hope of a brighter future in America, even as they felt intensely the gap between an idealized land of opportunity and the reality of a caste-ridden society.

The vision of a color-blind democracy, such as moved Father Divine, was a basic theme among activists and opinion molders in the black community. Leaders in the NAACP and the Urban League, numerous journalists, educators, and progressive clergymen worked from the premise that America could change for the better. This attitude found expression even among impassioned black writers who, especially in the years after World War I, sought to articulate the new pride and persistent anguish of an entire race. The brooding and brilliant poet Langston Hughes captured such sentiments in depicting America as

> The land that never has been yet —
> And yet must be —
> The land where *every* man is free. . . .
> Its dream
> Lies deep in the heart of me.[1]

If Father Divine traced the source of this dream to divine revelation, that, too, accorded with the cultural style of the black community. Jean Toomer's winding, rhapsodic verses in *The Blue Meridian* typify how the yearning of black people for a just America slipped naturally into a religious reverie:

> It is a new America,
> To be spiritualized by each new American. . . .

"The old gods," Toomer added in a verse that might have served as the text for many a sermon by Father Divine, ". . . [w]ithdrew into the distance and died" in favor of a new God, one who would help people become Americans, "Not to mouth the label but to live the reality."[2] Indeed, to Peace Mission disciples, Father Divine personified that active, caring deity, under whose guidance blacks and whites, together, would create the "New America."

Divine, Garvey and the Question of Black Nationalism

Father Divine's American nationalism distinguished him even from the minority of cultists who shared his focus on issues of race and oppression. While contemporary cults like the Nation of Islam and the Church of God (Black Muslims and Black Jews) retreated from white society, Divine pressed the integration of his followers into the mainstream of national life. Despite Divine's avowed faith in America, though, he was also known for attracting many former disciples of Marcus Garvey, the premier black separatist figure of an earlier era.

Garvey had shattered the outward complacency of the ghettos in the early twenties with his spellbinding appeals for black unity and the regeneration of the blacks' true homeland, Africa. But his imprisonment in 1925 (tracing to financial irregularities) and deportation two years later left thousands of disciples in every large ghetto craving a successor to his dynamic leadership. Some former members of Garvey's United Negro Improvement Association (UNIA) joined offshoots of their old movement or new separatist groups like the Nation of Islam. Other, dispirited ex-Garveyites entered nonideological movements such as Daddy Grace's House of Prayer. But perhaps the greatest bloc of former disciples turned to the Peace Mission,[3] although Divine abhorred the racial separatism Garvey encouraged.

This seeming paradox reflects both the complex motives for joining a social movement and the inevitable similarities between organizations responding to the common heritage and hardships of lower-class urban blacks. A contemporary writer on Harlem, Roi Ottley, speculated that the overlapping appeal of Garvey and Divine traced to common "escapist" elements in their movements,[4] an observation that captured a part of the truth. Yet while Divine's ministry built on the techniques through which Garvey had drawn the ghetto's masses, he directed their hopes in ways ultimately at odds with the black nationalist vision Garvey proclaimed.

The UNIA, like the later Peace Mission, was a multifaceted social movement with a pronounced evangelical Christian character. Chaplains were prominent among the UNIA leadership, Christian hymns were integral features of UNIA meetings, and members often remarked on the spiritual enthusiasm that the rallies generated. It was also widely noted that Garvey and his aides thoroughly entwined their pan-African exhortations with biblical imagery.[5]

The two movements also shared a cultlike devotion to their respective leaders. Garvey and Divine were both objects of frenzied adulation by their masses of disciples, and were equally zealous as well as skillful in encouraging such displays. Garvey, like Divine, a short but magnetic individual with a compelling speaking manner, mesmerized audiences and made his own personality the unifying center of his movement. It is true that Garvey did not hint at divinity as did Father Divine; in later years, as he saw many former adherents turning to the Peace Mission, he lashed out at Divine's "blasphemy" in setting himself up as a false god.[6] Yet in his prime Garvey had been his own best hagiographer. He freely superimposed the life of Jesus with his own career, noting their common radicalism and suffering.[7] He encouraged the crowds who hailed him as the savior of the Negro race and even wore colorful military attire, complete with decorative sword, to perfect the image of a liberating prince. That Garvey passed up the title of "God" in favor of "Provisional President of Africa" may well indicate not so much modesty as the relative emphases he accorded politics and religion.

Both Divine and Garvey drew upon their charisma to generate self-respect and a feeling of community among the most disadvantaged ghetto residents. Divine spoke often of how the need of "the most underprivileged" made them greatest before God, who "will hear their simplest cry."[8] Garvey, too, exhorted followers never to lose confidence in themselves, for "God Almighty created each and every one of us for a place in the world."[9] Similarly, the shared rituals of each movement reminded disciples that they were part of a much greater social entity that recognized their common humanity and worth.

Parallels between the UNIA and the Peace Mission extended to a concern, far exceeding that of most cult movements, to provide tangible benefits for their members. While the Peace Mission gained lasting loyalties by offering food and shelter, the UNIA filled the more conventional functions of black fraternal orders, drawing from members' dues to assure sums of money to their families in event of sickness or death. E. David Cronon quotes Garvey's widow, Amy Jacques-Garvey, in explaining that this arrangement "was the easiest means of reaching the common man, who wanted security in his distress; hand him this first, then tell him of the spiritual, racial benefits that would come in time."[10]

Uplift through economic enterprise also ranked high on the list of UNIA aims, foreshadowing Peace Mission concerns a decade later. The UNIA set up the Negro Factories Corporation in 1919, with a $1 million capitalization, to "build and operate factories in the big industrial centers of the United States, Central America, the West Indies and Africa to manufacture every marketable commodity."[11] Just as the Peace Mission in the thirties sought to give its members economic independence, so the earlier UNIA program asked members to support its cooperative enterprises "in order to insure steady and profitable employment for their sons and daughters."[12]

Beyond these specific similarities, the UNIA and the Peace Mission shared an ambivalent view of society that reflected their dual character as cults and reform movements. The cultlike qualities were evident not simply in the veneration of a charismatic leader but in the way each movement became the vital center of existence for many emotionally rootless converts. Typically the disciple derived his beliefs and values from cult preachings, planned his daily routine around cult meetings and projects, limited his social contacts to fellow members. Even his financial welfare was connected to the enterprises and largesse of the cult organization. In effect, the disciple offered total devotion to his movement in exchange for absolute security. Unsurprisingly, many former followers of the UNIA could move to the Peace Mission scarcely troubled by differences of doctrine, because the new affiliation required no adjustment in their basic mentality. Indeed, it permitted none.

At one level, then, the UNIA and the Peace Mission functioned like virtually every other cult: to insulate members from a society they found deeply troubling. On another level, they attempted much more. Each movement tried to guide its newly inspired disciples to raise their social status and to challenge the inequities that mired the great majority of members in second-class citizenship. Here one could see the same utopian passion at work in Garvey and Divine as they focused the often nebulous yearnings of their charges into ideologies of social change.

Divine shared with Garvey some doctrines of racial uplift often associated with black separatists — indeed, their range of agreement was far broader than either Garvey or Divine ever acknowledged. Both the Garveyites and the Divinites rejected traditional Western images of a white god, and rejected, too, the racist attitudes that fostered such images. They spurred disciples to cultivate both psychological and financial independence, and they envisioned a society free of racial oppression.

For his part, Garvey sometimes promoted his ideas on black progress in terms of conservative American values such as Father Divine later exalted. Garvey's advocacy of business development, for example, seemed on occasion as much a calculated homage to the booming twenties and the Gospel of Wealth as a call to race solidarity. Biographer Cronon notes a revealing stock circular for Garvey's most famous enterprise, the Black Star Line steamship company, that appealed to ghetto dwellers in terms that might have garnered warm approval from Andrew Carnegie: "The Black Star Line Corporation presents to every Black Man, Woman, and Child the opportunity to climb the great ladder of industrial and commercial progress. . . . The Black Star Line will turn over large profits and dividends to stockholders, and operate to their interest even whilst they will be asleep."[13]

In political matters, too, Garvey at least nominally included traditional civil rights aims in his eclectic political program. The UNIA's declaration of Negro rights, drawn up at a mass rally in New York in 1920 that anticipated the Peace Mission's Righteous Government Convention, added to its primary resolutions for pan-African unity planks condemning enforced segregation, lynching, and "limitations of political privileges of any Negro citizen in any part of the world."[14]

Perhaps the most significant common denominator of the two movements is that both advanced a theology of social action, enriching an aspect of Afro-American religion that had been muted but never extinguished. Garvey stressed that God never intended that any person "should descend to the level of a peon, a serf, or a slave. . . . These different classes God never created. He created MAN."[15] He told his disciples that because they were formed in God's image they had "the same common rights, and today I trust that there will be a spiritual and material resurrection among Negroes everywhere. . . ."[16]

Of course, the details of the two leaders' theologies reflected their divergent concerns and programs. Garvey justified black separatism and any action needed to free Africa by pointing to a common God and destiny for black people, while Divine emphasized interracial harmony and non-violence based on his view of mankind's common spiritual nature. As a minister with pantheistic leanings, Divine came to personify God for his followers and to see Providence in all events; Garvey, less sure of God's immanence, cast himself as intermediary for the divine will, while vacillating between depicting God as an unfailing ally of his cause and as interested in spiritual but not physical matters. "God does not interfere," he once distilled this latter, grimmer view of history, "and that should be the Negro's interpretation in this twentieth century of Christ's religion."[17]

Garvey was consistent, though in his theme of liberation rather than his theological framework. The important element in his religion, like Divine's, was to avoid the old passivity associated with the Negro church. "To lead and be spiritual," he preached, "does not mean that we must be all humility and obliging . . . we must resist, yet not resist; we must fight, yet not fight; we must be JUST."[18] Essentially, whatever encouraged the Negro to assert his rights was for Garvey good theology, whether that placed God in the remote heavens or at the head of a UNIA parade.

There were, in short, ample bridges of culture, doctrine, and outlook that aided passage from Garvey's UNIA to Divine's Peace Mission. Whether a person joined for evangelical ecstasy, escape (or more positively, independence) from society, self-esteem, racial equality—or likely some combination of these—the new disciple might find fulfillment in either organization.

Still, in terms of the impact the UNIA and the Peace Mission had as American reform movements, their conflicting perspectives of white, American society proved a crucial divide. Garvey's belief that blacks had to work out their aims apart from whites precluded vigorous pursuit of the integrationist goals central to most civil rights leaders, including Divine. His insistence on strictly black membership in the UNIA and investment in its financial projects further reduced his influence beyond the ghettos. It deprived him of a core of politically liberal whites such as provided needed skills and funds to the Peace Mission. In fact, Garvey courted as white "allies" mainly such extremists as the Ku Klux Klan, which he praised for candidly espousing the white man's view of blacks and for agreeing with his aim of sending blacks to Africa.[19]

Garvey's advocacy of racial separatism and his claims that Africa represented the only true home for black people checked his influence even in the black community. His program enjoyed far less black middle-class approval than Divine's, a weakness he exacerbated by intemperate exchanges with critics like W. E. B. Du Bois. Moreover, Garvey's focus on African colonization absorbed much of his time, money, and energy without ever achieving substantial black emigration.

While steep financial, diplomatic, and logistical obstacles all undermined Garvey's ambitious plans to transport millions to Africa, an underlying problem was his severe misreading of Afro-American attitudes. Many blacks cheered Garvey as a liberator, but of these only a few intellectuals fully shared his vision of restoring the black man's African heritage. The vast majority certainly had little desire to "return" to Africa. As a result, Garvey's resettlement projects developed importance chiefly as a symbol of black pride in the face of white racism, without ever having a reasonable chance of fulfillment.

By contrast, Father Divine's own colonizing venture, which he viewed as a symbol of his wider integrationist program, was at once less ambitious and more attuned to mass sentiment. In setting up rural communes on American soil, Divine aimed not to return to a particular land, thousands of miles and contingencies away, but to land *per se* — to decent living space for those in crowded slums, to farm work for those idle in the cities. In every way Divine built his utopian world out of conservative materials — careful investments by white and black members, avoidance of debt, self-sustaining economic communities, and an ideological heartland within driving distance of his disciples. Implicit in his direction of the entire interracial colonizing project, as in all his undertakings, was the faith that black Americans could free themselves of the ghetto without having to renounce their native land. In the last analysis, Divine appeared less an inheritor of Garvey's vision than a determined practical critic.

It remains to explain why Father Divine, rather than Garvey or other cultists concerned to improve black welfare, held such confidence in the American people and their political system. One possible reason is that Divine reached the height of his influence and formulated the bulk of his social tenets after 1932: that is, after the advent of Franklin Roosevelt and the New Deal, an upturn in civil rights activism, a rise in black political power generally, and a resurgence by the black church as a progressive social force. By contrast, the Garvey movement and most Black Jewish sects first flourished after World War I, when racism was resurgent and the rise of the ghettos seemed more salient than that of the civil rights movement. The Nation of Islam was a more recent creation, but its sullen, angry withdrawal from the larger society occurred in the first bitter and bewildering years of the Depression. Therefore, to the extent that the cults reflected their times, only the Peace Mission clearly derived its social attitudes from a relatively liberal political climate, one which increasingly took account of black needs and demands.

Father Divine's inveterate manic temperament, leading him to seek the positive in any situation or experience, offers a further clue to his confi-

dence that he could change America. It was characteristic of his temperament that while many black separatists rejected Christianity as a tool of
white American oppression, Divine found in it a source of inner strength
for ending all oppression. In the same way, his reading of American political documents like the Declaration of Independence did not simply produce cynicism at the disparities with actual conditions but inspired a fervent
belief that he could make those documents a living reality.

Personal circumstance also helped confirm Divine's optimism about
American society. He seems to have been highly anomalous among the
black cultists in that he had already acquired considerable success in
America before becoming a major religious and social figure. Suburban
comforts, an integrated environment, and, perhaps most important, the
respect of white neighbors—all were his a full decade before he extended
his ministry to the ghetto poor.

There is, finally, the factor of birth. It is perhaps significant that a high
proportion of black nationalist cult leaders—including Rabbi Wentworth
Matthew of the main Black Jewish sect, Wali Farrad of the Black Muslims, and of course the Jamaican-born Marcus Garvey—were of foreign
origin. On the one hand, this afforded a detachment helpful in discerning
and freely discussing the racial injustices that most black cultists ignored.
At the same time, their relatively brief immersion in the mythology of
the American dream left them without any sustaining vision of a country
ripe for reform. The misery of the ghettos likely seemed to them as indicative of a hopelessly racist society as any they had seen abroad. Therefore
these leaders either assumed a largely passive vigil for an American racial
apocalypse or worked toward a distant pan-African ideal of social change.

In contrast to Garvey, Farrad, and Matthew, Father Divine was American by birth, experience, and outlook. He once retorted, upon learning
of a southern senator's plan to send blacks "back" to Africa, that no other
group but the American Indian had deeper roots in this country than the
Afro-American.[20] The United States was his homeland and the source of
his social and cultural heritage. It was also, for a man who read Jefferson
seriously, a birthright to freedom and fair opportunity. Although often
denied in the past to those of his dark skin, it was nevertheless far too
precious to sell for a foreign-based ideal or simply give away in isolated
wait for a better day to come. Instead Father Divine made it the central
goal of his Peace Mission movement to bring that birthright to its full,
long-belated redemption.

Radical Reformers of the Depression

Father Divine's career best illustrates a recurring pattern in American
reform leadership, particularly among those seeming radicals who work

outside the two-party system yet invoke mainstream values and call for change through traditional institutions. This reform tradition encompasses groups as diverse as antebellum abolitionists, agrarian agitators of the late nineteenth century, and civil rights militants in recent times. All have blended moralism and a largely single-issue path to utopia with a conservative's faith in the basic soundness of American society.[21] Indeed, the exemplars of this pattern have often served as the moral shock troops for reform programs later adopted by more conventional partisan forces.

The durability of this reform tradition emerged with especial clarity during the trying years of the Depression. Despite fears for the survival of liberal capitalism in America, no extremist movement ever became a significant factor in national politics. Fascist groups, though numbering in the hundreds, generally consisted of "little more than a fanatic and a letterhead."[22] Left-wing parties made somewhat more of an impression, particularly among intellectuals, but they were too widely viewed as bearers of foreign, subversive doctrines to develop a mass following. The communists, in particular, failed to adjust to the domestic political pressures of American society, fatally conditioned as they were to observing the last *nyet* of Kremlin dictates.

By contrast, the most successful insurgent political movements of the Depression deftly balanced radical proposals with conservative rhetoric. Foremost was the network of Share Our Wealth Clubs, counting 6 million members and led by Senator Huey Long from Louisiana, who proposed to make all Americans affluent through redistributive income taxes. The National Union for Social Justice championed the way of monetary expansion under Father Charles Coughlin of Michigan, whose lilting Irish brogue came by radio into some 10 million homes weekly to discuss God and free silver coinage. Finally, a movement of several million dues-paying members lobbied for a pension plan offered by Francis Townsend, a California doctor, designed to end want and insecurity among the elderly.[23]

Each of these movements contended with daunting liabilities. Despite their national scope, they drew on a limited core constituency — Long's poor rural southerners, Coughlin's midwestern ethnic workers, Townsend's aged poor. Each of their programs suffered appalling deficiencies of economic analysis, ignoring the dangers of unchecked inflation and overrating the curative powers of narrowly based reform measures. And at least two of the three leaders were transparently unscrupulous and opportunistic: Long, who ran Louisiana like a dictator, and Coughlin, with his lightning changes of view and his forays into anti-Semitic lore. Yet as separate crusades and as joint sponsors of a presidential ticket in 1936, these movements overshadowed all other challenges to the major parties.

These three movements bid for respectability in American politics by offering repeated assurances that their aims accorded fully with national virtues and traditions. In contrast to the fascists, they expressed a concern for individual freedom. Unlike the communists and socialists, they proffered simple remedies, free of abstruse doctrine, for immediate and widely felt grievances. They also projected an optimism about the prospects for peaceful change that imbued them with an aura of political purpose and energy few other dissenting groups could match.

While Father Divine in no way compared with Long, Coughlin, or Townsend in influence or priorities, as a reformer he shared their concern to wrap even the boldest calls for change in a respect for national tradition. In particular, four crucial common values informed their welter of platforms and proposals, reflecting an underlying conservatism typical of native "radical" movements in the Depression. All of these leaders, including Divine, identified their aims with the larger cause of democracy itself; they accepted the broad outlines of capitalist enterprise; they extolled a special American destiny; and they tied a largely secular program to a broadly inclusive, Judeo-Christian ethic. If all of their movements were in some respects utopian, still they carefully adjusted their range of vision in order to appear as defenders of a distinctly American faith.

To elude the brand of "extremist," each of the three mass leaders periodically sounded the tocsin of imperiled democracy and offered himself as its firmest champion. Coughlin described his National Union for Social Justice as a nationwide "lobby of the people"[24] against a plutocratic conspiracy, while Long promised to guard the economic rights of 99 percent of the people against the depredations of very few fortune holders.[25] Francis Townsend similarly depicted his old-age pension plan not as an exercise in interest-group politics but as a "national recovery program" to promote democracy and benefit the entire American people. His plan would be enacted, he predicted, "when the citizenry . . . take charge of their government."[26]

Father Divine mirrored these efforts to convey an identity of aims between a specific reform program and American democratic principles. "By following the standard of my Righteous Government Platform, men have a righteous weapon of defense," he said, and quickly added: "and not only so, but they have the national sword of the Constitution and its amendments as their protection. By these two great documents combined, I am bringing all men on one common level."[27] He intended as well to give "a new birth" to the Declaration of Independence, which had often been treated as "nothing but a mockery, yet it is good and it is powerful."[28] Divine likened his methods to "evolution, not revolution," urging supporters to change America in the democratic way, "by the ballot, not by the bullet."[29]

Another imperative for any vaguely leftist group in the thirties seeking to escape an extremist image was to dissociate itself from any socialist and communist aims. Coughlin decisively overreacted to the problem by castigating the immensely popular president as a man under communist domination.[30] Huey Long's campaign book of "memoirs," *My First Days in the White House,* contained a passage given equally to surrealism and self-indulgence, in which John D. Rockefeller III warmly supported "President" Long's plan for redistribution of wealth as an inspired stroke to stabilize the capitalist order.[31] And the Townsend plan, which critics viewed as a blueprint for national insolvency, was publicized as an attempt to make capitalism function, since the profit system was "the main spring of civilized progress."[32]

Father Divine had once tied his political fortunes to those of the communists, yet by the mid-thirties he, too, began to identify himself as a champion of free enterprise, an especially curious role for the head of a network of communes. As role models for his followers, Divine selected some of the titans of corporate enterprise. Henry Ford, with his superabundant store of capitalist virtues, was a hero to the minister as much as to millions of other Americans.[33] As for Andrew Carnegie, the steel magnate whose lavish philanthropies traced to profits earned partly through ruthless management, Divine allowed that he was "as high as man in mortal consciousness and on a material plane could attain."[34]

Nationalism was a third key to mass approval, and Coughlin, Long, and Townsend all eagerly interwove their ideologies with unabashed patriotic romanticism. Coughlin hammered at the stark choice facing his listeners, not between silver coinage and alternate recovery measures but between American freedom and foreign bankers' tyranny. He urged, "Save America for Americans and give our Constitution a chance to operate. . . ."[35] Huey Long conjured up eminent patriots of different eras to laud the aims of his program, noting that "Jefferson, Jackson, Webster, Lincoln, Theodore Roosevelt and [William Jennings] Bryan have clamored to spread our work and our wealth among all the people."[36] In the same way an official in the Townsend movement declared at a mass rally, "Some day men will talk of Dr. Townsend and [his aide] Robert Clements as we now speak of George Washington and Alexander Hamilton or Abraham Lincoln and General Grant." They "no longer belong to themselves," he volunteered patriotically, "they belong to the American nation."[37]

Father Divine matched these ventures into nationalist sentiment. He regarded English as the most suitable universal language, and followers in foreign countries were encouraged to testify in English at banquets. Moreover, despite his disclaimers of any limiting national loyalties, the very first plank in his Righteous Government Platform of 1936 demanded "the immediate repeal of all laws, ordinances, rules and regulations, local and national, in the United States *and elsewhere,* that have been passed contrary to the spirit and meaning of the Constitution of the United States and its amendments."[38] Divine's vision of a just and harmonious world was, in effect, his reform program for the United States writ large.

Even the Peace Mission's endless invocations of divine sanction for its program, which might seem to put it in a church by itself among radical movements of the era, in fact represented one more facet of the reform tradition they shared. In part, this reflected a tendency for American politicians of nearly every persuasion to lash their values securely to a partisan Providence. Throughout American history the special needs of reform movements operating outside the two-party system have reinforced this tendency to dispense political wisdom in the form of moral and religious absolutes. On the one hand, an evangelical style has offered a way to stir crowds and contributions without aid of a strong, ready-made political apparatus. Further, the use of religious moralism to reduce complex problems to conflicts between good and evil have enabled reformers to obscure weaknesses in their political and economic thought.

All three mass leaders freely mingled piety and politics. Father Coughlin offered the clearest example, as a textbook case of evangelical populism returned to the land of the living, with an urban Catholic coloring. He cited papal statements favoring workers' rights and also echoed the fundamentalist rhetoric of past campaigns for free silver: "Long enough have we been the pawns and chattels of the modern pagans who have crucified us upon a cross of gold."[39] Huey Long also enlisted the deity to defend the vulnerable economics of his Share Our Wealth proposals. "I never read a line of Marx or Henry George or any of them economists," he flaunted his ignorance. "It's all in the Law of God."[40] It was perhaps fitting that his closest aide in spreading word of his program was a fiery evangelist, Gerald L. K. Smith, who, upon Long's assassination in 1935, assumed leadership of his movement. As for the Townsend movement, an official bulletin viewed its pension plan as forged in the spirit of "Christ, the reformer, who gave us the Christian principles upon which the United States of America was founded."[41]

Father Divine, too, employed a peculiarly American idea of Providence in tying his social program to a spiritual mandate. He viewed freedom as springing from a unified religious and political ideal, with each citizen "independent in Christ according to the Constitution."[42] Divine quoted Abraham Lincoln's hope that this nation, under God, might have a new birth of freedom, as illustrating the bond between faith, liberty, and American society.[43]

The religious overtones of these movements extended to the cultlike glorification of their leaders, evident among the three major radical groups as well as in the Peace Mission. While Huey Long was content to take Emperor Frederick the Great as a role model,[44] Townsend and Coughlin evinced higher aspirations. Townsend was deified by many followers, one of whom wondered aloud why no star had risen over Townsend's birthplace to guide the wise men of the generation to his side.[45] Father Coughlin perhaps came closest to matching Father Divine's role as a spiritual protector, as a journalist at one of his conventions recorded in 1936: "[S]peakers simply referred to Coughlin as Father: 'Father says . . . Father thinks . . . Father told us.' The woman who nominated him for president of the organization stated, to frantic applause, that 'for those of us who haven't a material father, he can be our father and we won't need to feel lonesome.' "[46]

All three leaders wished, however, to appear to be far more than personal father figures; out of vanity, vision, or shrewd ambition, they acted as folk heroes in a long tradition of larger-than-life patriots who led the nation through critical times. Thus Doctor Townsend once told an aide as he stood before the Lincoln statue in the capital: "Take this man for example; just a poor lawyer, no smarter than me and certainly not better educated than me, but just being at the right moment before the people with a plea to save the Nation from slavery . . . and now the world faces a fate worse than slavery and a lowly country doctor comes out of the West to save the world. It might be me sitting up there."[47]

Father Divine, of course, was of all these leaders best known for the personal veneration he received. Yet he was also the most insistent in placing his messianic role in the service of an American democratic mission. In late 1939 he issued an "international new year greeting" in which he announced to the world's masses the blessings that the United States, under his guidance, could bestow: "Do not think that I am a fanatic. I have stressed the Constitution and its amendments for many years so vividly until thousands and millions . . . have been converted into the spirit of this democracy. They are calling for deliverance; they are calling for a Deliverer!"[48]

These diverse evocations of conservative symbols — democratic, capitalist, nationalist, pious — yielded all these movements an enhanced popular appeal. It helped the three major radical movements to attract sympathizers nationwide and to stimulate more rapid action on several reform measures, including Social Security.[49] Then, too, when these movements briefly merged in 1936 as the National Union party, nominating Senator William Lemke of Nebraska for the presidency, his nearly 900,000 votes more than tripled those of the Socialist, Communist, and Fascist candidates combined.

Father Divine, while striving toward a far more modest level of recog-

nition, similarly achieved a stature vastly greater than any of his cult competitors. The praise civil rights leaders gave his political program and the
attention, if often reluctant, various national figures accorded him were
simply unparallelled among the cultists of his day.

In absolute terms the influence of the utopian movements was nevertheless scant. The Union party suffered the typical fate of third-party movements, as Franklin Roosevelt's landslide victory inflicted a blow from which
it never revived. This debacle reflected weaknesses in the Union party's
program (a strange pastiche of ill-fitting panaceas), personal squabbles
and liabilities among its leadership, and, above all, Roosevelt's peerless
political skill in keeping discontented Americans around his own banner.

The foundering of the Union party also suggests more fully the impos-
sibility of Father Divine's political ambitions, as a cult leader and as a
black man crusading for racial equality, than scarcely a cause to match
the appeal of curbing bankers, taking wealth from the Rockefellers, or
providing pensions to the aged. Still, the basic elements of Father Divine's
reform leadership—the obeisance to American ideals, the appeal to
religious sentiments, and the attempt to transcend a single-interest constituency—all marked him as sensitive to national values and political techniques. Divine remained, even more tenuously than his utopian contem-
poraries Coughlin, Long, and Townsend, on the margins of influence;
yet like them he was, by temperament and action, a reformer in a venerable
American tradition.

The Coming of War—A Test of "Americanism"

Father Divine's blend of democratic ideals and national loyalty emerged
most clearly in the late thirties and early forties, spurred by the challenge
of fascist aggression. The country's growing resolve to check the Axis
powers tested reformers like Divine by casting doubt on pacifist values
and diverting attention from domestic issues. Yet as the nation moved
toward war, Divine expressed his faith in America's special destiny more
forcefully than ever. Without directly renouncing nonviolence, he invested
the Allied cause with the status of a crusade for freedom and equality—
in short, the extension of utopian politics by other means.

After the joint German-Russian conquest of Poland in September, 1939,
Father Divine began to speak out frequently about the evils of totalitarian
societies. Fascist governments, he observed, kept their people in darkness
and did not tolerate religious minorities. Russia, too, seemed to him a
sorry society that, for all its professed idealism, suppressed its own citizens: "There is no difference between Germany and Russia in that respect.
The Russian people are not permitted to read what they like. They are
not permitted to do what they like. They are not permitted to think as

they like." Some Soviet spokesmen, Divine related, had explained to him that government control was necessary to guard against reactionaries and counterrevolutionists, "but I don't believe that anyone will still maintain that so many years after the revolution, there is any more reason [for repression]." He added that, had the Soviet Union been a democracy, the voice of the people would have kept its rulers from invading their Polish neighbor, "with whom they certainly should live in perfect peace and harmony."[50]

Father Divine increasingly identified his interests with a strong, assertive America, which he saw as a bulwark against the growing menace of the totalitarian states. In particular, he viewed Nazi Germany, with its antidemocratic, racist dogmas and expansionist policies, as the antithesis of his own values. This sentiment deepened in 1941, when a fascist journal editorialized that America had fatally weakened itself through racial integration and cited Divine's movement as an example. Divine retorted that a united democracy was the basis for America's unassailable strength, and predicted that American leadership would one day rule the world.[51]

Divine's actual ideas for checking the fascists were often so impractical as to hold significance chiefly for revealing the depth of his nationalist sentiment. This was particularly evident in the details of a proposal to "unite the Americas for hemispheric defense," an aim that signs announced in every Peace Mission hall. The minister wrote President Roosevelt in December, 1939, to advise that the United States incorporate all Latin American nations into its political system, if necessary by purchasing these countries outright.[52] When told of the intense resentment such a policy would engender, Divine replied that only the most egalitarian union was intended.[53] For him, the cultural, ethnic, and other historical divisions between peoples were so many transient and trivial bars to inevitable unity—the American way.

Still, Divine's unflagging concern to check fascist encroachments placed him in the forefront of national sentiment, moving tentatively away from isolation and neutrality. Even many in the black community, despite a disgust with Hitler's policies, conceded little difference between racist Germany and racist America, and asked why this country tended to seek the salvation of democracy on European battlefields rather than in Mississippi. But Divine, as he continued to digest news of the outrages perpetrated by totalitarian governments, seemed imbued with a heightened appreciation of America's existing freedoms: "We ought to be very glad and very happy that we are living in the United States of America. We are enjoying privileges and rights here that very few others enjoy. That does not mean that there is no room for improvement. . . . [but the persistence of injustices] is not as much the government's fault as it is the fault of the people themselves."[54] Thus, although prejudices remained to be over-come, Divine seemed most impressed that the democratic system worked in America—and deserved to be guarded against foreign enemies.

The entry of the United States into the war in December, 1941, after the bombing of Pearl Harbor, led most blacks to close ranks around the Allied effort while calling for a "double victory" over both foreign and domestic foes of democracy. As Roy Wilkins put it, "It sounds pretty foolish to be *against* park benches marked 'Jude' in Berlin, but to be *for* park benches marked 'Colored' in Tallahassee, Florida."[55] The double-victory ideal, tempering patriotism with continued civil rights protest, per-fectly captured the tenor of Father Divine's wartime attitudes, which his statements since the late thirties had foreshadowed.

In choosing to press the Allied cause, Divine had first to meet the chal-lenge of his own pacifist ideals. It was a problem common among Ameri-can clergymen, many of whom still carried guilt and horror over past chauvinist and militarist preachings while caught up in the nation's first crusade to make the world safe for democracy a quarter-century earlier. By contrast, substantially more ministers referred to American involve-ment in World War II only as a necessary evil; some entreated merely for an early end to the slaughter, and joined neutral groups like the Red Cross. Still, the number of pastors who preached nonviolence was very small; the contrary pressures of national sentiment and national security were simply too great.[56]

Father Divine's wartime ministry was at once more unreservedly parti-san and yet more faithful to nonviolence than typified his fellow ministers. He could take these seemingly polar positions because he firmly believed that a nation's strength lay not in its military but "in the moral force of its citizens."[57] When, after Pearl Harbor, he asked his followers to give their "mental and spiritual allegiance" to their country, "according to the plan and purpose of the Almighty,"[58] he considered this the highest con-tribution they could make to their nation's conflict with an ungodly power.

Peace Mission members nonetheless offered their nation more than prayers. They responded with alacrity to Father Divine's endorsement of war bond sales. "We do not have to kill a man by buying bonds,"[59] he explained somewhat ingenuously. He exhorted disciples to purchase bonds "for victory and a just and lasting peace; and for reconstruction, mass production, rescuing the perishing and to care for the dying."[60]

The Peace Mission scrupulously avoided any challenge to the Selective Service process. True followers were expected to declare themselves con-scientious objectors but in no way evade the draft rules themselves. "[I]f it were required," Divine said, "every American citizen would register to let the government know where he or she was, and then give the government the opportunity of investigating to find out" whether they were sincere.[61] Divine added that he had done as much himself during World War I, voluntarily registering with a draft board as a sign of patriotism and a matter of law, despite his resolve never to fight another man.[62]

As a final concession to the American war effort, Divine declined to categorically ban military service among his followers. He recognized that there were varying degrees of commitment to his tenets of nonviolence. Only the most devoted were truly prepared to abandon all physical self-defense on religious principle. These were indeed obliged to eschew military combat. But "if a person would fight for himself or another or use physical force in the defense of anything, he has a right to fight for his government and in the defense of his country."[63]

While Divine trimmed his pacifism to its sparest essentials, he refused to rein in his civil rights activity. His conduct at Brigantine in 1942 was characteristic. In guiding disciples to lease their hotel free to the military, but on condition that segregation be banned despite opposition by white neighbors, he epitomized the civil rights movement's theme of double victory.

In the same vein Father Divine served notice that the struggle he supported knew no national bounds. The true enemy was injustice and falsehood, "even if it is in one of us."[64] Even when predicting that the Axis powers would fall because they opposed God and righteousness, he refrained from crediting his own nation with unblemished virtue. The war was a chastisement for moral failings on both sides, and the Allies would triumph only by a renewed commitment to human rights. "The democracies," he warned, "are put to a hard test because they reflect to some degree, even to a great degree, the evils prevalent among the aggressor nations."[65]

If the war had any positive meaning, Divine believed, it was in quickening the advances by people everywhere to gain their rights. It was not enough for nations to claim to favor this cause based simply on their resistance to a worse tyranny. "England," he observed of America's closest ally and the world's greatest colonial power, "excuses her injustices and inhumanity to man by holding aloft the threat of Communism; but I say, mankind is no longer seeking Communism, Nazi-ism, Totalitarianism, or any other kind of ism; humanity is demanding liberty, equality and justice."[66]

Divine's recital of national obligations as well as virtues, even in the midst of a global crisis, reflects the deeper consistency of his patriotic sentiments in war as in peace. As a millennialist who saw all events as part of an ascent toward perfect justice, Father Divine was loyal to the United States because he believed it had a special role in this providential process. Blessed with a democratic heritage, this nation could be the first to perfect his vision of the good society while defending and advancing it throughout the world. In that faith Divine offered himself as a prophet of the "American way" while realizing that this ideal still existed, to a challenging degree, only in the realm of his moral imagination.

Notes to Chapter 9

1. "Let America Be America Again," in *The Poetry of the Negro 1746-1970,* ed. Langston Hughes and Arna Bontemps (New York: Doubleday, 1970), p. 195.

2. "The Blue Meridian," in ibid., pp. 107, 128, 130.

3. Roi Ottley, *'New World A-Coming': Inside Black America* (Boston: Houghton Mifflin, 1943), p. 82, writes that Father Divine "fell heir to the bulk of Marcus Garvey's thousands." Samuel Haynes wrote in the Garveyite publication *Negro World,* Apr. 15, 1933, that former Garveyites were moving by "thousands" to "new religious movements claiming to be associated with Garveyism." He noted with some bitterness that these ex-followers saw in Father Divine, Bishop Grace, and others the incarnation of Marcus Garvey. His comments are cited in Vincent, *Black Power and the Garvey Movement,* p. 222.

4. Ottley, *New World,* pp. 82-83. By contrast, Vincent, *Black Power and the Garvey Movement,* pp. 224-27, analyzes the movement from Garvey to Divine largely as a flight from a socially activist organization to an escapist one. That interpretation seems, to this writer, based on some valid but highly selective perceptions of the two movements that minimize their mutual ambivalence as escapist cults and militant reform movements.

5. The outstanding study on this facet of Garvey's movement is Randall K. Burkett, *Garveyism as a Religious Movement: The Institutionalization of a Black Civil Religion* (Metuchen, N.J.: Scarecrow Press and American Theological Library Association, 1978).

6. See the Garveyite journal *Black Man,* 1 (July, 1935):11-13, and 2 (Sept.-Oct., 1936), cited in E. David Cronon, *Black Moses: The Story of Marcus Garvey and the Universal Negro Improvement Association,* 2d ed. (Madison: University of Wisconsin Press, 1955), p. 163, and St. Clair Drake's Foreword to Burkett, *Garveyism as a Religious Movement,* pp. xxii-xxiii.

7. Marcus Garvey, *Philosophy and Opinions,* ed. Amy Jacques-Garvey (New York: Atheneum, 1977), 2:18, 87.

8. Sermon of Apr. 12, 1948, in *ND,* Aug. 4, 1973, p. 16.

9. Garvey, *Philosophy and Opinions,* 1:37.

10. Cronon, *Black Moses,* p. 61.

11. Ibid., p. 60.

12. Ibid.

13. Ibid., p. 52.

14. Vincent, *Black Power and the Garvey Movement,* p. 117.

15. Garvey, *Philosophy and Opinions,* 1:24.

16. Ibid., p. 90.

17. Ibid., 2:32-33. A sample of Garvey's more optimistic thoughts about God's role in history is found in ibid., p. 17: "Surely God will answer our prayers against the wicked and unjust and strengthen us for the great work that must be done in His name and to His glory."

18. Ibid., p. 53.

19. On Garvey and the Ku Klux Klan, see Cronon, *Black Moses,* pp. 189-90.

20. See Father Divine to Senator Theodore G. Bilbo of Mississippi, Mar. 15, 1940, in *ND*, Mar. 21, 1940, pp. 52-55; see also similar comments by Father Divine, in response to racist statements by Louisiana Senator Allen Ellender, in his sermon of Feb. 18-19, 1938, in *ND*, Feb. 24, 1938, p. 12.

21. There are, of course, exceptions within each of the groups mentioned. Abolitionist William Lloyd Garrison, for example, despite his commitment to nonviolent change, could hardly be described as an unqualified believer in the basic goodness of America or its political documents. Yet on the whole the abolitionists, like the bulk of populists and civil rights demonstrators, among other groups, fit within this mold of "conservative utopian," stressing one bold set of changes but otherwise accepting the fundamental status quo in American society. For an insightful treatment of this interplay of reform and conservative qualities, see Richard Hofstadter's *The American Political Tradition and the Men Who Made It* (New York: Alfred A. Knopf, 1948) and his *The Age of Reform: From Bryan to F.D.R.* (New York: Vintage Books, 1955), esp. pp. 23-130, examining the contradictions in populist perspectives.

22. David Bennett, *Demagogues in the Depression: American Radicals and the Union Party, 1932-1936* (New Brunswick, N.J.: Rutgers University Press, 1969), p. 5.

23. Bennett, *Demagogues,* offers an extremely perceptive appraisal of the interaction and the legacy of these movements.

24. Charles J. Tull, *Father Coughlin and the New Deal* (Syracuse, N.Y.: Syracuse University Press, 1965), p. 64. Coughlin further saluted American ideals of democratic tolerance by stressing that his new movement welcomed Jews and Christians alike, though his defenses of silver as the "gentile" metal and his increasingly open anti-Semitic accusations gave his interfaith overtures a hollow sound.

25. Huey Long, *Every Man a King* (1933; reprinted Chicago: Quadrangle Books, 1964), p. 291.

26. *The Townsend Plan National Recovery Program Ready Reference,* 2d ed. (Chicago: Old Age Revolving Pensions, 1936), pp. 3, 4.

27. Father Divine to Arthur J. Farmer, July 31, 1939, in *ND,* Aug. 3, 1939, pp. 87-88.

28. Sermon of Dec. 31, 1941–Jan. 1, 1942, in *ND,* Sept. 9, 1978, p. 10.

29. See, for example, sermon of Jan. 19, 1935, in *SW,* Feb. 9, 1935, p. 2, and sermon of Nov. 1, 1937, in *ND,* Nov. 11, 1937, p. 11.

30. Tull, *Father Coughlin,* p. 245. Although Coughlin at times suggested that capitalism was already too corrupted to be saved, he stated more typically that capitalism was "perhaps the best system of economics provided it does not run counter to the laws of morality" (cited in Bennett, *Demagogues,* p. 51).

31. Huey Long, *My First Days in the White House* (1935; reprinted New York: Da Capo Press, 1972), pp. 77-79.

32. Arthur Schlesinger, Jr., *The Politics of Upheaval* (Boston: Houghton Mifflin, 1960), p. 38.

33. See, for example, sermon of Nov. 7, 1936, in *SW,* Nov. 14, 1936, p. 7.

34. Sermon of Dec. 13, 1935, in *SW,* Dec. 21, 1935, p. 12.

35. Charles Coughlin, *A Series of Lectures on Social Justice, 1935-1936* (Royal Oak, Mich.: Radio League of the Little Flower, 1936), p. 109.

36. Long, *Every Man a King,* p. 296.

37. *The Townsend Plan Analyzed* (New York: Tax Policy League, 1936), p. 4.

38. See Father Divine's remarks on English as a universal language in an inter-

view with Professor Herman von Walde Waldegg of Harvard University, Jan. 12, 1940, in *ND,* Jan. 18, 1940, p. 49; italics added in text quotation.

39. Schlesinger, *Politics of Upheaval,* p. 19. Coughlin thus revived the words of William Jennings Bryan at the Democratic convention in 1896.

40. Ibid., p. 63.

41. *Townsend Plan . . . Ready Reference,* p. 39.

42. Sermon of July 2, 1935, in *SW,* July 13, 1935, p. 4.

43. Father Divine to V. C. Chessmore, Nov. 15, 1941, in *ND,* Nov. 20, 1941, p. 89.

44. T. Harry Williams, *Huey Long* (New York: Alfred A. Knopf, 1949), p. 492.

45. Schlesinger, *Politics of Upheaval,* p. 33.

46. Jonathan Mitchell, "Father Coughlin's Children," *New Republic* 88 (Aug., 1936):73, cited in Bennett, *Demagogues,* p. 62; citing Jonathan Mitchell, "Father Coughlin's Children," *New Republic* 88 (Aug., 1936):73.

47. Schlesinger, *Politics of Upheaval,* p. 39.

48. "International New Year Greeting," Dec. 28, 1939, in *ND,* Jan. 4, 1940, pp. 11-12. The immediate aim of this salutation was to interest Latin American republics in his proposal that all nations of the Americas become part of the United States.

49. See Bennett, *Demagogues,* pp. 308-9, for an appraisal of the achievements of the different movements; Bennett's overall evaluation of these movements is decidedly negative.

50. Sermon of Jan. 7, 1940, in *ND,* Jan. 11, 1940, p. 84.

51. *NYAN,* May 10, 1941, p. 13.

52. Father Divine to Franklin Roosevelt, telegram, Dec. 9, 1939, in *ND,* Dec. 14, 1939, p. 82.

53. Interview given by Father Divine to Professor Herman von Walde Waldegg, Jan. 12, 1940, in *ND,* Jan. 18, 1940, p. 49. As a final testament to Divine's well-intended chauvinism, he ascribed the continued refusal of Latin American peoples to merge with the United States to their resentment over American failure to enact an antilynching bill in 1940. After all, he allowed, why would Latin Americans want to enter a racist society? See sermon of Dec. 29, 1940, in *ND,* Jan. 2, 1941, p. 7.

54. Sermon of Jan. 7, 1940, in *ND,* Jan. 11, 1940, p. 85.

55. Roy Wilkins, "The Negro Wants Full Equality," in *What the Negro Wants,* ed. Rayford W. Logan (Chapel Hill: University of North Carolina Press, 1944), p. 130.

56. See Ray H. Abrams, *Preachers Present Arms: The Role of the American Churches and Clergy in World Wars I and II* (Scottdale, Pa.: Herald Press, 1969), esp. pp. 15-124, 259-74.

57. Father Divine to John P. Welch, Sept. 29, 1941, in *ND,* Oct. 2, 1941, p. 69.

58. Sermon of Dec. 23, 1941, in *ND,* Dec. 25, 1941, p. 83.

59. Sermon of Apr. 17, 1943, in *ND,* Apr. 22, 1943, p. 13.

60. Sermon of Jan. 12, 1944, in *ND,* Dec. 2, 1978, p. 9.

61. Father Divine to Cephas Gabriel, Apr. 18, 1942, in *ND,* Apr. 23, 1942, p. 99.

62. Sermon of Oct. 22, 1940, in *ND,* Oct. 24, 1940, p. 43.

63. Father Divine to Cephas Gabriel, Apr. 18, 1942, in *ND,* Apr. 23, 1942, p. 99.

64. Sermon of Dec. 23, 1941, in *ND,* Dec. 25, 1941, p. 83.

65. Father Divine to Mrs. C. Wesley Wood, May 1, 1942, in *ND,* May 7, 1942, p. 79.

66. Father Divine to G. G. Truesdale, Feb. 27, 1942, in *ND,* Mar. 5, 1942, p. 65.

Epilogue

From Cult to Corporation: The Peace Mission in Transition

The Peace Mission evolved after 1940 from a mass movement wholly dependent on its founding Father, to a formal sect featuring an elaborate bureaucracy. While such trends typically overtake charismatic movements sometime after the passing of the original leader, the Peace Mission was transformed while Father Divine still lived and firmly controlled its affairs. Under the pressures of advancing age and growing legal problems, Divine increasingly focused on building institutional guarantees for the movement he had once sustained through sheer vitality and seemingly endless ingenuity. The result of these changes was that the Peace Mission proved able to survive even the great trauma of Father Divine's death in 1965, but at the cost — exacted well in advance — of virtually all the movement's original social energy and impact.

The Peace Mission Church

The catalyst spurring the Peace Mission's conservative shift was a bitter court fight, spanning more than five years and exposing the fragility of the movement's financial and legal state. A former follower, Verinda Brown, sued in 1937 for money allegedly given to Father Divine in trust while a disciple. On the face of it, Brown had a dubious case: she had no direct evidence, she had obviously enjoyed numerous material benefits while a Peace Mission member for five years, and she implicitly admitted that Father Divine had never directly solicited anything from her. Yet a New York court ruled against Divine, placing the burden of proof on him and implicitly viewing his leadership as outside the full protection of the law. The judgment of some $7,000 was a trivial sum by the standards of Peace Mission finance, but Divine realized that payment would only tempt other disgruntled or greedy disciples to launch similar suits. As each of several appellate courts sustained the adverse decision, the weary cult leader prepared drastic action to ensure his personal freedom and the security of his kingdom.[1]

In 1941 Father Divine incorporated several key Peace Mission centers in the Northeast. This marked a decisive break with Divine's earlier stress on an "invisible" church. Yet for a movement plagued by damaging defections and litigation, this decision offered major advantages. It afforded the Peace Mission legal status on a par with other churches, providing at least a partial antidote to the tendency of trial judges to treat the Peace Mission as a barely legitimate "racket." Incorporation also entitled each official church to deed property in its own name, so that no disciples could claim any of the movement's assets on leaving the Peace Mission, as Brown was attempting to do.[2]

Unlike the Righteous Government Platform of 1936, which consisted of several dozen prescriptions for improving the world, the Peace Mission's new Magna Carta — its corporate by-laws — modestly confined itself to problems of institutional continuity. The document created individual church trusteeships, presidencies, and other offices to simplify questions of delegated leadership.[3] For the first time, then, Father Divine formally recognized a special bureaucratic class in the Peace Mission, despite his earlier denunciations of elitist practices. The necessities of the movement in "middle age" simply took precedence over Divine's egalitarian instincts.

The corporate charter's by-laws also formally enshrined the absolute leadership role of Father Divine. In earlier years Divine had nominally renounced any special privilege or rank. He was, in the polite fiction of his own rhetoric, simply serving as "a sample and an example" for those who wished to lead the life he advocated. The by-laws now explicitly listed him as "supreme spiritual authority" while stipulating that he be called by the various terms used to describe images of the Supreme Being.[4] Divine thus sought to embalm for all time the charisma that had marked his personal rule, just as the Peace Mission entered a new, more impersonal stage of its existence.

Incorporation improved the long-range legal position of the Peace Mission but could not deflect the menace that the Brown case posed. Those judicial proceedings were like a vise that squeezed ever more tightly the Peace Mission's operations, until by mid-1942 Divine faced the apparent choice of meeting Brown's claim or going to prison. Characteristically, though, he discovered a third, unforeseen alternative.

In July, 1942, Father Divine left New York permanently. Vowing never to pay an "unjust" judgment, he relocated with several hundred followers in Philadelphia, safely beyond the jurisdiction of New York authorities.[5]

He thus thwarted both Verinda Brown's demands and the threat of imminent imprisonment, though at the cost of isolating himself from the heart of his Harlem-based movement.

Father Divine's sudden self-exile from New York, coming just when renewed national prosperity and high employment were fast eroding the Peace Mission's economic appeal, led to a sharp decline in his following. Yet this appeared not to affect Divine greatly, for he was by then becoming absorbed with consolidating his corporate creation, to the increasing neglect of mass-based social activity.[6] The pattern behind his actions was not wholly unfamiliar, for throughout Divine's long ministry he had alternated between periods of activism and isolation. Now, after years of unrelenting work for reform, he seemed almost to welcome a new stage of serenity and withdrawal from an often hostile society. Then, too, by the time he quit Harlem, Divine was already entering old age, not so abruptly as to threaten his hold over the Peace Mission but inducing him nevertheless to measurably slow the pace of his leadership.[7] The years in Philadelphia therefore did not witness a resurgence of Divine's Peace Mission movement but rather its quiet consolidation, as old legal claims faded away and new social currents passed it by.

The Peace Mission's growing conservatism may also be viewed as the typical response by a socially militant cult when other organizations emerge to assume its activist role.[8] The fact that the Peace Mission's sharp turn from radical politics came just when civil rights groups were forging a strong national coalition appears, in this light, more than coincidence or sad irony alone. Rather, Father Divine may well have seen that the progressive aspects of his ministry no longer held a special attraction for ghetto dwellers and could be jettisoned without significant disruption of the movement. Such a perception, coinciding with Divine's need for tranquility, would have done much to ease his transition from active social reformer to secluded corporate planner.

The Peace Mission's search for accommodation with the wider society resulted, in part, in a pronounced rightward shift in its political rhetoric. During the Depression Father Divine's emphasis had been on making the United States a more democratic nation; in the years after World War II it was on guarding the existing society against subversive influences. In particular, tirades against communists and unions, often in combination, revealed Father Divine's utopian vision shading ever more fully into the most profoundly conservative prayers of the Cold War era.

By 1950 the man who once marched with Communist party members and endorsed their principles as virtually all commendable had come to portray communism as the ultimate evil. "I came here to free you from all Communism and from all infidelism," Father Divine reinterpreted his mission to cheering disciples. Communism, he explained in a sermon that might have been pieced together from contemporary July 4th speeches, was dangerous because it opposed the values he came to promote: Americanism, Christianity, Democracy, Judaism, and Brotherhood. These values were all "synonymous" because they affirmed the dignity and freedom of every individual under God, and had to be vigilantly defended against the infiltration of "Communistic propaganda."[9]

Unions fared little better in Divine's sermons than communists, nor did the Father always distinguish between the two. His relations with labor groups had long been tenuous, but when workers struck key railroads during the Korean War, it prompted Divine to release all his accumulating resentments against their "corrupt" and "undemocratic" practices. It might have been President Truman in an especially peppery mood who declared, as the outraged Father did in February, 1951, "I will not tolerate it, strikes, and such as that, to try to retard the advancement of our defense!" The unions, by striking against the railroads, were subverting the national security, "and I know it is Communistic!" Indeed, no subversive doctrine seemed to him beyond union intrigue. They were "inspired by atheism and Nazism and other isms that spell division, to undermine the foundations of our government, of which we all revere!"[10]

One suspects that while Father Divine truly believed that communism posed a dire threat to American values, his growing focus on that theme served more immediate purposes as well. Seeking "respectability" for his Peace Mission movement, Divine could scarcely have chosen a surer route than to expound the anticommunist rhetoric then at the heart of mainstream patriotic sentiment. Also, by speaking frequently on the subject, Divine could continue to take firm, even strident ideological stands, as in the thirties, but without incurring real controversy or committing his movement to any tangible political activity. On the contrary, Divine's relentless anticommunist diatribes formed the last camouflage for the fact that the Peace Mission had long since lost its political purpose and energy.

The decline of the Peace Mission extended to the economic realm. Its businesses sharply contracted during the forties, and most of them outside Philadelphia, Newark, and Harlem eventually closed down, including those in the vaunted "Promised Land."[11] The main problem, which worsened with the years, was not that the businesses were unprofitable; rather, the continued economic advantages of cooperation no longer seemed a widely compelling reason in these prosperous times to forsake all for Father Divine. In short, as converts diminished in number and old disciples left the movement or shifted from rural branches back to the cities, a flourishing, multimillion dollar cooperative network languished for lack of manpower.

As the Peace Mission lost its former scope and influence, it increasingly sought to enhance its status as a legitimate religious institution. There arose new orders of the devoted, each with its own elaborate code of conduct and special liturgical functions.[12] "Rosebuds" included young women disciples, "Lily-buds" somewhat older women, and "Crusaders" men of all ages. If one already lived a celibate life, as Father Divine advocated, it was not very difficult to attain membership in one of these orders: about half the active disciples belonged. Nor were these "privileged" orders except insofar as they were entitled to lead hymns of praise to Father Divine. Initiates did, however, wear special uniforms, brightly colored to distinguish them unmistakably from their brethren in the organization. It was a small move, perhaps, but it underscored the advent of the Peace Mission as an established church rather than simply a bustling and spontaneous evangelical assembly.

Another sign that the Peace Mission was seeking institutional stability, at the cost of its millennial fervor, was its thorough reinterpretation of the religious significance of death. Death had once seemed to Peace Mission members the ultimate disgrace, resulting from a sinful state of mind. "[I]f you die, you are not of me. If you are an invalid you are not of me," Divine had stated on many occasions.[13] This teaching was so ingrained in the Peace Mission's creed that when Pinninnah, "Mother Divine," died in 1937, Divine avoided informing his disciples for fear that the news might shatter their faith. Yet as the demise of veteran followers became too frequent for even the most devout to ignore totally, the movement grudgingly accorded death a less odious and more profoundly spiritual significance.

The new doctrine held that death was a natural process, even among the faithful, and signified that a person's spirit had sought to obtain a new and more perfect body. A letter from a female disciple in Panama, telling of her brother's passing, reveals how the rank and file adjusted to this teaching: "[It] was his desire that he go away in the belief that he would obtain a new body, free from all ailments and pure. We that were around him did not feel much distressed, but were in the realization that his passing was but the means to a happy end."[14]

In asking, in effect, "Death, where is thy stigma?" the Peace Mission made theological provision for its institutional future. It ensured that the passing of the whole first generation of disciples, who joined in the 1930s, would not discredit the movement's central tenet that God resides in every individual. The concept of immortality simply became more heavily spiritualized, a development that accorded well with the movement's general trend toward a more socially passive and aloof character.

It is symbolic of the Peace Mission's new, inward-looking character that

Father Divine's one brief return to fame came with a deeply personal act. In August, 1946, he appeared in his Philadelphia church with a beautiful, twenty-one-year-old white disciple called Sweet Angel, and announced that he had secretly married her more than three months earlier.[15] The interracial aspect of the marriage garnered headlines across the country, while astonished disciples tried to assimilate the news that their leader, after years of solitary rule, was now preparing to share the glory, if not the power, of his kingdom.

The marriage amazed all the more because the bride, born Edna Rose Ritchings in Canada, was scarcely known to anyone in the Philadelphia church before late 1945. At that time she made a pilgrimage by bus from a West Coast Peace Mission center to visit Father Divine. Although "Sweet Angel" left for Montreal when her numerous visa extensions were discontinued, she overcame both parental objections and bureaucratic barriers to return shortly after to Philadelphia. She recalled many years later, "I just wanted to come down to *see* Father," but the day after her arrival he married her. She laughed gently, in wonderment at the turn of events.[16]

If the marriage overwhelmed Sweet Angel, it also raised some difficult questions among the faithful. Why, after so many years of strongly discouraging marriage by his disciples, did Father Divine himself now wed? Why did he choose someone nearly fifty years his junior, who had only recently joined the Peace Mission, rather than one of many veteran loyalists? Perhaps most delicate of all, what had happened to Mother Divine, who had simply disappeared from public view in 1937? No one till now had dared question her whereabouts, but Divine's new marriage made at least some explanation necessary, to ensure the continued morale of followers taught to believe that the virtuous would never die.

Divine assured his followers that his was not a marriage in the conventional sense but a spiritual union to symbolize interracial harmony and uphold a standard of chaste conduct for others in the movement. In dealing with the thorny issue of Mother Divine's passing, he took the mystical tack that she had desired a new, more beautiful "Rosebud's" body—a somewhat prescient yearning, inasmuch as the Rosebud order of the Peace Mission was created after she had already died. Divine nevertheless maintained that the late Pinninnah and the vibrant Sweet Angel were really one and the same person. This was a particularly formidable concept for anyone who remembered the dark, corpulent form of the elderly Mother Divine and then looked at the blonde, youthful Sweet Angel. The disciples accepted their leader's assurances, however, that "Mrs. Divine presently, as you see her, is the reproduction and reincarnation of the spirit and the nature and the characteristics of Mother Divine!"[17]

One may appreciate Divine's explanation more readily, perhaps, by viewing it apart from its supernatural aura. The need for a close companion must have sharpened considerably with the move from Harlem. The old days of frenetic activity and high visibility were largely gone. In their place there was stability, routine, security. No longer did battalions of journalists press in upon him, for his Peace Mission movement had lost its dynamic and unpredictable qualities. In such circumstances the desire grew for a spiritual companion like Pinninnah, to ease the relative stillness of a ministry once in the vortex of constant challenge and change. Sweet Angel — personable, infectiously buoyant, and utterly loyal to the Father and his work — amply filled that need. She was, for him, Mother Divine returned to life.

The marriage likely also served a vital purpose in aiding the Peace Mission's transition from cult to church: it provided for a successor to Father Divine. This was an accomplishment carefully left unspoken, for disciples took their leader's continued existence as a certainty, nor could they then conceive of the Peace Mission except in terms of Father Divine's presence. Divine therefore could not broach the idea of succession explicitly without risking his followers' central, unifying faith in his own deity. But by formally elevating Sweet Angel as his "spotless virgin bride" who represented his "church" on earth, Divine effectively invested her with the mystique and authority needed to eventually rule in his stead.

Bolstered by Father Divine's encouragement and public praise, Mother Divine changed over the next decade from simply an adoring bride to an able, nearly coequal partner in running the Peace Mission. By the mid-1950s followers who once reflexively thanked "Father" for all blessings had learned instead to exclaim, "Thank you, Father and Mother!" Mother Divine may not have shared her husband's image as God on earth, but she increasingly came to act as his vicar for the Peace Mission's continued operation.

Elder Statesman

The move to bourgeois respectability in Philadelphia included a developing role for Father Divine as elder statesman to progressive ministers and aspiring cult figures. In Harlem Divine had been largely reviled by churchmen, who viewed him as a threat to traditional religious values and often feared him as a competitor. But time — and the fact that the Peace Mission no longer attracted many new disciples from other congregations — enabled Father Divine to appear in a more positive light. Increasingly, clergymen visited his Philadelphia residence in search of advice, inspiration, and aid. And some came to pay belated tribute to this aging cult leader, whose reputation for combining evangelism and reform assumed new meaning in an age of growing civil rights militancy by the black church.

Adam Clayton Powell, Jr., was easily the most noteworthy addition to the ranks of Father Divine's clerical admirers. Powell's mellowing view traced to his political needs as a candidate for the New York City Council in 1941. He made it known that Divine's electoral aid would be welcome, and the Peace Mission leader responded warmly, despite Powell's earlier disparagement of his work. A former Democratic party leader, Joseph Ford, recalled, "I got Father to give his endorsement to Powell and it proved very helpful to us in the campaign after he allowed Powell to speak at one of his dinners."[18]

As Father Divine continued to support Powell's political aims while conveniently fading in direct, competitive influence in Harlem, Powell began to describe him in admiring and even fulsome terms. In 1951 Powell took pains to distinguish Father Divine from the religious "racketeers" he so often denounced. Powell asserted his faith in Divine's incorruptible nature based on "an intimate personal knowledge of him and a deep friendship with him for twenty years." He added that Divine "has done a great good, although I do not subscribe to all his beliefs."[19] Of course, twenty years earlier Powell had scarcely heard of Father Divine, after which he had confined the acquaintance to polemics accusing the Peace Mission leader of every vice from deceit to megalomania. Yet Powell's sudden, politically induced amnesia appeared quite acceptable to the Father. He chose quietly to forget Powell's old slights, in order to maintain the public attention and respect of the country's leading black politician. As Divine's energies ebbed, this association provided a treasured, vicarious involvement with the civil rights movement he could no longer actively promote.

Leon Sullivan, today a noted civil rights activist and the pastor of Philadelphia's Zion Baptist Church, was still a young seminary student in New York in 1943 when he paid the first of many visits to the Peace Mission. The generosity and interracial fellowship he experienced left an indelible impression on him, and so did Father Divine's advocacy of a religion concerned with social justice.

Sullivan perceived Divine as a spiritual and social prophet, an inspiration to those entering the civil rights movement. In an interview with Divine in 1945 the young pastor alluded in wonderment to Divine's achievements and added, "Dr. [Adam Clayton] Powell and I and that bunch, think that we are doing something, and, gee whiz! — we haven't even scratched the surface!"[20]

During the fifties, as Sullivan became known as a versatile and highly effective civil rights organizer, he continued his close and reverent contact with Father Divine. In turn, at Sullivan's request Divine made exceptions in his generally passive approach to race-related issues during this period. In July, 1958, for example, Sullivan urgently asked Divine to aid the mass demonstration honoring Ghana's visiting Prime Minister Kwami Nkrumah, in order to show American solidarity with this "symbol of democracy and freedom in Africa." Divine directed his followers to rally in force, though this gathering was far from the spirit of the Peace Mission protest marches of the thirties. Rather, the tone of the event was epitomized by an appearance of the "Rosebud Choir" at the outdoor reception for Nkrumah.[21] The choir's selection of patriotic songs to regale the visiting African dignitary reflected the deep conservatism that marked even Father Divine's rare public actions. Divine looked hopefully to young leaders like Leon Sullivan to carry on the work of reform, but his own struggles with society were clearly past.

Rising cult leaders also courted Father Divine's favor. No longer the dominating charismatic figure he had been in the thirties, Divine appeared less as a formidable rival and more than ever as the grand magician to the new faces in the field. They journeyed to his haven and sought his blessings for their own ventures.

The major black cult leader of Detroit, known as "Prophet Jones," paid his respects to Father Divine in 1953. Although Jones claimed to be "Dominion Ruler of the Church of the Universal Triumph," with heavenly favor and a good deal of earthly splendor, he quickly accepted an invitation to help consecrate a new Peace Mission estate near Philadelphia. The question of how one spiritual potentate should treat another without sparking hostility or losing face taxed Jones's abilities and resulted in a small masterpiece of intercult diplomacy: "I herewith graciously, humbly and sincerely, yet royally, accept your invitation to attend."[22]

Jones visited with a truly royal retinue, including two valets, two secretaries, a hair dresser, two bodyguards, and a cook, as well as many followers and an array of suitcases containing some of his 400 suits and a $12,900 mink coat. But Jones was simply overawed by his view of Divine's wealth and the loyalty Divine commanded. His first experience of the Father's understated absolutism came with their meeting at the railroad station near Divine's residence: "[T]he ecstatic faithful piled in around them, crying, 'Peace, peace—it's wonderful, wonderful!' A long-armed policeman was helpless to restore order. Then Father Divine raised his arm. 'Peace, kindly move back,' he said, and the crowd parted like the Red Sea."[23]

The two leaders exchanged warm greetings that constituted an encouraging exercise in mutual respect, given the delicate situation of having two supreme deities in the same suburb. "I am happy to meet you, Your Holiness," Divine ventured, to be outflattered by Jones's effusion, "God bless you, Your Godliness. It's a pleasure and an honor."[24] Jones toured the estate and later hinted to reporters of possible future collaboration with Divine, though he could not specify just how. Nothing concrete emerged from the meeting, however, except to confirm Divine's stature as *eminence gris* among American cult figures.

Another self-declared prophet by the name of Jones visited the Peace Mission center in Philadelphia several times during the late fifties. Jim Jones was a young, struggling minister in Indiana when he first came to Father Divine, hoping to find answers to the financial problems, congregational apathy, and outside intolerance that plagued his People's Temple. Jones appeared at once awestruck and envious upon seeing the affluence and the unreserved veneration Father Divine enjoyed. In this and subsequent visits Jones paid limited attention to the spiritual and social principles underlying the movement, but he took exacting note of the techniques by which Father Divine maintained dominion over hundreds of willing subjects.

During his early visits to Philadelphia Jones testified repeatedly on the adversity he had encountered and, in an audacious analogy with Father Divine's ministry, he suggested to the Peace Mission followers that he also knew the pain of being a great but largely unappreciated leader. Yet, for all his wishful comparisons, Jones idolized Father Divine as a prophet with vastly more honor than he. Jones believed that his experiences at the Peace Mission marked a turning point in his life, for "I came and saw the reality of things that I had known for years."[25]

The reality Jones claimed to have discovered was apparently both a spiritual state and a successful model of chaste communal life. Pushed to the edge of despair by setbacks in Indiana, Jones looked at the Peace Mission's achievement and believed that he, too, could bring his utopian plans to fruition. He freely acknowledged his debt to Father Divine for the faith that now surged through him. "You have been responsible for that!" he exclaimed at a Peace Mission banquet. ". . . Father Divine's ministry — God in this place gave me the inspiration just at the very time when I could have given the whole thing up and become defeated; I came to the Peace Mission and gained new zeal and new power!"[26]

Jones also displayed unusual insight into the reasons why countless imitators of Father Divine had failed to equal the Peace Mission leader's record of enduring accomplishment. Too many of these "tremendous divine healers," Jones told a Peace Mission audience, had tried to win a mass following as a "personality minister" without any real concern to improve the lives of other people. "I never have any confidence," Jones warned, "in somebody that wants to accept all the glory." But Father Divine succeeded because "he shares what he has with you! He wants you to come into his likeness! . . . I have heard him say, 'What I am, you can be!' "[27]

The speech reflected a side of Jones that was still principled and optimistic. He believed that an effective ministry had to embrace more than manipulative technique; that only a leader who, like Father Divine, was moved by ideals larger than his own ego could create a movement of lasting spiritual and social value. Jones's speech was also astonishingly prescient, for it unconsciously prefigured the deterioration of his own career two decades later, as a "personality minister" cynically and singlemindedly seeking "all the glory." Unlike Father Divine, his intended model, who combined a will to power with constructive purpose, Jones ultimately made power alone the center of his cult role. When that power, too, began to dissolve, there were no further supports to sustain his life or movement. In this sense, his words at the Peace Mission banquet may well be read both as an encomium to Father Divine's distinctive ministry and as Jones's own tragic epitaph.

"I Need Not Say More"

The key decision of Father Divine's reign in Philadelphia—to sharply reduce his work for reform in favor of consolidating the Peace Mission's organization—took on a new aura of wisdom as he continued to decline physically. His once frequent travels, which had made him appear literally omnipresent to his followers in the Northeast, nearly ceased by the 1950s. Without the efficient and loyal bureaucracy Divine had earlier established, his movement would scarcely have maintained itself during his deepening isolation from disciples and outsiders alike.

As Father Divine became ever more reluctant to leave the Philadelphia area, the Peace Mission adjusted by investing his headquarters with greater physical splendor and symbolic import. In 1953 a veteran disciple named John Devoute donated for Father Divine's personal use a thirty-two-room mansion just outside Philadelphia, overlooking a seventy-three-acre garden-filled estate of breath-taking beauty. While the main Peace Mission centers in Philadelphia continued to function, the Woodmont estate came to serve as Father Divine's primary home. As if to justify his stationary life by exalting his immediate surroundings, he proudly referred to this property as "the mount of the house of the Lord." Although he still occasionally reminded his followers of the old tenet that Heaven was not a geographic location but a spiritual condition, he tended to portray Woodmont as, at the least, the leading jewel in creation.

Beginning in 1955, the aged cult leader held the attention of the outside world chiefly for reasons of uncertain health. He went into prolonged periods of seclusion without explanation, prompting speculation that he was ill or dead; his rare public appearances tended to fuel rather than dispel the gossip of his failing health. On these occasions he spoke in a low, hoarse voice or was even strangely silent, permitting Mother Divine to make announcements and handle questions.[28]

A more serious setback to Father Divine's image of vitality occurred in 1960, with the revelation that he had been in Bryn Mawr Hospital, suffering from diabetic coma. Unable to conceal his identity, Divine responded by denying he was ill in the conventional sense. Rather, he had taken the infirmities of the world upon himself in order to save it.[29]

Also in 1960, although aides stressed that Father Divine was spiritually as efficacious as ever, he ceased altogether to speak in public. Divine reassured the faithful in letters that explained his silence as the result of having already given the world all the wisdom it could receive. His messages assumed a wistful quality, as if he were already making his farewells to the world he had entered some eighty years before. An excerpt from one such letter, frequently reprinted in the *New Day,* reveals a nostalgic tone typical of his mood during this time: "You have often heard me say, 'I need not say more'; and it is true. I have already spoken much more than fifty years in advance of our present civilization. Had I not done so, humanity could not have been saved, for I have laid the cornerstone of a new nation, not only conceived by God but builded by him . . . and you have seen it unfolding in the lives of men everywhere."[30]

By the time of this valedictory, the daily administration of the Peace Mission had fallen to Mother Divine, working closely with Father Divine's able secretarial staff. Although not an innovator or social crusader as Father Divine had been in his prime, Mother Divine had already proven herself well suited to lead the Peace Mission in its search for spiritual purity and organizational stability. She made an impressive, intelligent, demure presence at Peace Mission banquets, and a graciously effective diplomat to guests from all walks of life. It was clear that Father Divine's earlier social radicalism was to be merely revered, not revived, but within the Peace Mission's own centers the Father's vision of a chaste, integrated communal society would go on as before.

Father Divine survived into the sixties only as a feeble remnant of his once vigorous body. His last public appearance was in 1963, and on that occasion he merely watched as Mother Divine gave the banquet sermon and welcomed visitors. In September, 1964, after his absence from a major event—the annual Woodmont dedication anniversary—his secretaries publicly hinted that his death was not far off. Three of his closest aides reported that they saw Father Divine daily but that they were prepared for the day when he would not be continually with them.[31]

The civil rights movement entered its zenith during these years, but the Peace Mission's involvement in the cause had by then diminished to a wholly passive state. In the absence of new reform initiatives from the ailing Peace Mission leader, his disciples simply celebrated the harmony they had always known in their Father's kingdom. As one follower, Blessed Mary Love, explained in 1964, "Father has freed us from within."[32]

There were signs that Father Divine himself was not nearly so content to ignore the nation's social turbulence. Possibly frustrated by his inability to play a personal role in the civil rights struggles, he compensated by taking credit for developments he approved of, without having participated in them directly. In that vein, he suggested that his spirit had inspired the actions of the freedom riders and the sit-in demonstrations, as well as other civil rights campaigns.[33]

The continued force of Divine's interest in civil rights became fully evident after President Lyndon Johnson delivered a ringing speech in March, 1965, urging passage of the voting rights bill. This measure would provide the federal government with much stronger powers to enforce the voting rights of any citizen, regardless of race, creed, or color; it was a step Divine had urged for three decades. Despite his extreme frailty, Divine rallied his reserves of physical strength to convey his heartfelt support for the president's commitment. Divine's message is particularly illuminating, in view of critics' unrelenting charges that he spoke only in obscure terms, held scant interest beyond self-aggrandizement, and stood outside the mainstream of black concerns. He wrote to Johnson:

> I highly commend you on your wonderful speech before the Joint Session of Congress. It is with profound gratitude I have witnessed this great ship of state being steered into a new world of unity and dignity for all mankind. If this "so great a people" will now stand together just as Americans in the unity of spirit, of mind, of aim and of purpose, there is nothing that can prevent the establishment of a universal Utopian democracy in which all men, everywhere, shall enjoy the reality of life, liberty and happiness. May I extend my blessings as my life to you in this effort.[34]

Within six months, Father Divine died. He was then in his eighties and convinced that the interracial utopia for which he had so long yearned was at last coming to pass. Whatever the accuracy of that judgment, the evidence does suggest that in the cause of racial harmony and equality he had indeed, with considerable effect, extended his blessings and his life.

Notes to Epilogue

1. See *Times,* Mar. 1, 1941, p. 17, for the ruling of New York Supreme Court Justice Phillip J. McCook, mandating that Father Divine pay the disputed judgment or suffer imprisonment; the article also contains a vehement statement of protest by Father Divine. Other key judicial rulings on this case are recorded in

Times, Jan. 18, 1940, p. 14; Mar. 9, 1940, p. 1; Nov. 2, 1940, p. 13; Mar. 1, 1941, p. 17; Mar. 6, 1941, p. 23; June 9, 1942, p. 16; June 11, 1942, p. 15.

2. See Zwick, "Father Divine Peace Mission Movement," p. 120.

3. Burnham, *God Comes to America,* p. 74.

4. Ibid., p. 107, reprints the bylaw formally deifying Father Divine.

5. *NYAN* reports Father Divine's departure, July 25, 1942, p. 1, and analyzes it, Aug. 1, 1942, p. 5. Father Divine spoke about his motives in his sermon of July 19, 1942, in *ND,* July 23, 1942, pp. 6-7; and in his sermon of Aug. 11-12, 1942, in *ND,* Aug. 13, 1942, pp. 6-7. For information on Father Divine's continued, but vain, appeals of his court sentence, see *Times,* Aug. 14, 1942, p. 34; Oct. 3, 1942, p. 17; Dec. 11, 1942, p. 27. Also see Charles Breitel (counsel to Governor Thomas E. Dewey of New York) to Father Divine, Jan. 28, 1943, in *ND,* Feb. 4, 1943, p. 21, declining Father Divine's request for Governor Dewey's intervention and stating that authority in such matters was vested solely with the appellate courts.

6. Although the Peace Mission's participation in protest campaigns declined markedly, there is evidence of sporadic activism through at least the mid-forties. See, for example, the *Afro-American* (Philadelphia ed.), Nov. 13, 1943, p. 2, and *Times,* May 6, 1946, p. 10.

7. Father Divine contracted diabetes sometime during his later years, though this fact was concealed from the public until 1960. It is perhaps significant, in this regard, that beginning in the late 1940s Divine mentioned the disease frequently in advising others on general health problems. See, for example, interview given by Father Divine to an unnamed female follower, Feb. 22, 1948, in *ND,* Sept. 23, 1972, p. 12.

8. See the penetrating analysis of this phenomenon in Peter Worsley, *The Trumpet Shall Sound: A Study of 'Cargo' Cults in Melanesia,* 2d ed. (New York: Schocken Books, 1967), p. 232.

9. Sermon of Dec. 25, 1950, in *ND,* Jan. 7, 1978, p. 4.

10. Sermon of Feb. 6, 1951, in *ND,* Dec. 2, 1978, p. 7.

11. Zwick, "Father Divine Peace Mission Movement," pp. 129-30, insightfully examines why the Promised Land declined.

12. See Burnham, *God Comes to America,* pp. 84-96, for a description of the various religious orders, and Zwick, "Father Divine Peace Mission Movement," pp. 108-9, for a provocative discussion of why they were created. Zwick views them essentially as more conducive to Father Divine's supreme authority over his followers than the order of "Angels," which was discontinued during this period.

13. See, for example, sermon of Sept. 12, 1938, in *ND,* Sept. 15, 1938, p. 76.

14. Disciple identified as "E.E.M." to Father Divine, Feb. 5, 1959, in *ND,* Feb. 28, 1959, p. 21.

15. See *Times,* Aug. 8, 1946, p. 23, and Aug. 9, 1946, p. 19.

16. Interview with Mother Divine, Woodmont, July 2, 1977.

17. Sermon of Aug. 21, 1946, in *ND,* Aug. 24, 1946, p. 17.

18. *NYAN,* Sept. 18, 1965, p. 7.

19. Adam Clayton Powell, Jr., "Sex in the Church," *Ebony* 7 (Nov., 1951):29.

20. Sullivan's statement, Aug. 24, 1945, in *ND,* July 31, 1971, p. 13.

21. Leon Sullivan to Father Divine, July 21, 1958, and Father Divine to Leon Sullivan, July 23, 1958, both in *ND,* Aug. 2, 1958, p. 29; see also *ND,* Aug. 9, 1958, p. 23.

22. "Cosmic Lubritorium," *Time* 62 (Sept. 21, 1953):79.

23. Ibid., p. 80.

24. Ibid.

25. Jones's banquet speech, Philadelphia, July 20, 1958, in *ND,* Aug. 2, 1958, p. 19.

26. Ibid., p. 21.

27. Ibid.

28. Zwick, "Father Divine Peace Mission Movement," p. 60.

29. *Times,* May 14, 1960, p. 14; *NYAN,* May 21, 1960, p. 1; *Philadelphia Evening Bulletin,* May 13, 1960, p. 1; *ND,* May 21, 1960, p. 1.

30. Father Divine to disciple identified as "S.P.," Jan. 26, 1960, in *ND,* Feb. 6, 1960, p. 19.

31. *Times,* Sept. 13, 1964, p. 53.

32. R. W. Apple, "Father Divine Shuns Rights Drive," *Times,* May 10, 1964, p. 65.

33. In 1961, as "freedom riders" extensively tested southern compliance with court rulings against segregation in interstate transportation, a headline in the *New Day* referred to "The First Freedom Rider, Father Divine." See *ND,* July 1, 1961, p. 7. Divine reinforced this image with frequent statements like the following: "You can see the work of my spirit moving among men in all parts of the world . . . I am stirring up the racial issue in Africa; and in the deep South of this country I am bringing about a true democratic feeling of mutual understanding concerning the same rights of each and every inhabitant of this nation." See Father Divine to F.K., May 17, 1961, in *ND,* June 3, 1961, p. 8. Similarly, he claimed that his braving of thirty-two lynch mobs to sow the seeds of democracy was now bearing fruit throughout the land; see, for example, Father Divine to "J.H.," June 15, 1961, in *ND,* July 1, 1961, p. 7.

34. Father Divine to President Lyndon Johnson, telegram, Mar. 17, 1965, in *ND,* Mar. 27, 1965, p. 1.

Sources

A. Primary Sources

The indispensable sources for examining Father Divine's Harlem ministry are the two major journals of the Peace Mission, the *Spoken Word* (Oct. 20, 1934–July 31, 1937) and the *New Day* (May 21, 1936 –). These weekly (and in some years semiweekly) journals contain stenographic records of Divine's statements in over 10,000 sermons, letters, interviews, and office talks. The journals also offer a running commentary on the events in which Father Divine participated and the programs he created or aided. In addition, testimony by disciples and visitors often appears in these papers, shedding considerable light on the composition of the membership and the nature of Father Divine's appeal and influence. Although cross-checking with other sources reveals that the *New Day* and the *Spoken Word* transcribe statements by Father Divine and others with great accuracy, the student of Peace Mission activities should be aware of certain editorial peculiarities. All words relating directly to race, for example, "white" and "Negro," are replaced by such euphemisms as "light-complected" and "so and so" race. Certain "negative" words with religious connotations are often bowdlerized and, in some cases, replaced by their antithesis: thus the "devil" becomes the "other fellow," and "Amsterdam" Avenue becomes "Amsterbless" Avenue. The style of capitalization used by these journals is also highly idiosyncratic; in text quotations it has been changed to standard usage for purposes of clarity. In all other respects quotations from these journals are reproduced with complete fidelity.

Contemporary news accounts in various national journals provide a rich store of information on Father Divine's activities. The major newsweeklies *Time* and *Newsweek* and the large New York dailies, including the *Times,* the *Herald-Tribune,* the *Daily News,* the *Post,* and the *Daily Mirror,* reported frequently on Divine, though seldom favorably. The journals emphasized, for the most part, his flamboyant personality and legal difficulties while only occasionally touching upon his social activism. The

224

Times, however, does offer some valuable accounts of Divine's efforts to integrate white neighborhoods and his programs for economic and political change. William Randolph Hearst's *New York Evening Journal* crusaded against Divine's ministry during the thirties, branding Divine a demagogic menace. Its extensive reports are so biased as to be of only slight use, beyond reflecting the considerable hostility many northern whites harbored toward Father Divine.

The black newsweeklies of the Depression era covered Father Divine's leadership more thoroughly and sympathetically, though also frequently capitalizing on his exotic image to stimulate sales. The *New York Amsterdam News,* an essentially local journal attentive to the flourishing cults and sects in Harlem, routinely featured Father Divine on its front page during the mid-thirties. The *Baltimore Afro-American,* the *New York Age,* the *Pittsburgh Courier,* and the *Chicago Defender* also devoted considerable space to Divine's ministry. A humorous, even sensational tone pervades many of these accounts; yet overall, both the news reports and editorials are vastly more respectful of Divine's progressive leadership than most of the white-owned newsweeklies and dailies.

Several dozen interviews with current members of the Peace Mission movement supplemented the above materials in the preparation of this study. Among the leaders who gave interviews are the following: Mother Divine, in Woodmont, July 2, 1977; the secretarial staff to Mother Divine (collectively), in Philadelphia, July 2, 1977; Heavenly Rest (former personal secretary to Father Divine), in Tarrytown, July 4, 1977; Paul DeLap (director of the Newark Peace Mission and former aide to Father Divine), in Newark, July 1, 1977; and Mr. Patrick (personal chauffeur to Mother Divine and former personal chauffeur to Father Divine), in Woodmont, July 2, 1977. Attendance at banquet services in Philadelphia (July 2, 1977) and Tarrytown (July 4, 1977) also proved of value, though students of the Peace Mission should exercise caution in comparing the bureaucratized, middle-class movement of today with Divine's gatherings of forty years ago.

The following interviews with those outside the movement were particularly helpful in illuminating aspects of Father Divine's ministry: Preston Williams (professor of religion at Harvard Divinity School), in Cambridge, Mass., June 24, 1977; Owen Dodson (author in 1938 of the acclaimed play "Divine Comedy," sharply satirizing Father Divine), in New York, June 28, 1977; and Clyde Ferguson (professor of law at Harvard Law School), in Cambridge, Mass., Feb. 29, 1980.

B. Secondary Sources

Three biographies of Father Divine, each tending to emphasize the exotic aspects of his Peace Mission movement, form the standard introduction to his career. The most comprehensive treatment of Divine's rise and the state of his movement during the 1930s is Robert Allerton Parker, *The Incredible Messiah: The Deification of Father Divine* (Boston: Little, Brown, 1937). Despite the lack of formal documentation (particularly regrettable given the uniquely detailed narrative of Divine's early years), this is a serious, often moving effort to explain Divine's appeal in terms of the deplorable conditions in Harlem. Parker argues plausibly that the racism and poverty afflicting ghetto residents created a yearning for messianic figures that cult leaders like Divine tried to satisfy. Yet Parker is less persuasive in concluding that Father Divine was little more than a petty tyrant who offered "an unconscious satire" of the fascist leaders then menacing Europe. Part of the problem is Parker's insufficient attention to Divine's social idealism and to black perspectives of Divine's work. Lacking a full appreciation of the Peace Mission's dedication to human rights and racial equality, Parker instead stresses the emotional and cult features of the movement. The result is a portrait that harshly caricatures Divine as a cynical demagogue while implicitly disparaging his reform activity. Although the book is free of overt racism, John Jasper, reviewing Parker's work for the *Afro-American* magazine (May 15, 1937), asserts that the author seemed clearly alarmed that so many white persons were venerating a black man. "Calling them names," Jasper adds, "probably salves his Anglo-Saxon pride." With these caveats in mind, one can still profit from consulting Parker's vivid and wide-ranging study.

Any bias in Parker's work is dwarfed by that in John Hoshor, *God in a Rolls-Royce: The Rise of Father Divine, Madman, Menace, or Messiah* . . . (New York: Hillman-Curl, 1936). Hoshor frequently produces group slanders like the following: "Unlike most blacks, Baker was not lazy." He writes genially of "broad-shouldered bucks" and "high yallers," and knows that "nothing else tastes as good to a negro" as fried chicken. He seems, in short, to find blacks fit subjects for ridicule, not simply as part of a wider human comedy but because they are black. Yet, despite his racism, Hoshor is also the most original of Divine's biographers, and when his prejudices are sifted from his insights, much of value remains. He claims, rightly, that Father Divine centered all his energies on the goal of complete racial equality. He also argues vigorously, if more questionably, that Divine's tenet of celibacy was chiefly a measure to defuse objections to integration in both North and South. Hoshor's emphasis on Divine's sense of social mission gives his informally written book a much sounder perspective than Parker's more somber and erudite work. Yet ultimately Hoshor's tendency to burlesque all blacks trivializes Divine's ideals and achievements. The resulting picture of Divine, though less harshly drawn than Parker's, is therefore equally comical, and misleading.

The third biography is by Sara Harris, with the assistance of Harriet Crittendon, *Father Divine,* enl. ed. (New York: Collier Books, 1971; original ed., New York: Doubleday, 1953). The book covers the latter period of Father Divine's life, when he was relatively inactive, though Harris praises his longstanding concern for equal rights. The author is a trained social worker and her detailed, insightful case studies of individual Peace Mission members contribute greatly to understanding the movement. Nevertheless, this work often seems intent on sensationalizing an already distinctive movement, as confirmed by the book's original title, *Father Divine: Holy Husband.* The focus throughout is on the alleged sexual pathologies of Peace Mission disciples, rumors of sexual indiscretions by Father Divine, factionalism among officials in the movement, and the fanatical adulation accorded Father Divine. The tone of the book mixes fascination with revulsion and, toward Divine, much sarcasm. One reviewer, who thought that even this treatment was too kind to Father Divine, nevertheless noted that while Harris was highly sympathetic to white followers, she at times accorded black disciples an "Amos and Andy" treatment. (See Tom Posten, "Shepherd of Fantasies," *Saturday Review of Literature* 36 [Nov. 14, 1953]:19.) In all, Harris offers a rare intimate portrayal of life in the Peace Mission, but her focus on gossip unfortunately obscures the larger purpose and accomplishments that marked Divine's leadership.

Most contemporary essays on Father Divine's Peace Mission movement during the Depression mirror the cynicism and condescension evident in the major biographies. The best written and most influential of these accounts is a three-part series by St. Clair McKelway and A. J. Liebling, "Who Is This King of Glory?" *New Yorker* 12, pt. 1 (June 13, 1936):21-28; pt. 2 (June 20, 1936):22-28; pt. 3 (June 27, 1936):22-32. The first two parts afford valuable information on Divine's early evangelical career; the concluding essay details the financial workings of the Peace Mission "kingdom." A. J. Liebling expresses his negative view of Father Divine still more explicitly in a review of John Hoshor's biography, in *Saturday Review of Literature* 14 (Oct. 3, 1936):11. Liebling criticizes Hoshor's emphasis on Divine's idealism and suggests instead that Divine was simply a businessman who dealt in religion and made a staggering profit for his efforts.

Among other contemporary accounts of special value, Hubert Kelley, "Heaven Incorporated," *American Magazine* 221 (Jan., 1936):40-41, 106-8, perceptively analyzes several white leaders in the Peace Mission and vividly describes banquet testimonies of "divine cures." Henry Lee Moon, "Thank

You, Father So Sweet," *New Republic* 88 (Sept. 16, 1936):147-50, theorizes about the possible sources of Divine's income. Jack Alexander, "All Father's Chillun Got Heavens," *Saturday Evening Post* 212 (Nov. 18, 1939):8-9, 64ff., contains important information on Divine's expanding rural centers.

Various psychological profiles of Peace Mission members tend to argue that the movement did not effectively fit its disciples for life in the outside world. The major exponents of this position include James Brussell, "Father Divine, Holy Precipitator of Psychosis," *American Journal of Psychiatry* 92 (July, 1935):215-24; Laura Bender and Zuleika Yarrell, "Psychoses among Followers of Father Divine," *Journal of Nervous and Mental Diseases* 87 (Apr., 1938):418-49; Lauretta Bender and M. A. Spalding, "Behavior Problems in Children from the Homes of Followers of Father Divine," *Journal of Nervous and Mental Diseases* 91 (Apr., 1940):460-72; and Hadley Cantril and Muzafer Sherif, "The Kingdom of Father Divine," *Journal of Abnormal Psychology* 33 (Apr., 1938): 147-67.

Accounts in religious journals of Father Divine's leadership are, as might be predicted, almost uniformly deprecatory. "Seven Day's Survey," *Commonweal* 26 (May 7, 1937):46, terms Divine's doctrine "singularly devoid of intellectual or doctrinal content." Edwin T. Buehrer, "Harlem's God," *Christian Century* 52 (Dec. 11, 1935):1590-93, evinces compassion for those in the movement but clearly reveals a sense of horror at the proceedings. Frank S. Mead, "God in Harlem," *Christian Century* 53 (Aug. 26, 1936): 1133-35, scarcely displays any ambivalence about Divine ("He says nothing. As a preacher, he's Public Failure Number One; theologically, there is no rhyme or reason in him.") or about the "500 stupefied fanatics" with whom the author attended a Peace Mission banquet. Books examining religious behavior similarly cite Father Divine as an example of religious demagogy or blasphemy. Raymond J. Jones, *A Comparative Study of Religious Cult Behavior among Negroes with Special Reference to Emotional Group Conditioning Factors* (Washington, D.C.: Howard University Press, 1939), views Father Divine as a cult "showman" in the manner of more primitive witch doctors and tribal priests. V. F. Calverton, *Where Angels Dared to Tread* (New York: Bobbs-Merrill, 1941), pp. 328-43, expresses some admiration for Divine's frugal way of life compared with certain other religious figures, but he also deplores Divine's preaching as a study in "consummate incoherence."

Black writers placing Divine's leadership in the context of black communal needs offer varying evaluations but, on balance, are far more favorable to Divine than white authors. Roi Ottley, *'New World A-Coming': Inside Black America* (Boston: Houghton Mifflin, 1943), pp. 82-99, expresses serious reservations regarding Divine's flamboyant leadership but carefully distinguishes him from his unsuccessful competitors in Harlem, such as Daddy Grace, who sought to take from the masses without giving in return. Divine, by contrast, was a good provider. He was also "a Baptist fundamentalist at heart and in precept," who inherited Marcus Garvey's thousands by taking to new limits the worship of all things black. One should note that Divine himself would have denied this vehemently, for he stressed the essential meaninglessness of complexion. Nevertheless, as Ottley demonstrates, many former Garveyites were undeterred by such nuances. Claude McKay, "There Goes God! The Story of Father Divine and His Angels," *Nation* 140 (Feb. 6, 1935):151-53, adopts a similarly ambivalent view of Divine, which he amplifies in *Harlem: Negro Metropolis* (New York: E. P. Dutton, 1940), pp. 32-72. McKay openly admires Divine's ability to outmaneuver his adversaries, and he takes note of Divine's wide-ranging activities in Harlem. Yet McKay stresses the sensational, cult features of the Peace Mission movement, and seems to view Divine's ministry as a series of tactical coups without a unifying philosophy. A more categorically positive analysis is George Streator, "Father Divine," *Commonweal* 31 (Dec. 15, 1939):176-78, who praises Father Divine's social leadership and defends his celebrated banquets as partaking of a venerable American ritual of communion. Streator emphasizes that Divine did much to ensure black welfare against the depredations of slumlords and other exploiters. Arthur Huff Fauset, *Black Gods of the Metropolis: Negro Religious Cults of the Urban North* (Philadelphia: Philadelphia Anthropological Society, 1944; reprinted Philadelphia: University of Pennsylvania Press, 1971) is an outstanding work, free of cultural prejudice and exceptionally observant in recording Divine's religious ideas and Peace Mission rituals. Fauset also notes that Divine's movement was by far the most socially and economically progressive of the cults in the ghetto.

The 1940s witnessed the decline of Father Divine's social activism and the end of his personal reign in Harlem. Accordingly the literature on his ministry greatly diminished in volume. Yet, perhaps because he appeared more innocuous to white society, the writings during this time revealed a new appreciation for his religious teachings and personal integrity. Charles Samuel Braden, *These Also Believe: A Study of Modern American Cults and Minority Religious Movements* (New York: Macmillan, 1949), pp. 1-77, is perhaps the finest single essay ever written on the Peace Mission movement. It is a model of tolerant observation, combined with a rare lucidity in explaining the principles of the movement. Another work in this sympathetic vein, of particular value for its revealing anecdotes about Father Divine, is Marcus Bach, *They Have Found a Faith* (Indianapolis: Bobbs-Merrill, 1946), pp. 162-88.

The rehabilitation of Father Divine and the Peace Mission has progressed considerably in recent years. Kenneth E. Burnham, "Father Divine: A Case Study of Charismatic Leadership" (Ph.D. thesis, University of Pennsylvania, 1963), draws extensively on quotations from the *New Day* to convey the Peace Mission's religious principles. His view of the Peace Mission as a serious movement is also evident in recent writings: "The Father Divine Peace Mission," in *Black Apostles: Afro-American Clergy Confront the Twentieth Century,* ed. Randall K. Burkett and Richard Newman (Boston: G. K. Hall, 1978), pp. 25-47, and *God Comes to America: Father Divine and the Peace Mission Movement* (Boston: Lambeth Press, 1979), a revised and updated version of his doctoral study.

Stephen Zwick, "The Father Divine Peace Mission Movement" (Senior thesis, Princeton University, 1971), is a highly insightful, scholarly treatment that emphasizes the changes in the movement since Divine's death in 1965. While remaining a dispassionate critic of the Peace Mission, Zwick also recognizes that Divine built a complex and constructive movement. He concludes his pioneering work: "Father Divine may not have been God, but he was certainly a great man who deserves far more attention than he has received from American historians."

Joseph R. Washington, Jr., *Black Sects and Cults: The Power Axis in an Ethnic Ethic* (New York: Doubleday, 1973), suggests that Father Divine was the most constructive of the black cult leaders who sought power for an oppressed people, if mainly through spiritual means. Washington praises Divine's philanthropic work and asserts that he might have done yet more had he possessed a broad vision for reform. In fact, Divine had a comprehensive reform vision that was at the center of his theology and his movement's activities. Yet given the predominant view of Divine as the leader of an essentially escapist cult movement, Washington's thesis marks a bold step toward explaining the Peace Mission as a vigorous agent for social change during the Depression.

The following works also treat aspects of Father Divine's life:

Barnes, Roma. "Blessings Flowing Free": The Father Divine Peace Mission Movement in Harlem, New York City, 1932-1941." Ph.D. thesis, University of York (England), 1979.

   The dissertation has not been examined by this writer, but an abstract suggests that it treats the Peace Mission as a movement "impelled by social conflict and directed toward social change."

Boaz, Ruth. "My Thirty Years with Father Divine." *Ebony* 20 (May, 1965): 88-98.

   Article claims not to be "a petulant outburst of an embittered former follower"; it is, however. The author's main charge is that she was once Father Divine's mistress.

Crumb, C. B. "Father Divine's Use of Colloquial and Original English." *American Speech* 15 (Oct., 1940): 327.

Denlinger, Sutherland. "Heaven Is in Harlem." *Forum* 95 (Apr., 1936): 211-18.

"Divine Judgment." *Literary Digest* 123 (May 1, 1937): 6-7.
Summarizes Divine's legal troubles.

Faithful Mary. *"God," He's Just a Natural Man.* New York: Gailliard Press, 1937.
A scandalous exposé, of doubtful veracity, by a leading Peace Mission member who defected to form her own cult in 1937. She, like Ruth Boaz, claims to have been Father Divine's mistress and charges that he was a totally unprincipled demagogue. In 1938 Faithful Mary rejoined the Peace Mission and completely recanted her widely publicized statements.

Faris, Robert E. L. *Social Disorganization.* New York: Ronald Press, 1955, pp. 584-89.
Interprets the Peace Mission movement as reflecting the desire of rural Negroes for a sense of security and stability.

"Father Divine Enters Politics." *Christian Century* 53 (Oct. 7, 1936): 1334.

Flynn, John T. "Other People's Money." *New Republic* 89 (May 26, 1937): 73-74.

Garrison, W. E. "Security at Any Price." Review of *Father Divine: Holy Husband,* by Sara Harris. *Christian Century* 70 (Nov. 11, 1953): 1297-98.

Harkness, Gloria. "Father Divine's Righteous Government." *Christian Century* 82 (Oct. 13, 1965):1259-61.
Reports on eighteen pages of notes taken at a meeting of Father Divine's movement in 1936.

Howell, Clarence. "Father Divine: Another View." *Christian Century* 53 (Oct. 7, 1936):1332-33.
Defends Father Divine as a coherent religious thinker whose main sources of inspiration were Oriental: Divine Science, New Thought, and Christian Unity.

Johnson, Guy B. "Notes on Behavior at a Religious Service at the Father Divine Peace Mission." Appendix D to "The Church and the Race Problem in the United States," by Guion G. Johnson and Guy B. Johnson. Manuscript prepared for the Carnegie-Myrdal study of the Negro in America. Schomburg Collection of the New York Public Library.

Levick, Lionel. "Father Divine Is God." *Forum* 92 (Oct., 1934):217-21.

McKay, Claude. "Father Divine's Rebel Angel." *American Mercury* 51 (Sept., 1940):73-80.

   Interprets the defection of Faithful Mary, her failure as an independent cult leader, and her abject return to the Peace Mission as illustrating the dependence of all the movement's disciples on Father Divine's inspiration.

Moseley, J. R. *Manifest Victory.* New York: Harper and Bros., 1941, pp. 106-9.

   Contains invaluable references to the author's early encounters with Father Divine.

"New Mrs. Divine." *Life* 21 (Aug. 19, 1946):38.

Palmer, E. Nelson. "The Father Divine Peace Mission." Appendix C to "The Church and the Race Problem in the United States," by Guion G. Johnson and Guy B. Johnson. Manuscript prepared for the Carnegie-Myrdal study of the Negro in America. Schomburg Collection of the New York Public Library.

"People." *Review of Reviews* 95 (June, 1937):23-24.

Powell, O. G. "Divine and Lung Power." *Forum* 92 (Nov., 1934):x-xi.

"A Prophet and a Divine Meet." *Life* 35 (Sept. 28, 1953):103.

Randolph, Richard V. *God Is on Earth Today.* Los Angeles: Society of the Sacred Seven, 1952.

   A rhapsodic exploration of Father Divine's teachings by a dedicated follower.

Rasky, Frank. "Harlem's Religious Zealots." *Tomorrow* 9 (Nov., 1949): 11-17.

Schroeder, Theodore. "A Living God Incarnate." *Psychoanalytic Review* 19 (Jan., 1932):36-45.

Stewart, Ollie. "Harlem God in His Heaven." *Scribner's Commentator* 8 (June, 1940):20-26.

Streator, George. Review of *The Incredible Messiah,* by Robert Parker. *Opportunity* 15 (Oct., 1937):314.

   Streator views Divine as an "innocent" pawn of newsmen looking for banner headlines.

Thomason, John W., Jr. "Father Divine's Afflatus." Review of *God in a Rolls-Royce,* by John Hoshor. *American Mercury* 39 (Dec., 1936): 500-505.

Warmsley, V. Review of *God in a Rolls-Royce,* by John Hoshor. *Crisis* 43 (Nov., 1936):348-49.

Williams, Chancellor. *Have You Been to the River?* New York: Exposition Press, 1952, pp. 200-224.

   Uses fictional setting for a provocative foray into the world of black religious leaders, including Father Divine.

Index

Abolitionists, 197
Abyssinian Baptist Church, 25
Africa, 126; and Marcus Garvey, 190, 192, 194-95; viewed by Father Divine, 196
The Afro-American. See Baltimore Afro-American Age. See New York Age
Alexander, Jack: on Father Divine and the law, 95
Allen, A. A., 42
Allen, James Egert, 119, 184
Allied powers, 204-5
All People's Party, 145-46, 165
American Federation of Labor (AFL), 136, 137, 140
American League against War and Fascism, 149, 169
Amsterdam News. See New York Amsterdam News
Antebellum era, 157, 197
Antilynching legislation: advocated by Father Divine, 7, 153, 157-61, 164-68 *passim,* 184; campaign for, 157-61; and Franklin D. Roosevelt, 166-68 *passim. See also* Lynching
Apex News and Hair Company, 118, 132
Arata, Joseph, 47
Arias, Julia, 48
Atlantic City, N.J., 115, 118
Austin, J. C., 182
Australia: disciples of Father Divine in, 71
Axis powers, 202, 205

Baker, George, 9, 10, 16-20, 27, 52. *See also* Father Divine: early years
Baldwin, James: on storefront churches, 22; on segregation, 114

Baltimore: early residence of Father Divine, 10, 16-20
Baltimore Afro-American, 53
Barbour, R. C., 108-9
Barton, Bruce, 28, 124
Becton, G. Wilson, 43-44
Better Schools (journal), 99
Bill of Rights, 119, 158
Black Belt, 11-15 *passim,* 23. *See also* Blacks: in the South
Black Jews, 108, 190, 195
Black Muslims (Nation of Islam), 12, 94, 108, 145, 190-91, 195-96
Black religion: as reflection of community values, 3; conservative features of, 3-5, 14-15, 17, 24-25, 37-46, 103, 141-42, 145, 182-83, 187; and social activism, 3, 5, 7, 24-25, 45-46, 145, 146, 181, 186-87, 216; changes in, during the Depression, 5, 8, 37-46, 181, 186-87; segregated character of, 6, 30, 108-9; importance of, in rural South, 14-15; importance of, in Northern ghettos, 22-24; Carte Woodson on, 38; W. E. B. Du Bois on, 183-84; Jean Toomer on, 190. *See also* individual churches, cults, and ministers
Blacks: in the South, 3-4, 10-15; urban migration by, 4, 22, 125, 180; economic impact of the Depression on, 4-5, 133-34; and Pan-Africanism, 4, 191, 193; and economic cooperation, 6, 122; and Franklin D. Roosevelt, 7, 166-68; and education, 13, 14, 96, 171; businesses of, 102, 124, 131-32; and New Deal agencies, 107-8, 130-31; and Communist party, 148-50; and elections, 150, 162, 164, 166; American

A Note on the Author

Robert Weisbrot was born in New York City and grad-
uated, summa cum laude, from Brandeis University in
1973. He was a Fellow of the Du Bois Institute for Afro-
American Research in 1979-1980 and received a Ph.D.
in history from Harvard University in 1980. He is
presently on the faculty of Colby College in Waterville,
Maine. His other publications include the book, *The Jews
of Argentina: From the Inquisition to Perón* (1979).

Blacks in the New World